# Feminism, Inc.

# Feminism, Inc.

## Coming of Age in Girl Power Media Culture

Emilie Zaslow

palgrave
macmillan

FEMINISM, INC.



First published in hardcover in 2009 by
PALGRAVE MACMILLAN®
in the United States—a division of St. Martin's Press LLC,
175 Fifth Avenue, New York, NY 10010.

Where this book is distributed in the UK, Europe and the rest of the world, this is by Palgrave Macmillan, a division of Macmillan Publishers Limited, registered in England, company number 785998, of Houndmills, Basingstoke, Hampshire RG21 6XS.

Palgrave Macmillan is the global academic imprint of the above companies and has companies and representatives throughout the world.

Palgrave® and Macmillan® are registered trademarks in the United States, the United Kingdom, Europe and other countries.

ISBN: 978–0–230–11996–3

Library of Congress Cataloging-in-Publication Data

Zaslow, Emilie.
Feminism, Inc. : coming of age in girl power media culture / Emilie Zaslow.
p. cm.
Includes bibliographical references and index.
ISBN 0–230–60814–0
1. Teenage girls. 2. Mass media. 3. Feminism. I. Title.

HQ798.Z37 2009
305.23082'0973090511—dc22 2009021753

A catalogue record of the book is available from the British Library.

Design by Newgen Imaging Systems (P) Ltd., Chennai, India.

First PALGRAVE MACMILLAN paperback edition: November 2011

10 9 8 7 6 5 4 3 2 1

Printed in the United States of America.

**Transferred to Digital Printing in 2011**

*For Eric, Sam, and Zoe*

# Contents

# ACKNOWLEDGMENTS

THERE ARE MANY PEOPLE TO WHOM I OWE A TREMENDOUS AMOUNT OF GRATITUDE. It is their support and encouragement that made this book possible. I began the work for this book as a graduate student in the Department of Culture and Communication at NYU. JoEllen Fisherkeller has been a mentor and a friend. Her dedication to listening to the voices of young people is inspiring. Radha Hegde and Susan Murray were generous with their time and provided valuable feedback. I was also lucky to learn and work beside some outstanding colleagues and friends. Allison Butler, Eric Saranovitz, and Nancy Silverman were my anchors. Allison Butler has been amazingly generous with her close reading of this book and her constructive advice.

Earlier in my academic career there were two people who shaped my scholarship and had a great impact on the direction of my work. At Oberlin, Camille Guerin-Gonzalez once wrote, "We need you," in response to one of my papers. Though I am certain she does not know, these lovely and ambiguous three words have made a huge impact on my sense of self as a scholar. At SUNY Buffalo, Liz Kennedy unknowingly led me down the path of girls' studies when she introduced me to the American Girl Collection.

Pace University has been a supportive environment in which to write this book. I am grateful to my colleagues—Satish Kolluri, Barry Morris, Mary Ann Murphy, Bill Page, and Abbey Berg—for their words of encouragement. Mary Stambaugh has been giving with her time, laughter, and optimism. My students at Pace, especially those in the Gender and Media courses, have kept me current on popular media and shared their enthusiasm about my research questions. Another Pace student, Joe Glover, deserves sincere gratitude for his outstanding artwork that graces the cover of this book. At Palgrave, Burke Gerstenschlager and Kaylan Connally have made this as smooth a process as possible.

Though I cannot thank them by name, I would like to express my gratitude to the seventy girls who participated in this study as well as the adults who helped to coordinate the focus groups at schools and Girl Scout troops.

I owe a great deal to the twenty-five girls who spent additional time with me discussing their lives, their media experiences, and their futures; I was amazed time and again not only by the girls' willingness to share their experiences but also by their awareness of the social construction of gender and the articulateness with which they spoke about femininity and feminism.

There are no words to express the gratitude I have for my family. My parents, Lucy and Richard Zaslow, taught me how to write, taught me that my voice had impact, and taught me that teaching was a political act. In the past few years, they have taught me about a generosity that goes unmatched. They are the most giving people I know; I can only hope to be the kind of parents and grandparents they are. My sister, Carrie Zaslow, has been a role model throughout the years, demonstrating not only what it means to follow your heart, but also what it means to be passionate about the work you do. Gail Braverman has graciously given her time and energy to reading this book several times and made delicious meals to feed my brain. Special thanks to Laurie and Stan Diamond who have provided me with support and inspiration. The rest of my family–Wendy & Rob Michnoff, Alan Braverman, Pete Quattromani, the extended Zaslow, Diamond, and Kryzak-decended families—have provided laughter and support. I have been lucky to have wonderful friends throughout my life and during the writing of this book. Judy Schoenberg who knew me as a girl, and who shares my belief in the importance of studying girls and women, has been a true kindred spirit. I have also enjoyed sharing my work with—as well as being distracted from it by—Jun Egawa, Jen Stumpf, Heidi Burbage, Maya Zelio, Nancy Rosenbaum, and Jonathan Mayers.

Eric Braverman has been nothing short of the "partner in marriage" he pledged to be. Not only has he read this book with great care and interest, he has been my greatest supporter throughout the entire project. It is his love, humor, hard work, and amazing parenting that have made this manageable. There are no words to express my most sincere appreciation for him. Sam Zaslow-Braverman and Zoe Zaslow-Braverman have smiles that make me feel lucky every day. Seeing the world through their eyes has given me greater focus and their genuine love of life is always an inspiration. This book is for the three of them, my loves.

At an earlier stage, this work was supported by an American Dissertation Fellowship from the American Association of University Women. Chapter 4 of this book has appeared in a slightly different version in *Girlhood Studies* vol. 1, no. 2 (2009).

INTRODUCTION

# A Decade after Spice: Girl Power Media Culture in the New Millennium

## Shrink-Wrapping Femininity and Feminism: The Girl of Girl Power

In 2000, the WB network premiered *The Gilmore Girls*, a television dramedy about a single mother, Lorelai, and her teen daughter, Rory. In the first episode viewers learned that Lorelai, now the thirty-two-year-old manager of a New England inn, shocked her wealthy family when she left home at age sixteen with a baby in utero and a determination to support herself without financial assistance from her parents. The series revolves around the mother-daughter relationship casting it as primarily democratic, with Lorelai offering Rory dating advice and flavored lip balm, while still imposing the occasional discipline.

In an episode that first aired in the winter of 2001, Rory and Lorelai are joined by Dean, Rory's teen boyfriend, as they watch a repeat of the 1960s domestic sitcom, *The Donna Reed Show*. On the episode they watch, Donna is disappointed that her husband has not called to tell her that he will be home late from work even though she has spent hours preparing his dinner. At the end of the program Donna forgives her husband, teasingly claiming that after ten years of marriage she has finally learned to accept that he is not really late for dinner but rather early for breakfast. As they watch the show, Lorelai and Rory create their own dialogue that mocks Donna Reed's complacency and submissiveness. Dean has a different perspective on Reed's role as a housewife: "I don't know—it all seems kind of nice to me . . . families hanging together. I mean, a wife cooking dinner for her husband. And look—she seems really happy." Dean recalls that his mother made dinner for his father before she started working and that she still prepares the family's weekend meals; defensively, he asks whether Rory would consider his mother an oppressed housewife. Rory explains to Dean that the difference between his mother and the women of the 1950s and 1960s, like Donna Reed, is choice. Dean's mother has a choice to cook or not, whereas Donna Reed was *expected* to thanklessly serve her family and look beautiful while doing it.

Later in the episode, sixteen-year-old Rory, who is house-sitting for her neighbor, invites Dean to keep her company. Wearing pearls and a vintage 1950s-style dress, Rory welcomes Dean and reveals that she has prepared a meat and potatoes dinner for him. As she serves dessert, Rory realizes that she forgot to make the dinner rolls. Mocking the perfection expected of the prefeminist wife, Rory jokes that she will have to turn in her pearls if the oversight is caught (presumably by the "good wife" police). Though Dean appreciates the meal, he lets Rory know that he does not expect her to be like a woman from the 1950s. Rory, known for being quite studious, then reveals that she has been researching Donna Reed and discovered that the actress "*did* do the whole milk and cookies wholesome big skirt thing, but aside from that, she was an uncredited producer and director on her television show, which made her one of the first women television executives. Which is actually pretty impressive." The script leaves a sense of ambiguity behind Rory's intentions; she never reveals whether the performance of the doting homemaker was to please Dean with the postwar wifely role he admired or if it was to teach him a lesson about female liberation by reminding him what the postfeminist Rory brings to the relationship.

The playful border crossings between girlishness and female empowerment, the offer of demureness and the demand for independence, and the ambiguity surrounding feminist intention, all depicted in this episode of the *Gilmore Girls*, are characteristic of girl power media, or media produced for girls and women after the late 1990s. Over the past nearly twenty years, girl power has represented an expansive media culture that encourages girls and women to identify both as traditionally feminine objects *and* as powerful feminist agents. Girl power media culture has well-defined characteristics that are visible across media and have continued to be relevant over time. Rooted in a neoliberal language of choice, girl power offers girls and women a sense that they can choose when to be girly and when to be powerful, when to be mother and when to be professional, when to be sexy for male pleasure and when to be sexy for their own pleasure. These states are both stable and liminal; one is always powerful as a girl, and yet this story about girlhood suggests that girls can play with power taking it on and off at will.

The term "girl power" entered our everyday lexicon when the short-lived, but overwhelmingly, successful British pop singing group, The Spice Girls, proclaimed that girl power was a way to identify with feminism without having to use what had become a "dirty word."[1] The Spice Girls, composed of five female performers each representing a different manufactured identity—Scary, Posh, Baby, Sporty, and Ginger—promoted a notion of girl power that was both feminine and feminist; they celebrated the athletic beside the cute and the spicy rage at being oppressed beside the desire to be decorated with the trimmings of femininity. Decked out in miniskirts, plunging necklines, and go-go boots, The Spice Girls sang of female solidarity, demanded the ability to control their relationships, and voiced their sexual desires.

The Spice Girls made the term a household name but girl power quickly moved beyond a catchy slogan to represent a cultural moment in which girls not only had an increase in purchasing power but also required industry executives to create a new consumer profile. Teen girls have long been attractive as a market because they have disposable income, more leisure time than adults, and are associated with adolescent looseness and experimentation.[2] But after a postwar boom in market interest in teen girls,[3] "the American public [began] to shift its focus away from the figure of the teenage girl" whose identity became more complicated as perceptions of sexuality and gender changed in the 1960s.[4] By the late 1990s, however, advertisers and media producers were again starting to take note of teen girls' market potential.[5] Teenagers, especially girls, were seen as an ideal target market that spent an estimated eighty-five billion dollars per year.[6] Between 1997 and 1999, *Adweek*, *Brandweek*, *Fortune*, and *Time* magazines all published articles declaring the late 1990s the era of girl power. *Fortune* devoted six pages to "Girl Power" claiming that "the teen girl [was] back with a vengeance" and that she was attracted to advertising that depicted girls and women in male-dominated fields, "kick[ing] butt" on the sports field, and being in control of style trends.[7] Suddenly, girls were everywhere— on the cover of *Spin* magazine's "The Girl Issue," buying newly launched magazines specifically marketed to them,[8] starring in well-received teen television dramas and sitcoms,[9] serving as leading characters in animated shows,[10] headlining in Lillith Fair, an all-women's summer music festival, and featuring on the big screen in movies.[11] The girls in these girl power media texts were different from the girls of yore. These girls were not demure, vulnerable, and passive;[12] girl power girls had a "take-charge dynamism."[13]

Unlike the pop group who brought the term to the fore, girl power itself was not a passing trend. Girl power culture extends far beyond the Spice Girls or any other individual texts, characters, pop stars, or celebrities; it is diffused through all media, especially media addressed to, or engaged with, by girl audiences, in a postfeminist era.[14] Girl power defines a new model of girlhood replete with a postfeminist system of values and practices.

The girl represented in girl power media attempts to shrink-wrap feminist sensibilities with feminine styling. She believes that she should be treated as an equal to her male peers, that she should be in control of her own body, that she is entitled to play tough and be smart, that she can, and will, support herself financially, and that her future should be self-determined. Furthermore, she believes that she has a core of inner (girl) power on which to draw as she combats oppression and directs her own life. But the girl of girl power culture also feels she has a right to enjoy her sexuality, to revel in the desire she elicits, and to have a future in which the care of a child, and sometimes a husband, is of central importance. The girl of girl power shifts our conceptualization of femininity so that the cultural narrative about what it means to be a girl is upset and rewritten. A simple profile of the girl of girl power culture is easy to construct, but *Feminism, Inc.* extends beyond this two-dimensional character sketch, exploring how teen girls growing up in girl power make sense of what it means to be female, feminine, and feminist in this era.

Drawing on interviews with seventy teen girls, I explore the negotiative processes in which girls engage as the transgressive and commercial girl power cultural discourses they encounter in media collide with the constrained social, political, and economic realities of their lives. In this moment, when media adopts feminist rhetoric and images of strength, independence, and career success to code characters, pop music stars, and other celebrities as quintessential women, how do girls navigate their own encounters with gender discrimination, social impediments to economic advancement, and political barriers to equity? As girl power simultaneously reifies gendered social roles and rejects the cultural dualisms of masculinity and femininity, how do teen girls imagine their futures as adult women?

## GIRLS' STUDIES ON GIRL POWER

Feminists from various disciplines including media studies, sociology, psychology, English, and education have all contributed to the growing field of girls' studies, a field that has, of course, been interested in girl power.[15] Key scholars have begun to question the transformative potential of girl power media culture; Catherine Driscoll has queried: "Can feminism be a mass produced... product, and can merchandised relations to girls be authentic?" while Angela McRobbie has pondered whether it is possible for media to "incorporate the political aims of feminism... while pursuing an aggressive capitalist pathway."[16]

Grounded in a Marxist critique, Meenakshi Gigi Durham has noted that girl power will not—indeed cannot—fully challenge hegemonic paradigms of sexuality, beauty, and femininity because it is essentially a product located, produced, and distributed in a capitalist economy. Because the capitalist imperative requires that the worth of a cultural expression is based on its exchange value in the market rather than what it can contribute to the cultural commons or social progress, Durham concludes that girl power will benefit corporations who profit from girls' culture but will not serve girls themselves.[17] Writing for the popular press as "women, moms, and teachers," developmental psychology professors Sharon Lamb and Lyn Mikel Brown agree with Durham's position on girl power, describing it as a monster-strength media discourse that parents must protect girls from because it "only makes girls feel powerful when they are conforming to the cute, sweet, hot little shoppers [marketers] think girls should be."[18] In her more nuanced critique, Anita Harris argues that, as a commodity, girl power serves as a seemingly easy, but inauthentic, pathway to the type of success and agency previously denied to women. Girls can consume a (feminist) identity—purchase powerful clothing, buy CDs that contain pro-women lyrics, or learn a rhetoric of empowerment, for example—but girl power does not require an investment in social change.[19]

Though it cannot be denied that the market benefits from the mass production of feminist rhetoric, Catherine Driscoll has argued that pop feminism may have social potential worth analyzing and should not be dismissed simply because it is a lucrative discourse. She contends that the very fact that feminist politics is present, and generates huge income, in mainstream media makes evident a shift in dominant ideologies.[20] Most academic accounts of The Spice Girls, a girl power media text that has been widely analyzed, note that while the band is a commodity, formed through the corporate music machine (rather than emerging in a more "authentic" manner as in the quintessential garage band), that has garnered huge sums of money for the music and related industries, they offer a challenge to traditional narratives of femininity and "sell feminism as compatible with many traditional roles for girls."[21] As five young women, with five different personalities, the Spice Girls, according to Dafna Lemish, provide fans with a nonessentialist model of femininity. From this perspective, the Spice Girls encourage a postmodern approach to identity where gender is multiple and shifting, and in which all forms of femininity are "possible and legitimate."[22] The Spice Girls' presentation as women who return and manipulate the male gaze is also viewed as a challenge to sexual objectification. While typical femininity is associated with (sexual) passivity, The Spice Girls demand the ability to control their relationships by insisting in their lyrics, "I'll tell you what I want, what I really, really want."[23]

Similarly, *Buffy the Vampire Slayer*, a televisual media text often touted as a girl power series, is widely celebrated by media scholars as an example of how feminist politics can thrive in mainstream media. *Buffy the Vampire Slayer*, which debuted on television in 1997, told the tale of Buffy, a blonde, White, thin, middle-class teen girl whose destiny it was to protect the world by killing vampires.[24] The show's creator, Joss Whedon, is reported to have said that he wanted to create a female hero who was able to use her personal power to protect herself, unlike typical blondes in the horror genre who were usually weak victims.[25] Existing in a lineage of television women who successfully fought evil with their physical prowess and their mastery of weapons, Buffy was significant because unlike *Wonder Woman*, *Charlie's Angels*, and *Bionic Woman*, she was a teen.[26]

Consistent with her critique of girl power media in general, Durham argues that Buffy may be an atypical representation of a physically powerful teen girl but she is not an oppositional character because she does not challenge normative beauty, sexuality, or class and racial hierarchies.[27] Yet, like the Spice Girls, *Buffy* is frequently praised for its representation of a teen girl who denies the femininity/feminism divide and insists that one can be sexy/femme while still being strong/resistive.[28] Buffy serves as a site on which feminist activism and its backlash are both negotiated and repudiated; her embrace of fashion, normative beauty, and other girly acts work alongside her physical power and her warrior stance to create a hybrid female identity that challenges both the normative binary of femininity as well as that of feminism.[29] While this position may only be available to the Buffy character whose transgressions are tempered by her normative identity as heterosexual, middle class, White, and thin, Helford claims that Buffy's embrace of fashion, beauty culture, and other girly acts work alongside her physical power and her warrior stance to create a hybrid female identity that challenges the binary of femininity and feminism. *Buffy* may not be a feminist text but it is certainly laden with transgressive potential because it challenges gendered relations and requires viewers to negotiate perspectives on femininity and power.

The concern over girl power's social potential and its relationship to feminism is an important discussion, one that has not yet been exhausted. Yet investigations into girl culture demand a nuanced analysis not only of girl power texts but also of the impacts of living in the girl power era. As Aapola, Gonick, and Harris have asked, what happens to girls "when the value of self-determination and individuality becomes the new cultural ideal of femininity" without regard to girls' economic, political, and social realities?[30]

Harris begins to answer this in *Future Girl*, which moves beyond an analysis of specific girl power texts to provide a rich examination of the social and cultural landscape in which twenty-first-century girls are coming of age.[31] Situating girl power within neoliberalism, Harris theorizes that as our cultural imagination begins to position girls as power-brokers and self-determined citizens, and as girls, in actuality, become more visible as consumers, students, and employees, they may become vulnerable to increasing scrutiny and regulation from governments, educators, and market analysts who seek to know and control the girls they "manage" and in whom they invest. Moreover, this visibility may lead to a shift in how girls understand their social role. Neoliberalism raises individuals as pinnacles of civilization and suggests that individualism will thrive in a free-market economy rather than in a society whose foundation is one of social welfare.[32] In this scenario, power emerges from the choice-making of individuals rather than from structural supports or systemic change and the emphasis on personal responsibility leads to increasing attempts at self-improvement and self-monitoring. With Aapola and Gonick, Harris argues, "The neo-liberal incitement of individualism, rational choice, and self-realization bumps up against discourses of femininity creating contradictory and complex positions for girls."[33] Harris's analysis calls for additional research into the experience of growing up in girl power media culture. Her study paints a broad stroke over girls' varied social environments in Western nations, rather than exploring the specificity of either the American experience or the experience surrounding the mediascape. Moreover, there have been no in-depth studies exploring how girls in girl power media culture experience shifts in the conceptualization of power, sexuality, and gender identity. Indeed, Aapola, Gonick, and Harris advocate for further study of the ways in which neoliberalism impacts girls' lives: "A new phase of 'girls' studies' is needed; one which grapples with theorizing the changing conditions under which young women's diverse self-making occurs."[34]

In *Feminism, Inc.* I explore the lived experiences of seventy urban teen girls who are growing up in the girl power era. As the girls speak about contemporary media—with a distinct focus on television and music—I listen to their articulations on gender identity, class, sexuality, womanhood, and feminism. I analyze the disjuncture between the ways in which girls talk about their own lives, the ways in which media scholars have talked about girls' lives, and the ways in which popular media talks to and about girls. In doing so, I argue that girl power media culture is rooted in a neoliberal discourse in which urban teen girls come to understand female power as an individualistic stance rather than a collective achievement. Yet, girl power media culture also allows girls to engage with counter-normative discourses about female expression, sexual desire, and self-determination. Coming of age in girl power culture, girls experience a cultural discordance that arises in the tension between the neoliberal empowerment language and narratives that they adopt, and their real social and emotional experiences of gender, race, and class inequities. Paradoxically, while they employ a language of choice and encounter a revised narrative of female identity many of the girls in my study, particularly those from low-income communities of color, describe feeling confined in their style, voice, sexuality, and imaginings of the future.

The girls in this study have a far more complex relationship with the language and politics of girl power than we are led to believe by Durham's suggestion that girl power's "challenges to patriarchal interests are subsumed within a powerful discourse of complicity with dominant norms of femininity, sexuality, race, class, and the disciplining of the female body, all in the interests of capital."[35] Girl power *is* a watered-down feminist position available as a stylish accessory, but it is also a meaningful and widespread embodiment of some feminist positions that girls draw upon as they create their gender identities.

## Growing Up in Girl Power: The Organization of This Book

Before embarking on the lived experience of girl culture, which is the core of this text, the first chapter is dedicated to understanding the social, cultural, and political environment in which girl power media culture emerged and thrived. Chapter 1 provides a history of girl power, analyzing the cultural moment in which the discourse emerged. This chapter explores how girl power arose from conflicting, competing discourses, as a pro-girl, pro-sex, anti-oppression, in-your-face, cultural moment that was well suited for the consumer market. It investigates the moment in which cultural producers realized that by using the girly, pro-individual style adopted by the third-wave feminist and riot grrrl movements, they could profit from the fears of mothers whose daughters faced the "crisis" of growing up in a sexist society as well as from the guilt faced by mothers who were scapegoated by the feminist backlash.

Exploring the experience of growing up in girl power media culture requires a decentering of the media text and a focus onto the ways in which teen girls integrate, struggle with, negotiate, and embrace girl power media culture. In chapter 2, readers are introduced more fully to the methods employed and to the participants included in this project. Throughout this chapter I posit that one of the missing elements in the study of girls, media, and identity is research that combines an analysis of the cultural with the social. Analyses that focus on text and content, while a critical component of media studies, do not explore the complex relationship between media culture and audiences' interpretation and use of media. The large body of research on youth and media does not account for the social processes through which girls incorporate culture into their narratives of self nor does it enable an investigation of the ways in which girls weave media experiences with "real life" experiences to form gendered identities. The chapter ends with an introduction to the girls in this book and the environments in which they are coming of age.

Each of the subsequent four chapters explores how girls experience, make sense of, and negotiate gender identities in dialogue with notions of sexuality, style, independence, and feminism in girl power media culture. Chapter 3 explores how the girls in this book make sense of the images they see of female sexuality as a powerful and profitable commodity in pop music. This chapter queries: How do audiences determine who is a sexual subject and who is a sexual object in a contradictory mediascape? How do audiences make sense of a woman who presents herself as an agent in sexual encounters yet maintains a sexual image that is rooted in a stereotypically male-coded fantasy? In chapter 4, girls' everyday experiences with style are positioned beside their media experiences with girl power discourse about style. The findings of this chapter challenge cultural studies research that has celebrated the ways in which girls actively subvert dominant discourses about femininity and gender through knowledge and selection of fashion, adornment of the body, and subcultural communities surrounding style. Chapter 5 turns the analytic eye to girls' dreams of the future, and of what it means to be an independent woman. I ask how girls imagine creating a balance between career and family interests. This chapter finds that as the girls in this book think about their futures as mothers and as professionals, they experience a cultural discordance between the real experiences of the women in their lives and the girl power discourse of choice and self-determination. Grounded in discussions about diverse media texts such as Oprah Winfrey, *The View*, Jennifer Lopez, and *Saved by the Bell*, chapter 6 explores how girls in an era of girl power media define feminism. Is feminism still a movement for social change or does it become a stylish identity marker? In a media culture that normalizes female power, who is a feminist? Finally, the conclusion addresses the cultural discordance experienced by many girls as the mediated narrative of girlhood conflicts with the girls' social and economic realities and with the more localized cultural narratives they encounter about gender.

This book owes a great deal to the seventy girls who spent time with me discussing their lives, their media experiences, and their futures; Though I am aware that in both structure of the research process and in the production of this text, the power to name, to give voice to, and to analyze is imbalanced, I have attempted to build my critical analyses around the local and specific ways in which the girls understood their own worlds—both cultural and social. I encourage readers to do the same.

CHAPTER 1

# GROWLS AND WHIMPERS: THE ROOTS OF GIRL POWER DISCOURSE

BEFORE EMBARKING ON THE LIVED EXPERIENCE OF GIRL CULTURE, which is the core of this text, I dedicate this chapter to understanding the social, cultural, and political environment in which girl power media culture emerged and thrived. If the Spice Girls are responsible for introducing the expression to popular media, it was a convergence of four social and cultural movements that created the environment for girl power to emerge as a central organizing discourse in media culture. The soil became fertile for a girl power media culture in the late 1990s at the apex of the popularization of feminist psychosocial studies of girls, the conservative backlash against second-wave feminism, third-wave feminism, and the subcultural riot grrrl movement.

As discussed in the introduction, girl power discourse has been aptly linked to a neoliberal turn in which individualism and choice are prized. Gonick has produced an outstanding discussion linking the increased interest in girls to "an expression of the uncertainties, tensions, fears, and anxieties elicited by the rapid social, economic, and political changes taking place due to neoliberal policies."[1] Here she details how this social movement toward personal responsibility, and away from social welfare, leads to an increasing scrutiny of young people who are the individuals on which the future depends. Her summation of girls' import in this future dependency, which cites Erica Burman, is worth quoting at length:

> This development may be credited to the replacement of manual production with service work—a feminized sector—as the mainstay of the neoliberal economy. Relatedly, the shift in the economy from that of production to consumption privileges the feminine through women's and girls' long-standing association with consumption. Burman suggests that the proliferating psychological culture promoting emotional literacy (and therefore self-responsibility) also contributes to the feminization of neoliberal subjectivity. (362)

If changing girls' role in a new economy created interest in and desire to control girlhood, the four movements discussed later, all of which emerged within neoliberalism, worked within and beside this new role to create a moment ripe for girl power.

## The Tightening of the Psychosocial Corset

In the early 1990s, parents, teachers, advertisers, and other adults interested in girls' lives were suddenly barraged with academic and institutional reports that warned against a growing crisis in girls' lives. These reports cautioned that as girls approach adolescence, the experience of living in a patriarchal culture catches up with them; this male-dominated culture leads to the development of low self-esteem and silences girls in interpersonal relationships and classrooms. The academic reports were followed closely by parenting advice books and magazine articles guiding parents to protect their daughters and shield them from a "girl poisoning" culture.[2]

In 1992, Carol Gilligan and Lyn Mikel Brown of Harvard's project on Women's Psychology and Girls' Development published a groundbreaking study tracking the psychosocial development of seven- to eighteen-year-old girls at a private day school in Cleveland, Ohio. The researchers found that as girls near adolescence they lose confidence in themselves, feel a growing confusion about their own emotions and desires, find their voices constricting, and lose the ability to articulate their experiences and thoughts.[3] Deeming the experience a "relational impasse," Gilligan and Brown raised concern about girls' emotional health; if girls were shutting down, being less than honest with themselves and their peers, unable to communicate about their experiences, how could they develop into psychologically stable women?

One year earlier, similar findings had been reported by the American Association of University Women (AAUW) whose researchers polled three thousand young women between the ages of nine and fifteen on their feelings about themselves, their families, friends, and schools.[4] Their study, *Shortchanging Girls, Shortchanging America*, found that as girls approach the teen years they have a difficult time retaining their self-esteem and feeling comfortable with who they are. According to Peggy Orenstein,

> The results confirmed what many women already knew too well. For a girl, passage into adolescence is not just marked by menarche or a few new curves. It is marked by a loss of confidence in herself and her abilities, especially in math and science. It is marked by a scathingly critical attitude toward her body and a blossoming sense of personal inadequacy.[5]

While the Harvard Project's research had focused almost entirely on economically privileged White girls, the AAUW report included African-American girls and Latinas. *Shortchanging Girls, Shortchanging America* found that White and Latina girls have a more difficult time retaining their self-esteem than do African-American girls who "maintain a stronger sense of both personal and familial importance."[6]

In 1992 the AAUW followed its report on self-esteem with *How Schools Shortchange Girls*, declaring that girls and women were nearly absent from school curricula. The report suggested that a consistent lack of role models, and the continually repeated and silent message that women's histories and experiences are unworthy of attention, may contribute to girls' diminishing self-esteem. Moreover, the report raised concern over girls' participation in math and science, areas that they did well in as young girls but felt they were not good at, not interested in, or not suited for, as they grew older. Two years later, Myra and David Sadker published *Failing at Fairness: How America's Schools Cheat Girls*. The pair, whose earlier studies of gender bias in education had centered on unfair teaching practices and sex-segregated courses, now focused on the "more powerful hidden curriculum that surfaced in the way teachers treat children and children treat one another."[7]

Based on observations and interviews, the Sadkers concluded that teachers interacted more with male students, asked male students more complex questions, and provided male students with more specific feedback. In addition, they found that boys mistreated their female peers with little institutional consequence or punishment. The Sadkers' findings were identical to those of the other researchers. They found that girls' self-esteem, level of academic achievement, and future goals are strong during elementary school but weaken as adolescence approaches. They used the metaphor of a corset tightening around a waist to describe how "adolescence closes around these precocious, authoritative girls... [who] begin to restrict their interests, confine their talents, [and] pull back on their dreams."[8]

The early discussions on girls' development may have reached a relatively small group of academics, feminists, and youth development workers but in 1994 two books published by the popular press placed the crisis in girls' lives on the national radar. In *School Girls: Young Women, Self-Esteem, and the Confidence Gap*, journalist Peggy Orenstein documented the year she spent as an observer of girls in two California middle schools. Influenced by the AAUW study on self-esteem, Orenstein opted to spend half of her time at a mostly White suburban school whose students were from a variety of class backgrounds, and the other half at an urban school populated almost entirely by students of color raised in low-income families. Combining documentary sketches of girls at the two schools, along with research from the AAUW report, Orenstein confirmed that in schools and homes girls were being silenced as well as rewarded for compliance while their male counterparts were praised for their assertiveness and aggression. *School Girls* drew national attention; it was well received by major newspapers and excerpted in *The New York Times Magazine* as well as in *Glamour* magazine.[9]

Pushing the conversation even more rapidly from the halls of academia to those of secondary schools and homes was the 1994 release of Mary Pipher's *Reviving Ophelia: Saving the Selves of Adolescent Girls*. A *New York Times* bestseller for three years, *Reviving Ophelia* used a plethora of case studies that ultimately painted a bleak picture of adolescence for American females. Based on sessions with clients she had met with in therapy, and interviews with other girls, Pipher found that "with puberty, girls face enormous pressure to split into false selves."[10]

Using dramatic metaphors, Pipher positioned girls as "saplings in a hurricane," "vulnerable trees that the winds blow with gale strength," and "planes and ships that... crash and burn in a social and developmental Bermuda triangle."[11] She argued that parents, educators, and other concerned adults must intervene to save and empower girls.

Pipher's work has been rightly criticized for pathologizing teen girls without a rigorous body of knowledge to report on,[12] but as a bestseller it brought cultural attention to girls' psychosocial development in a patriarchal culture and led the way for a girl power discourse and market that focused on reclaiming the innocence of girlhood while empowering teen girls to fight against a hostile social environment.

Following the mass interest in *Reviving Ophelia*, girls' social and psychological development became a popular discussion topic in parenting magazines. *Parenting* magazine ran a "Special Report" on raising daughters; *Time* magazine called *Ophelia* a sacred text for parents of adolescent daughters.[13] Book publishers followed suit, releasing scores of books for girls and their caregivers, including:

- *Power: Young Women Speak Out* (1995)
- *No More Frogs to Kiss: 99 Ways to Give Economic Power to Girls* (1995)
- *Growing a Girl: Seven Strategies for Raising a Strong Spirited Daughter* (1996)
- *Raising Strong Daughters* (1996)
- *Celebrating Girls: Nurturing and Empowering Our Daughters* (1996)
- *How to Raise an Independent and Professional Successful Daughter* (1997)
- *Brave New Girls: Creative Ideas to Help Girls Be Confident, Healthy, and Happy* (1997)
- *Sugar in the Raw: Voices of Young Black Girls in America* (1997)
- *Girls Speak Out: Finding Your True Self* (1997)
- *The Girls' Guide to Life: How to Take Charge of the Issues that Affect You* (1997)
- *33 Things Every Girl Should Know: Stories, Songs, Poems, and Smart Talk by 33 Extraordinary Women* (1998)
- *Any Girl Can Rule the World* (1998)
- *Girls Seen and Heard: 52 Life Lessons for Our Daughters* (1998)

- *Does Jane Compute? Preserving Our Daughters' Place in the Cyber Revolution* (1998)
- *Stay True: Short Stories for Strong Girls* (1998)
- *Deal with It! A Whole New Approach to Your Body, Brain, and Life as a gURL* (1999)
- *Everyday Ways to Raise Smart, Strong, Confident Girls* (1999)
- *How to Mother a Successful Daughter: A Practical Guide to Empowering Girls from Birth to Eighteen* (1999)
- *200 Ways to Raise a Girl's Self Esteem: An Indispensable Guide for Parents, Teachers, and Other Concerned Caregivers* (1999)
- *Girl Boss: Running the Show Like the Big Chicks* (1999)
- *Ophelia Speaks: Adolescent Girls Write about Their Search For Self* (1999)
- *Cool Careers for Girls* series (1999–2002)
- *Be True to Yourself: A Daily Guide for Teenage Girls* (2000)
- See *Jane Win: The Rimm Report on How 1,000 Girls Became Successful Women* (2000)
- *Toolbox for Our Daughters: Building Strength, Confidence, and Integrity* (2000)
- *Picture the Girl: Young Women Speak Their Minds* (2000)
- *Body Outlaws: Young Women Write about Body Image and Identity* (2000)
- *Girls Rule* (2001)
- *Raising Confident Girls: 100 Tips for Parents and Teachers* (2001)
- *Go Girl! Raising Healthy, Confident, & Successful Girls through Sports* (2002)
- *Every Girl Tells a Story: A Celebration of Girls Speaking Their Minds* (2002)
- *GirlWise: How to be Confident, Capable, Cool, and in Control* (2002)
- *Girls Will Be Girls: Raising Confident and Courageous Daughters* (2003)
- *The Girl's Guide to Loving Yourself* (2003)
- *Ophelia's Mom: Loving and Letting Go of Your Adolescent Daughter* (2003)
- *Dealing with the Stuff that Makes Life Tough: The 10 Things that Stress Teen Girls Out and How to Cope with Them* (2004)

- *Real Girl, Real World* (2005)
- *You Go, Girl* (2005)
- *Stressed-Out Girls: Helping Them Thrive in the Age of Pressure* (2006)
- *Raising Girls: Why Girls Are Different and How to Help Them Grow Up Happy and Strong* (2006)
- *All You Need to Know about Raising Girls* (2007)
- *My Feet Aren't Ugly: A Girl's Guide to Loving Herself from the Inside Out* (2007)

While an early feminist child-rearing book bearing the title *How to Raise an Independent and Professional Successful Daughter* was published in the late 1970s, it was not until girls' development research became a part of popular culture that the wave of girl-rearing books focusing on empowerment hit the shelves. The number of publications on the topic in a few years demonstrates the public preoccupation with girls as well as the belief that girls and their parents were a new market to grab, and one which would respond to the concept of empowering themselves and "saving" their daughters.

These parenting and self-help books spoke about the loss of esteem girls met at adolescence, the hatred girls felt for their bodies, the self-mutilation (from cutting and eating disorders) girls inflicted on themselves, and the failure girls experienced in schools. They used terms such as empowerment, success, confidence, and voice to speak about alternatives to traditional femininity. Many of these books instructed parents to help challenge this crisis for girls by critiquing and changing the stories that girls heard and the images that girls saw of themselves and of adult women. For example, in *200 Ways to Raise a Girl's Self-Esteem*, Will Glennon suggests that young women be encouraged to do a "media inventory" where they examine the mediated images of women.[14] These parental guides sometimes suggested that parents introduce their daughters to books and movies that depicted girls and women as strong, powerful, successful, and proud. Barbara Mackoff, for instance, devoted a section in *Growing a Girl* to listing authors who write books for young people that "celebrate women and girls."[15] She also encouraged parents to select movies with strong female role models for their daughters, sighting a 1976 study on sex role development, which she wrote suggests that "equal sex-role models in movies produced a *more* enduring change than similar models in picture books."[16]

In *Reviving Ophelia*, Pipher also linked the crisis in girls' development to "the pressure [that] comes from schools, magazines, music, television, advertisements and movies."[17] She explained that, while the voices of women and girls had been silenced throughout American history, in today's mass media–saturated society, girls are surrounded by "sophisticated advertising in which [they hear] that happiness comes from consuming the right products."[18] In her estimation, these advertisements, along with other mass media influences, are filled with messages that teach girls that they are not valued in society and that in order to be acceptable they must look, smell, dress, speak, and think in culturally approved ways. Pipher determined that today's girls are growing up in a "girl-poisoning culture."[19] The crisis—and its supposed girl power solution—received state legitimization in 1997 when the Department of Health and Human Services launched the aptly named "Girl Power": a public health campaign aimed at boosting girls' self-esteem and self-awareness to reduce their risky behaviors.

Though the public mind was already made up about the crisis in girls' lives, academic research began to explore the nuances of girls' development, specifically focusing on the ways in which race and class influenced the experience of growing up as a girl. These studies sought to further investigate what was suggested in the AAUW's findings about the differences in responses from Latina, White, and Black girls, as well as Gilligan and Brown's speculation that girls who "live in the margins, who are so clearly at odds with the dominant models of beauty and perfection, [may be able to] reveal the cultural hand behind these standards."[20] Erkut et al. argued that "race or ethnicity, social class, and urbanization of residence... mediate gender in ways that produce qualitatively different 'female' experiences for girls and young women" so that the racial, class, and regional contexts in which development occurs must be given equal attention to its gendered environment.[21]

Niobe Way found that the multiracial urban high school girls she interviewed did not constrict their voices, as did the girls in Brown and Gilligan's study, but rather used their voices to remain in connection with parents and same-sex peers. The girls relied on these relationships for guidance and support and felt secure enough in them to express disappointments and differences. The young women in her study were more likely to silence themselves in relationships with boys, which Way speculated was a result of associating with men who did not listen to them and/or had been violent toward them. Even in this silence, however, the girls appeared not to turn inward. Rather, as they got older and more mature, the girls seemed to feel more comfortable in their voices. Way suggested that urban girls, especially those from working-class families, learn from their mothers that they must use their voices or they will disappear in a world that does not seem to value them.[22]

Lyn Mikel Brown who had worked with Gilligan on *Meeting at the Crossroads* also turned to study the instances where girls' voices appear strong and clear. In *Raising Their Voices*, Brown explored how class contributed to the development of voice, self-knowledge, and peer relationships in two communities of girls in Maine, one from a working-class region and the other from a middle-class region. She found that the girls from the working-class community were outspoken in relationships, distrustful of authorities, loud and brazen, while their middle-class peers were preoccupied with where they fit into the social and material hierarchy of school and society. This preoccupation led them to suppress the views they feared would cause them to be ostracized. Thus they silenced themselves and turned inward rather than forging connections with one another. Ultimately the competition of the middle-class girls—over who would be closest to the top of the hierarchy—threatened and broke the collectivity they tried to form. Like Way, Brown found that girls who are already outside of the margins, who could never achieve "perfect girl" status, are more likely to be connected to themselves and others.[23]

Although these studies complicated the field of girls' developmental psychology and offered more complex views about girls' lives, what made its way into the mainstream press and solidified in the psyche of American girls and their parents was primarily the image of the victimized girl, or the girl in crisis. Combined with the backlash against second-wave feminism, the emergence of third-wave feminism, and the riot grrrl movement, the concern over the crisis in girls' lives created the perfect moment for the creation of a new market and the perfect moment for girl power media culture to emerge.[24]

## The Backlash against Second-Wave Feminism

At the same time as patriarchy was being blamed for the supposed crisis in girls' lives, mothers were being blamed for a whole other set of problems that girls (and boys) were experiencing. According to conservative critics, it was not growing up in a "girl-poisoning" culture but rather the decreasing involvement of mothers in the lives of their children that was at the root of the troubles. In this "undeclared war against women," mothers who worked outside of the home were blamed for the supposed breakdown of traditional family values and became scapegoats for the decline in educational scores, the rising crime rate, and the increasingly early involvement of youth in drugs and sex.[25] In addition they were told to fear the unhappiness and solitude that they had supposedly earned alongside their economic and social progress.[26] Women were accused of having been victorious in their battle against patriarchy but ultimately dissatisfied, lonely, depressed losers in life.[27] Apropos of the neoliberal turn, the feminist backlash of the 1980s and 1990s blamed individuals—women, in particular—for social ills that resulted from governmental policies enacted during the Reagan-Bush presidencies. These conservative administrations withdrew economic support for education, welfare, job training, sex education, and youth programming all while touting a return to "family values." Underlying this dichotomy was the philosophical belief that government is not responsible for social welfare but rather responsible for protecting individual rights and the free market. As such, individuals are responsible for their own economic and social well-being. The backlash was an attempt to divert public scrutiny and blame from governmental policy and toward individual choices made by women.

Historically, successes in movements for equal rights have been followed by conservative backlash. However, scholars argue that the backlash of the 1980s was unique in that it couched antifeminism in a "language of liberation."[28] Representations of women took a new turn in which the "good" woman was both feminine and seemingly feminist. Advertisers picked up on this and used "feminist rhetoric [such as sisterhood] to market policies that hurt women or to peddle the same old sexist products or to conceal anti-feminist views."[29] The backlash against feminism took its toll on all women—feminists and nonfeminists alike. The backlash had policy impacts, such as decreasing support for women's reproductive freedom, as well as social impacts, such as stifling women's career advancement. Less frequently addressed, the backlash had emotional impacts; it created in some women a sense of failure, personal ineptitude, and guilt.[30]

Marketers were quick to pick up on the guilt and vulnerability that mothers faced as families shifted to two incomes in increasing numbers.[31] For businesses of all kinds, working women's guilt, the increasing consumer market, and the change in family structures created new business prospects.[32] Companies that had previously targeted homemakers began to market their products toward working women by changing the tone of their advertising and the images of women in them. "Guilt Marketing" is aimed at "working parents... who are said to feel constantly culpable about never having enough quality time to spend with their kids."[33] This advertising targets caretakers whose "vulnerability arises from a double bind: a desire to work hard, achieve, and make money, and an equally strong desire to be with their families.... The emotional hook is guilt."[34] In the media and toy industries, this change in women's roles meant a new focus on selling educational products to mothers who had limited time to spend with their children but who, nonetheless, wanted them to learn certain values and skills.[35] By the early 1990s, guilt-marketing experts in the toy industry began to capitalize on the fear of a crisis in girls' lives. They identified a new market of parents, especially mothers, who sought out nonsexist toys and consumer products for their children.[36] Still marketed as educational, girl power media and toys were said to empower girls to break out of traditional positions and to "save them" from becoming victims of the crisis.

One well-known example of a girl power toy is the American Girl Doll. American Girl was introduced to the market in 1986 as a doll that gave girls the equivalent of "chocolate cake with vitamins" by providing them with a beautiful doll that also celebrated girlhood throughout American history.[37] In the collection, which started with three dolls but now includes fourteen, each doll is accompanied by a series of books that situate her within a particular era, region of the country, and ethnic identity. Created by Pleasant Rowland, a Wisconsin educator and entrepreneur, the collection was created as an antidote to Barbie, who Rowland felt was too sexual for young girls, and Cabbage Patch, the popular baby dolls of the era.[38] Where Barbie encourages girls to step into the role of a teen or adult women, and baby dolls encourage girls to position themselves as nurturing mother, the corporate website explains that American Girl Dolls—each of whom is nine when her series begins—allows girls to "enjoy girlhood" and shows "girls today that they can do great things if they believe in themselves and each other."

The stories that accompany these dolls position girls as key players in the everyday life of American history. Felicity demonstrates bravery by rescuing a male apprentice who is trying to break his work contract to fight in the American Revolution; Addy escapes from slavery and helps her mother to make a life in freedom; and Julie uses Title IX to fight for a spot on the boys' basketball team. Critics note that the American Girl series largely perpetuates dominant ideologies by creating stories in which the dolls engage in typically feminine activities and hold conservative views on womanhood and femininity.[39] Moreover, the American Girl catalogue (with its endless choice of doll clothes and hair care products) and store (which includes a doll hair salon and doll ear piercing), promote traditionally feminine play such as doll grooming and dressing.[40] These dolls, sold as much to mothers as to little girls, were marketed as nonsexist and embodied the contradictions of girl power: a healthy doll body and a spunky girl story accompanied by a push for endless consumption and a focus on grooming and style.

## The Other Backlash: Teen Pregnancy and Criminalizing the Black Teen Body

Shortly before the country began to talk about the White, middle-class girl in crisis, it had been discussing the African-American female teen who represented an altogether different kind of social problem. White middle-class girls were portrayed as hurting themselves, losing connection with one another, mutilating their own bodies, and falling into depressive states. Pop psychologists and government officials brainstormed over ways to save these girls. In essence, these White, middle-class girls were portrayed as victims. Their African-American peers, however, were caught in the middle of a racist, anti-change, conservative backlash. Although they, too, were portrayed as being caught in a crisis, they were more often depicted as being deviants who *caused* a social, economic crisis. Demonized, these girls were imagined to be hurting the nation as they hurt themselves.

Teen pregnancy became part of a national conversation in the mid-1970s when Senator Kennedy proposed the National School-Age Mother and Child Health Act. This legislation, which did not pass, expressed a concern that there was an increase in teen pregnancies and that such pregnancies played a pivotal role in the growing rates of welfare dependency and high school dropouts. Repeatedly, throughout the late 1970s, teen mothers were talked about as a drain on the welfare system and a cause of national poverty. Law- and policy makers overwhelmingly believed that in order to fight this growing problem, there should be increased access to contraception and abortion for young, poor women.[41]

In the 1980s, however, with the rise of neoliberal policies enacted by the conservatives in federal government, the story changed. Kristin Luker documents that gradually, "[t]he problem was not teenagers' pregnancies but their sexual activity; the remedy was not contraception but chastity; and thus attention should not be devoted to the young woman but to her family, who needed help in regaining its control over her."[42] The courts began limiting girls' control over their own bodies; they passed parental notification or consent laws and upheld the Hyde Amendment, which banned the use of public funds for abortions unless the life of the mother was at stake.[43]

Neoliberal discourse made teen mothers—particularly African-American teen mothers—the scapegoats for the social and economic problems facing the nation just as it had with adult working mothers who benefited from feminism. Deborah Tolman elaborates:

> On the body of the Urban Girl, social context becomes confused and confounded with race: she is a girl of color, and so she must be poor.... She is a daughter of a single mother. She is incapable of delaying gratification, fails in school, does not secure employment, and most of all she is sexually promiscuous, lacking in morality or family values, and out of control. She is at risk and at fault. She embodies the problem of teenage pregnancy.[44]

This picture was disturbing in many ways. It blamed African-American teen mothers for reproducing poverty, rather than casting a skeptical eye on a conservative administration that decreased funding for social welfare programs and supported "trickle down" economic policies. Moreover, it was historically inaccurate; in reality, overall teen pregnancies had actually decreased in the 1970s and 1980s, as had births among unmarried African-American teens. In fact, the group for whom there was a rapid increase in birthrates after the mid-1980s was unmarried White teenagers.[45] Though the teen mother population was not directly addressed by the girl power market, it represents yet another discursive construction of the female adolescent in neoliberalism and demonstrates Gonick's proposal that the increasing cultural interest in teen girls—and thus the development of girl power media culture—is rooted in the ambivalence and fear arising from the neoliberal politics and practices of the 1980s and 1990s.[46]

## Sisters and Girls: Third-Wave Feminisms

While conservative pundits were battling it out with academic feminists, young women were contributing their own voices to debates over these issues—declaring themselves initiators of a third-wave feminist movement committed to many of the same core issues as second-wave feminism.[47] Second-wave feminism (approximately 1960s–1980s) took on many forms, but a common goal was "to intervene in, and transform, the unequal power relations between men and women."[48] In general, second-wave feminism provided a critique of women's social, political, and economic positions within the social structure. Major focal points in discussions of feminism were issues of the body (objectification, violence, reproductive rights, sexuality, sports, and work), difference (between women and men, as well as among women in terms of sexuality, race, class, ethnicity, and nationality), and the public versus private (work and home, personal and political). These same issues continue to be relevant to third-wave feminists, yet third wavers are determined to use different strategies than their feminist fore-sisters as they attain gender equality. Indeed, strategies for transforming "unequal power relations" and creating a more equitable social structure have been in debate through the history of feminist struggles for equity and justice; however, the themes of "the personal is political" and "sisterhood is powerful" were central to the second-wave feminist movement. Rather than focus on a critique of femininity and a unification of all women, third-wave feminist politics has focused on an embrace of femininity and girliness as well as a celebration of diversity among women.[49]

"The personal is political" served as a capstone phrase and strategy for second-wave feminists. This broad statement served two purposes: it allowed women to see that the oppression they personally experienced in the home, in relationships, and in the workplace was part of a structural patriarchy that organized women's lives, and it challenged women (and men) to reflect upon the political implications of their personal choices. As such, this approach to politics encouraged women to fight collectively for social change and also to work individually to make changes in their own lives that reflected a feminist ontology. One of the most visually stimulating, and therefore most media-friendly, activist stances marked by this philosophy, was feminists' rejection of aesthetic femininity. Feminists who chose to let their body hair grow freely, to burn their bras, or to dump their makeup challenged the patriarchal positioning of women as objects of a male gaze.

While third-wave feminism supports the notion that "the personal is political" it challenges the second-wave critique of femininity often associated with this motto. Jennifer Baumgardner and Amy Richards, easily the most vocal third-wave spokeswomen, argue that what marks the third-wave movement is not a new philosophical understanding of gender, but a new feminist strategy in which the feminine is celebrated, accentuated, and consciously performed rather than dismissed as a source of oppression. As a way of explicating this revaluation of the feminine, Baumgardner and Richards offer the case of makeup. Instead of understanding beauty products as "a sign of our sway to the marketplace and the male gaze," third wavers believe that wearing makeup can be "sexy, campy, ironic" or decorative.[50] The "girlie culture rebellion" of third-wave feminism insists that a woman can be sexual and stylish without being exploited.

Equally important to second-wave feminism was the notion and the title of an early compilation of feminist writing "sisterhood is powerful."[51] This movement-defining mantra imagined a united collective of women who would fight against gender oppression. The expression suggested that women shared certain experiences as women and that together women could engender change. Rather than focusing on difference or on individual moments of empowerment, "sisterhood is powerful" drew upon the commonalities of women and their ability to coalesce around common oppressive conditions.

By the early 1980s, feminists of color and working-class feminists began to question the notion of "sisterhood" in feminism. Pointing out that the middle-class White women who dominated the feminist movement had not relinquished class and race privilege, did not include a critique of racism or classism within the feminist critique of patriarchy, and did not acknowledge that there was not just one female experience, feminists of color challenged the notion of universal "sisterhood."[52] This analysis reminded all feminists that women cannot be, and are not, defined solely by their gender and thus cannot take for granted that they share an experience of gender oppression. Still, the notion of collectivity and unified struggle remained important to many second-wave feminists, including feminists of color.[53]

For third-wave feminism, collectivity is not necessarily a central strategy. Though Heywood and Drake mark coalition as central to third-wave politics,[54] Baumgardner and Richards suggest that a defining characteristic of third-wave feminism is the sense that while girls are not necessarily activist in their feminism they are "living feminist lives"—which is exemplified by their "righteousness" and "sense of entitlement."[55] From this perspective, third wavers have attempted to carve out a unique social movement in which the feminist philosophy of gender equity of the second wave is enacted, rather than fought for, by third-wave feminists. In this model, feminism already exists and is available for women to enter into at will. Feminism does not insist upon a unified struggle to resist patriarchal oppression but may be an individual choice to embrace one's feminist inheritance.[56] In this, third-wave feminism is also well suited for an era of neoliberal politics; it is consumerist (or at least not anti-consumerist) and accepts, if begrudgingly, the "living of feminist lives" as opposed to the collective struggle for social, economic, and political change, as the mark of a feminist.

## Girl with a Growl

Riot grrrl, a movement that emerged out of the punk scene of the early 1990s, is often considered to be the authentic predecessor to a commercial girl power media culture. The riot grrrl movement was a "young feminist (sub)cultural movement that [merged] feminist consciousness and punk aesthetics, politics, and style."[57] This community of young women formed itself through self-produced publications, music, web pages, and meetings that challenged patriarchal ideologies and celebrated female identities. Using low-end, low-cost technologies to spread their messages and to solidify their movement, riot grrrls' control over cultural production in an age of increasing media consolidation was overtly political.[58]

Riot grrrl lore has several versions of the movement's emergence, but it is widely accepted that riot grrrl began when, after hearing about race riots, members of the female punk bands Bikini Kill and Bratmobile declared that the punk scene would benefit from a "girl riot." The band members began imagining ways to orchestrate this "riot" and their first step was to create a community of women and girls in the alternative music scene. Relying on the punk DIY (Do It Yourself) ethic, members of these bands began creating "zines" and feminist consciousness-raising groups.[59] Organized around demarginalizing young women in the punk scene (or what was often referred to as "Revolution Girl-Style Now!"), the movement gained momentum when more than fifty female bands performed on "Girls' Night" at the 1991 International Pop Underground Convention.[60]

When word of riot grrrl reached the mainstream press, Bikini Kill's Kathleen Hanna lied to an *LA Weekly's* reporter, claiming that riot grrrl had chapters in several cities across the country. This lie, told to generate such chapters, worked; within several months new groups formed across the country and the movement eventually became international.[61]

Riot grrrls' political quest was rooted in the second-wave feminist sense of the "personal as political." Many zine articles, songs, poems, stories, and art pieces challenged traditional cultural perceptions of beauty and body image, confronted the pervasiveness of sexual abuse, and displaced "compulsory heterosexuality." Girls spoke openly about their pain and anger in relation to violence committed upon them physically, politically, socially, and emotionally.[62] Moreover, their loose regional and national networks maintained through zines, records, and web sites "challenged ideological constructions of public and private space" by broadcasting the voices of girls and young women.[63] Riot grrrl was also rooted in a radical feminist belief in separatism as a strategy for cultural change. As Kearney argues, "[I]n order to establish their own sociopolitical identity" grrrls separated from "males to act on behalf of females... from adults to act on behalf of youth and... from the mainstream to act on behalf of radical culture and politics."[64]

As with third-wave feminists, celebration of iconic femininity was also central to the riot grrrl conversation. Riot grrrl styles ranged from alternative and androgynous to overtly playful and mockingly feminine. Girly dress codes—including babydoll dresses, makeup, barrettes, and knee socks were used by riot grrrls in "an ironic (dis)play and disruption of the signifying codes of gender and generation."[65] For riot grrrls, gender was the signifier around which discussions of oppression and empowerment revolved. As such, the riot grrrl movement was criticized both by insiders and by those who did not identify with the project as being essentialist and based in White, middle-class ideologies.[66]

In its early incarnations, riot grrrl was a prominent topic in mainstream media. In fact, mainstream media unwittingly helped create the national riot grrrl network and moved it beyond the realm of the punk music world. Many girls across the country came to know of riot grrrl through mainstream media outlets. One of the most prominent outlets was *Sassy* magazine, which "featured band/celebrity interviews, record reviews, and a monthly feature of zine addresses."[67] *Sassy* began to use the term "girl" with pride and incorporated some of the political mores of riot grrrl zines alongside their stories of cute skater boys.[68] *Sassy* presented the movement sensitively and to the satisfaction of most members.[69] However, in 1992 and 1993, several articles in *Seventeen* ("It's a Grrrl thing"), *Newsweek* ("Revolution Girl Style Now"), the *New York Times* ("Riot Act"), and *Rolling Stone* ("Grrrls at War") were felt to have misrepresented the movement by presenting the riot grrrls as immature, insincere in their political message, man-hating separatists, and as imitative of male punk bands or older women in rock.[70] Based on these articles, the "riot grrrls initiated a press blackout in 1993 and now refuse to speak with or be photographed by anyone associated with the popular media."[71] Although riot grrrl groups continue in some parts of the country and a few of the original zines and bands remain intact, the movement is not only largely underground but it has largely disintegrated.

Some of the disintegration of the riot grrrl movement has to do with internal rifts—debates over the role of men in feminist struggles, the importance of making race, class, and ethnicity central to the discussion of oppression and empowerment of grrrls, as well as the wisest position to take via mainstream media and corporate record labels. Another aspect of the disintegration is that the messages of riot grrrl were translated by the mediascape into a commodified feminism that "watered down the political message" and focused on the image and style.[72] Riordan argues that while media coverage of riot grrrl helped to popularize the celebration of girls *qua* girls, it also converted what was a use value (feminist thought emerging among young women) into an exchange value (commodities sold to young women that suggest use will bring them empowerment). Indeed, as Hebdige has argued of subcultures generally, the market recuperated the "semantic disorder" created by riot grrrls.[73]

## Convergence: Girl Power

Girl power is the culture industries' response to these social movements. Advertisers, media producers, retailers, and product designers quickly realized that by using the pro-girly, pro-individual style adopted by the third-wave and riot grrrl movements they could capitalize on the desire to solve the "problems" caused by both feminism and gender oppression, as well as the guilt faced by mothers who were scapegoated by the feminist backlash.

Girl power media culture represents a specific discursive moment in girls' cultural history and provides a contemporary example of how the promises of social movements are incorporated into hegemonic cultural production. While individuals and subcultural groups are involved in creating new social movements and the visual styles associated with them, corporations have long appropriated these movements and styles in order to keep current and make profits.[74] Thus, the capitalist imperative is such that audiences may be active agents in the creation of meaning, but the market does not allow for their meaning to further develop before it repackages and commodifies dissent (perhaps voided of resistive authenticity, if such a thing exists). David Harvey explains that "even though consumers are highly dispersed and have more than a little to say in what is produced and what... values shall be conveyed," it is the "sheer power of money," rather than democratic control, that serves to dominate late capitalism.[75]

In the lives of teens, this has meant that youth culture has become even more highly commercial; one cultural critic argues that youth began to feel they were "victims of a predatory marketing machine that co-opted [their] identities, [their] styles, and [their] ideas and turned them into brand food."[76] The concern for girls is that the onslaught of girl power media culture, a culture that sells feminist ideas through style, has reduced oppositional consciousness to symbolism so that feminism becomes something one can take on and off like a fashionable coat rather than a political movement or system of values.[77] Indeed, Riordan argues that with the commodification of these feminist messages, girl power becomes "neutralized" and "the radical message about structural change is lost."[78]

In contrast, Catherine Driscoll asks that we take seriously the tension between agency and complicity that is, and will indefinitely be, at the core of girls' media, particularly in girl power media culture.[79] In concert with Driscoll, I argue that as hegemonic discourse becomes more and more adept at mimicking the style, language, and tone of feminism, it becomes increasingly important for researchers to ask what happens when critical discourse is commodified and how commodified critical discourse is experienced. This book takes up the later question: If girl power is the promise of a feminist social movement incorporated into hegemonic cultural production, how do girls begin to parse the political from the commercial? How do they negotiate the inherently contradictory messages of girl power? (How) do they learn to enact feminist social change?

CHAPTER 2

# When Asked to Talk: Qualitative Research with Teen Girls

SITTING IN A CAFÉ IN QUEENS, New York, seventeen-year-old Razia is very serious as she tells me her views on life, feminism, and being a Muslim girl in the United States. With her long hair blown dry, and gloss punctuating her lips, Razia wears a loose-fitting T-shirt and a pair of jeans. During the week of our interview, Razia has taken over the household duties—cooking for the family, caring for her brother, and cleaning the house—while her mother stays with family in Pakistan preparing mentally for the great challenge of her pending divorce. The divorce, initiated by her mother, is a major and unconventional event in the Afghan Muslim community of which her family is a part, but Razia supports her mother's desire to be happy and to be free of a husband whom she considers selfish and controlling. She feels strongly about a woman's right to be independent and reveals that she "never wants to be in the position" that her mother is in. Instead, what Razia seeks for her future is to "be in control" of her own life, to study international relations, to be an ambassador, and, eventually, to marry a husband whom she wants but does not need. Presently, Razia does not feel in control of many aspects in her life: she is required by her father to conform to a strict dress code that does not include skirts, tank tops, T-shirts that fall above the hips, or tight jeans; she feels compelled to follow another unspoken dress code, upheld by peers, that insists on clothes, shoes, and handbags of specific brands at high price points; she experiences pressure from peers and media images to maintain a certain body weight; and she lives with the fear that a marriage will be arranged for her before she turns twenty, as was her sister's fate.

Feeling she needs to maintain command over something in her life, Razia is currently involved in two projects to regain control of her body. The first is a school project for her social science research class. For this class Razia developed and conducted a survey on beauty and body issues. She hopes that through this project she will understand what compels women to "follow the rules" as she herself feels compelled to do. Of engaging in this project she says, "I hope I will have more understanding of where I should be and what really does matter and what I've been taught is the right thing versus what isn't right."

The other project Razia has created to gain control over her body is one in which she limits the amount of food she puts into her body. Although Razia does not use the term "eating disorder," she describes the way she uses food as a means to control her world and limits her consumption in order to get closer to the body type she and her peers admire:

> I look in the mirror; I don't like anything about myself. I look at myself and I wish I could lose ten pounds, twenty pounds, or I look at myself and, I'm like, "I wish my fingers were a lot thinner than what they are. Why do I look so out of proportion?" Or, why can't I wear a certain outfit that I should be able to wear because it looks nice and because everyone wears it? I put myself in that situation a lot.... There's times, I sort of have an ulcer where I go through this phase, where there was a point where I didn't eat because I was so worried about what I would eat and what I wouldn't eat. And because I didn't eat too much, the times I did eat, there was like a burning in my lining, so sometimes now I have to deal with that. I still, like, if I have to suffer for anything, I won't suffer for not getting up and taking a shower and wearing nice clothes, but I'll take it out of my eating time.

Razia says that as a Muslim she believes a woman "doesn't need her body to express herself," but she admits that she "loves" pop singer Christina Aguilera, not primarily because she is a talented singer but because "she's so tiny and so pretty." She believes that women should be taken seriously and she admired singer Mariah Carey when she performed in conservative suits, rather than skimpy dresses. Yet Razia laughs when her male friend misinterprets the research interview as a job interview and sends her a text message saying, "Good going, smart girl. Wear a short skirt and lick your lips a lot and you'll definitely get the job."

Razia is determined to be both a counter-normative independent woman and a woman who fits the normative standards of attractiveness and slenderness. She admires female celebrities for their talent but also for their looks; she expects to be taken seriously but thinks it is funny when a friend demeans her by suggesting she use her looks to get a job. Razia's identity is formed in her interactions with her local Afghan Muslim family living in Queens, New York, and also in a larger, expansive girl power culture. Her story exemplifies the conflicted nature of gender identity within girl power media culture.

Throughout this study I situate girl power media culture as one of the many discourses encountered by girls as they work to make sense of their gender identities. Rather than argue that there is a causal relationship between media and the formation of girls' perceptions of gender (an argument I would surely be unable to prove),[1] I explore the important role of girl power media culture in the social experiences and identity projects of girls.

## MEDIA, IDEOLOGY, AND IDENTITY

Researchers of girls' culture have long been concerned about media's power to shape girls' perceptions of what it means to be female and feminine. Rooted in social constructionist, Marxist, and postmodern theories, studies of girls' culture begin with the assumption that identity is not a fixed category but a shifting one produced in relationship with cultural ideologies, institutions, and practices. Identity is produced through a continuous dialectical relationship between the self and the world. Put succinctly, there is no core-self waiting to be discovered or formed; rather shifting identities are created through social interactions and institutions.[2] The self is something we create as we experience the material world around us. Geertz argued that humans are "incomplete" and finish themselves "through culture."[3] He argued that our identities, values, practices, and affects are all cultural products that are manufactured rather than naturally assigned.

We are not free to create any identity we select but rather one that reflects the reality of our material conditions and the ideologies in which we come to know the self.

Ideologies, or "the system of ideas and representations which dominate the mind," are internalized and provide a guide for an individual as she constructs her identity.[4] According to this approach, ideology creates a situation in which people cannot see themselves as interpellated subjects or, put in another way, it creates a population that believes dominant ideology is common sense and in its interests rather than constructed and oppressive. Stuart Hall explained that Althusser believed that ideology "moved constantly within a closed circle, producing, not knowledge, but a recognition of the things we already knew. It did so because it took, as already established fact, exactly the premises which ought to have been put into question."[5] Mass media, as a system that can turn ideologies into cultural common sense and transmit them widely, hold the power to make ideologies "appear universal, natural, and coterminous with reality itself."[6]

Individuals are neither fully autonomous, nor living scripted lives. Rather, individuals negotiate identities in dialogue with ideologies, social positions, and cultural ideologies. Young people are no exception; Buckingham and Bragg have noted that in their study of sexual and gender identities, young people described an identity that was always in process and formed through personal acts of gender and sexuality rather than one that was fixed.[7] In these models, ideology plays a central but nondeterministic role in how people make sense of media, what people take away from their media experiences, and how media is used in the construction of the self. We become girls as we engage with culture, in this case media, and come to understand the ways in which gender is constructed in our world and the ways in which we, as girls, are expected to act in the world.

Once we encounter and understand our normative gender roles in society, we naturalize these norms and reify socially constructed values as we perform our selves for public consumption. According to Erving Goffman, when people present themselves to others, their "performance will tend to incorporate and exemplify the officially accredited values of the society..."[8] At the same time, the performative nature of self-presentation allows for the shifting of selves. Since there is more than one set of social norms, the performer may shift his/her presentation depending upon the approved expectations and values of the audience. Identity, then, is not static or fixed; it is mercurial. Thus, our social performances of self are reflective of (or at least in response to) what we learn through our engagement with media.

Postmodernism need not work against this modernist view of the self but can be seen as a friendly amendment: individuals do not become socialized through an encounter with a singular identity. Rather, individuals perform multiple selves as they wade through a world of competing and often contradictory cultural discourses, texts, institutions, and social practices that they negotiate, embrace, weave through, and reject.[9] Angela McRobbie argues that postmodern thought does not demand the end of the subject or the self but requires that we consider how this self is constructed throughout the life cycle and how "subjectivities [are always] in process, interacting and debating."[10] The "feminist social self," in particular, "is an amalgam of fragmented identities formed in discourse and history and called into being both by the experiences of femininity and by the existence and availability of a feminist discourse..."[11] Thus, analysis of girls' media sheds light on the various pathways through which girls come to understand shifting notions of sexuality, body, style, and power.

## GENDER, MEDIA, AND IDENTITY

A great deal of scholarly research on children and media has presented the relationship as an ongoing war between innocent children and powerful commercial media where children's identity is threatened by prevailing ideologies. It is not uncommon for cultural critics to use monster-like metaphors to describe media's power over children, such as in the introduction to their edited collection of articles where Shirley Steinberg and Joe Kincheloe write that "given their power to sink their tentacles deep into the private lives of children, the corporate producers of kinderculture constantly destabilize the identity of children."[12] Moral panics abound, lamenting the loss of "a less commercialized youth"[13] and blaming media's power over children for: creating a world of materialist consumers who have no sense of social value;[14] the supposed diminishing creativity in children;[15] and increasing rates of illiteracy,[16] obesity, anxiety, and attentional disorders.[17]

In particular, there has been substantial analysis of the ways in which femininity has been produced in children's media texts. Such studies—of texts, not audiences—often insinuate that girls are enculturated through their engagement with these limited media portrayals of girlhood and womanhood. Studies of Barbie, for instance, suggest that the doll has been encoded with a message of stereotypical femininity including normative beauty, domesticity, sexual objectification, heteronormativity, and consumptive excess.[18] These studies argue that while Barbie is in one sense just molded plastic, she also serves as a symbol for ideologies about gender, race, class, and consumption. Rejecting the notion of polysemy and situated meaning-making, Steinberg argues, for example, that "multiple readings aside, Barbie does operate within the boundaries of particular cultural logics. She does celebrate whiteness—blonde whiteness in particular—as a standard for feminine beauty; she does reify anorexic figures coupled with large breasts as objects of male desire. She does support unbridled consumerism as a reason for being."[19] Such studies imply that the embodied text determines conceptions of gender and is not negotiated by girls who are invested in a collection of contradictory discourses about femininity.[20]

Beyond Barbie, there has been limited but significant analysis of the ways in which girls have been represented in and targeted by commercial media. For example, in her study of the American Girl Collection books, which address a preteen audience, Inness focuses on the textual transmission of ideologies asserting that the dolls engage in typically feminine activities and hold conservative views on womanhood and femininity.[21] In the same edited collection on girls' culture, Scanlon argues that the dating genre of girls' board games socialize girls to believe that male attention and heterosexual romance will complete them as individuals.[22] Examining two contemporary series books for teens, Pecora finds that the genre privileges heterosexual romantic relationships and party-life over independence and planning for the future.[23] And, in her expansive content analysis of television programs, music videos, films, magazines articles, and both print and television advertisements, Signorielli concludes that "the priorities and activities of women in the media may send girls the implicit message that relationships are more important for women than occupations or careers."[24]

Some cultural critics have argued that there is a direct causal relationship between mediated images and girls' body image and eating disorders. Jean Kilbourne, best known for the documentary *Killing Us Softly*, suggests that advertising contributes to a social epidemic of eating disorders, violence against women, and self-loathing. Although she makes clear that she does not believe junk food and diet product advertising is solely responsible for high rates of obesity, anorexia, and bulimia, she does argue that the promotion of food and diet programs are a "significant part" of the problem because these industries "need to normalize and glamorize disordered and destructive attitudes toward food and eating."[25] Similarly, although from a more highly theoretical perspective, Bordo argues that media, advertising in particular, profits from creating and perpetuating female self-hatred, desire for thinness, and a desire for control over the body.[26]

These studies make important contributions to our understanding of girls and media, but they also bring to the fore the need for ongoing qualitative research with girl audiences. Is it, as Inness claims, "*impossible* to escape ideology in girls' books?"[27] Is it the case, as Pecora argues, that readers of the series books she analyzed "*will* learn of an academic life that reflects the 1950s when a woman's college career goal was an MRS?"[28] It often becomes bandied about with little, or weak evidence, that there is a proven causal relationship between mass media and girls' self esteem: "The effect of the media in developing the self-concepts of young women cannot be underestimated."[29] However, qualitative audience studies have suggested that although ideology is certainly a key arbiter in the construction of girls' gender identities, research on young people and media has historically overemphasized the role of media in the formation of girls' identity projects because it relies exclusively on textual analysis or content analysis, both of which place an emphasis on what has been encoded in a text and tend to overlook the decoding process of diverse audiences.[30] Such claims separate media from everyday activity; they overlook the relationship between the cultural and the social. In these studies there is no clear understanding of how interactions between media and girls play out on a sociocultural level or how a range of situated identities impacts media engagement and interpretation.

## Cultural Studies/Qualitative Methodology

Cultural Studies has demonstrated that while commonly encoded with dominant ideological perspectives, media messages are not interpreted in the same way for all individuals and audience groups.[31] As such, studies of media and identity that are rooted within Cultural Studies often move beyond textual analysis and explore how people make meaning from media,[32] the pleasures people experience in their media interactions,[33] and the ways in which audiences have resisted or subverted the dominant ideological narratives offered by mainstream media.[34] From this perspective, the flexibility of identity gives individuals and subcultural groups the ability to create new discourses and make new meanings that may exist outside of dominant ideologies.

Feminist methodology, by which this study is equally informed, has often argued that in order to move women's and girls' experiences from the margins to the center, researchers must listen to them directly and create theories based upon their standpoints.[35] Privileging experience can be useful in identifying commonalities and differences between girls and the ways in which subjectivities are constructed in particular environments.[36] My focus on experience is rooted in the assumption that teen girls' identities are hybrid and constructed through a variety of shifting, partial, social locations.[37] The self is continually produced and reproduced through an engagement with language, texts, and institutions. As girls wade through a world of texts, institutions, and social practices, they negotiate the competing and often contradictory cultural discourses they encounter.[38]

While textual analysis is important in that it provides a close reading of encoded meaning, starting with everyday experience, and exploring media as one of what De Lauretis calls "the conflicting investments" with which people make sense of gender, enables broader and less deterministic examinations of the role of media in social experience.[39] Analyses that decenter media provide us with a methodological approach that does not obfuscate the moments in which media users' social experiences collide with, disarm, and/or reflect their cultural experiences.[40]

As Cultural Studies scholars who use qualitative methods have demonstrated, young people do not simply soak up the dominant ideologies offered to them.[41] Rather, young people engage critically, and sometimes ambivalently, with media and culture through selection of genres, texts, and styles, talk about media and integration of media and consumer goods into their personal arsenals of life strategies.[42]

Paul Willis and Dick Hebdige, for example, have each demonstrated that individuals and subcultural groups use their bodies to express ideas and create new modes of thinking. Examining the dress, music, gestures, language, and styles of British working-class boys, they theorized that the creation of new styles and codes of conduct disrupted the "naturalized codes" that enabled a mainstream culture to function and allowed for the creations of new collective identities.[43] Hebdige, in particular, used the theory of bricolage to examine how individuals and subcultures used, appropriated, and reappropriated various cultural symbols to distort the power of commodities and produce new, counter-hegemonic identities. McRobbie celebrates girls' agency and the ways they engage in playful challenges to normative social roles.[44] In her discussion of the ragmarket and the appropriation of old clothes by young women, McRobbie suggests that the recycling of clothing demands we shift our analysis of consumer culture to acknowledge girls' participation in a redefinition of style as well as a new pattern of consumption.[45]

Likewise, studies of media selection, interpretation, and use have demonstrated that the textual meanings intended by producers of both youth and adult television do not necessarily match the meanings ascribed to the texts by young people.[46] For Buckingham and Bragg, ideology is not fortified and social learning does not inevitably occur through a unidirectional flow. They argue that "the media may intend to teach; but how and what children actually learn from them is a rather more complex matter."[47] It is through play and social interaction that media begins to form meaning in the lives of children. As children select which shows to watch, select which shows to discuss with friends and with researchers, consider how to speak about television, and contemplate their relationship to media texts, they make sense of their worlds and their own roles within it.

JoEllen Fisherkeller, for instance, found that the urban, middle school students she spoke with used their local cultures as they developed goals and dreams for the future. They then used these "guiding motivations" to inform their media selection processes and interpretive skills. These young people actively sought out television characters that offered them "'imaginative strategies' for acting on these dreams and hopes for the future, and for coping with social dilemmas."[48] Susan Murray also explores the meeting of the social and cultural in her analysis of girls' participation in a chat room devoted to the TV show *My So Called Life.* Murray found that girls who were struggling with self-identity in their schools and homes found salience in the show's protagonist who experienced a similar struggle. These girls took pleasure in seeing a representation of someone like themselves on television and ultimately formed a community of viewer-protesters when executives threatened to pull the show because of low ratings. Here, pleasure and fandom led to the development of a new collectivity for girls who had been isolated and to the creation of a space in which ambiguities about identity could exist in comfort.

## Case: Teen Girl Magazines, Ideologies, and Girls' Reading

Much of the academic research on girls and media has reflected market realities in which girls have been an audience for written materials—specifically magazines and series books—and in which reading has been believed to be a female activity.[49] Therefore, a great body of literature on teen girls and gender addresses the content of teen magazines because this medium has a long history and a clearly defined mode of female address.[50] Overwhelmingly, these studies have argued that teen girl magazines provide girls with limited and oppressive models of femininity. *Seventeen* magazine plays a central role in these studies because it has a history dating back to 1944 and has long dominated the teen magazine market.[51] These studies have discovered that despite minor shifts in content during social periods in which feminism was in vogue,[52] *Seventeen* has focused on beauty and fashion,[53] encouraged heterosexuality and other traditional sexual practices,[54] positioned girls as sexual objects for the pleasure of boys and men,[55] and linked sexuality to the display of a thin, White, voluptuous body.[56] *Seventeen* is, of course, not alone in its perpetuation of dominant hegemonic ideologies. Angela McRobbie's seminal work analyzing the British magazine *Jackie,* upon which many of the *Seventeen* studies were based, found that editorial content suggested that girls' energies should be focused on finding normative heterosexual romance, sustaining romantic relationships, and consuming beauty products in the interest of maintaining the self as an appealing partner in the romantic relationship.[57]

While recent studies suggest that these magazines also create mixed messages, offering girls a critique of gender normative femininity, they conclude that teen girls have little room for the construction of transgressive gender positions.[58] Dawn Currie, who complemented her content analysis with ethnographic research, argues that teen magazines do not offer young women a handful of epistemologies, behaviors, and identities with which to experiment. Instead, she claims, media "normalize the dominant order as it is experienced through [everyday life]."[59] In her view, as a young woman reads magazines that discuss her peers' experiences with gender oppression (e.g., having to worry about looks or feeling nervous about sexual relationships) and her experiences overcoming it (e.g., purchasing new clothes or trying new makeup), the young woman's own experiences growing up in a patriarchal society are normalized. Thus, media cultures reify the hegemony of gender oppression.

However, ethnographic research on teen girls, magazines, and reading suggests that while patriarchal ideologies dominate in girls' reading material, girls are active readers who do not always blindly accept the dominant readings of teen magazines. In one of the earliest reception studies with teen girls, Frazer interviewed the readers of British teen magazine *Jackie*, and found that they actively negotiated meaning as they read the texts so that "ideology [was] undercut... by [their] reflexivity and reflectiveness."[60] Moss further argues that theories of ideological persuasion do not stand up to the reality of girls' lives in which tastes, interests, and social practices shift rapidly.[61] These changes reflect an ability to navigate various media messages and experiment with various identity positions.

In her study of teen's talk about shopping Malik found that, for the girls in her study, teen magazines were less significant in influencing girls' identity constructions than was local culture and that magazines sometimes served to expand girls' perceptions of available identities beyond those in their local environments.[62] Local cultures were also evident in the interpretative process in Lisa Duke's study of Black and White teen magazine readers. Duke found that Black teen readers did not always share the same interests, and therefore did not always have the same interpretations of teen magazines as their White peers. Black girls were more likely to be interested in stories and images of "real girls" than of models and they did not personalize nor pay close attention to the beauty and fashion tips as they found these to be reflective of White cultural values and norms.[63]

Margaret Finders positions media consumption as a social act and uses Radway's *Reading the Romance* as her model.[64] Radway concluded her study of romance readers with the belief that "the romance-reading process gives the reader a strategy for making her present situation more comfortable without substantive reordering of its structure..."[65] Similarly, Finders argues that while the social queens of the school she observed used teen magazines as a "yardstick to measure how [they] were progressing into womanhood,"[66] and generally considered them to be authoritative sources on "woman stuff,"[67] their social reading practices enabled the girls to form a tight-knit social group, gave them a sense of authority (being the girls in school who knew what was "cool") and a sense of stability in an adolescent moment of confusion. Finders explains, "At a time when all the rules and rituals appear to be in flux, when even her body forsakes her, the early adolescent can turn to the pages of a teen zine for control. The illusion of stability provides a sense of power and control in a world that is often perceived as out of control."[68] Thus Finders concludes that while ideologies regarding beauty, body images, and appearance are reinforced by the act of reading teen magazines, ideologies of authority and status may be challenged by this same act.

* * *

## Conducting the Project: Method[69]

At the onset of this project, I thought I could best conduct ethnographic research in its classic sense of engaging in participant observation. I imagined becoming a "pal" to students, hearing girls' intimate conversations as I sat at their lunch table, and shopping with cliques of girls after school and on weekends. However, I came to understand that my questions could better be answered through interview-based research. I had been conducting informal participant observation for years through my work with young women at several youth programs.

I had been a teacher, a counselor, and a confidante to some of the girls with whom I had worked. However, I had not heard girls discussing what it meant to be female, feminine, and—most certainly not—feminist. Girls that I knew discussed their favorite singers using the term "hot" or talked about the previous night's episode of a sitcom as "so funny," but they rarely probed each other to think through what constituted "hot" or "funny," and they almost never discussed how their own feelings and personal experiences helped them to create meaning from these media texts. I suspected that listening to girls, without guiding them to discuss issues that were relevant to them (but about which they rarely spoke with peers), was going to be a project that yielded little significant data.

What I did know, from my experiences as a teacher, was that when asked to talk teenage girls have a lot to say about gender identity. When I taught a year of high school English, I asked the students in the class to prepare a speech. I must admit that I cannot remember what the boys spoke about because the speeches given by the girls—about their experiences with sexual violence, discrimination, sexuality, and gender role expectations—were so moving that one day there was a mass exodus of crying girls from the classroom to the bathroom. It is not that girls do not want to talk about gender identity; they often are not given the opportunity to do so.

I also knew that I did not want to limit this research to one or two groups of girls. This method, used by many of the outstanding and pioneering books in the nascent field of girls' studies and youth media studies, has been effective in capturing in-depth, nuanced snapshots of experiences of small groups of young people.[70] Yet, few of these studies have been able to draw comparisons among the experiences of diverse groups of girls. I wanted to explore this issue from a range of situated locations and to draw connections and distinctions among girls from varying socioeconomic, racial, and ethnic backgrounds.[71] Because media culture cuts across racial, ethnic, regional, and class lines and "provides a shared repository of images, characters, plots, and themes [and] the basis for small talk and play . . . on a national, even global scale,"[72] qualitative, multisited ethnographic research yields a more robust analysis.

Marcus argues that multisited ethnography enables researchers to move beyond the local and explore the ways in which culture circulates through various communities.[73] This study, though situated in the single site of New York City, explores how girls from diverse regions, racial and socioeconomic backgrounds, and institutions (churches, schools, and Girl Scout troops) make sense of the widely circulated girl power discourse in similar and distinct ways. Although I do not attempt to make generalized conclusions about "all girls" or even "all girls from New York," I do aim to demonstrate that there are similarities and differences that emerge as I unpack the girls' discussions of style, sexual representation, mothering, and feminism. While I identify the impact of race, social class, and region[74] on girls' aspirations and definitions of independence and strength, I also demonstrate that there are common understandings of feminism and the role of the female in American society that are not unique to one socioeconomic, racial, ethnic, or regional group, but that appear to be a part of the collective experience of growing up in a media culture that promotes girl power.

I conducted eight focus groups in seven locations as well as twenty-five individual interviews with girls between twelve and eighteen. I chose this age group for several reasons: the adolescent years are those that have been widely discussed as the years of crisis;[75] girls ages twelve to seventeen are the target audience for teen-related media production;[76] and the U.S. Census Bureau projects that there are twenty-four million teens between the ages of twelve and seventeen, making this one-third of the total youth market.[77]

I began this research with focus groups because they are particularly beneficial in research that aims to understand young people's media experiences and the relationship of these media experiences to identity production. Focus groups are also particularly well suited for feminist research because they encourage researchers to "focus on the multivocality" of participants' lives and articulations.[78] Focus groups are also beneficial because they can shift the power dynamic between the researcher and participants.[79] When participants worked together to name an experience—challenging each other and building on each other's articulations along the way—it was a reminder that there was not a singular "girl" whose experience I could capture, but rather that there were multiple positions explored and embraced by the many girls in the study.

The ability to watch the girls discuss and debate allowed me to see how they struggle both with defining femininity and feminism and with investing in certain discourses about what it means to have power as a female. As Hodge and Tripp argue, meaning is produced not just in the context of viewing but also in social interactions in which media meanings are discussed, interpreted, and used to make sense of the world.[80] Likewise, David Buckingham suggests that "talk about television serves to define the self in relation to others."[81] As young people select which shows to discuss and how to speak about them, they make sense of their world and their own roles within it. As I did not tell my participants which television shows, celebrities, or musicians to discuss, their understanding of gender identity emerged in their articulations of certain performers and characters.

In each focus group, the participants were recruited from the same site to increase their level of openness and trust with one another. Homogenous interview groups are more productive and participants feel safer communicating with people with whom they share common ground.[82] Since my groups were composed of girls who were connected with the same institution (school, Girl Scout troop, or circle of friends), the participants generally shared similar socioeconomic backgrounds as well as social and educational levels, and in some cases cultural backgrounds. These shared subject positions may have increased the level of trust girls experienced in the focus groups, made it more comfortable for girls to discuss tough issues, and allowed the possibilities for disagreement between the participants.

At the conclusion of each focus group, all of the girls were asked to volunteer as individual interview participants in the project. In each case, more girls than necessary opted to continue and I had to select interview participants based on girls' level of participation and social location. Generally, participants who freely spoke about media and self were selected for interviews, although girls who made only a few stimulating remarks but seem hindered by the focus group dynamics were also identified as candidates for in-depth interviews. As it was also important to me to have a diverse pool of participants, I considered girls' race, class, neighborhood, and first language when I determined who would be called for follow-up interviews. Through individual interviews, I was able to probe further and "recycle" my analysis back through the respondents—often asking them about ambiguities, confusion, or debates that arose from the focus groups.[83]

Readers will meet these girls throughout the book, but I will briefly introduce the group selected for more in-depth study to give a sense of the diversity of the participants. Six of the girls lived in and attended school in Brooklyn, nine lived in and attended school in the Bronx, nine lived in and attended school in Queens, and two attended school in Manhattan (though one of these girls lived in the Bronx). Seven of the girls identified as White or Caucasian; four participants identified as Chinese or Taiwanese; five participants identified as Black or African-American; five participants identified as Latina or Hispanic; one girl identified as Guyanese; one girl identified as Panamanian-Jamaican; one participant identified as Afghan; one participant identified as Nigerian; and one participant identified as Japanese-Brazilian. The girls were from a variety of educational and economic backgrounds with four attending a private school, two attending Catholic schools, and twenty attending public schools. It is highly difficult to name the socioeconomic status of individual girls, as this category is a complex one determined by numerous factors. However, fourteen of the girls had two parents working in white-collar careers or middle-income positions; three of the girls had one parent working in a middle-income position; five girls had single mothers/female guardians working in low-paying positions; and three girls had mothers/female guardians who do not work out of the home.[84] In addition, the percentage of individuals living below the poverty level in each girl's zip code can also be helpful in determining the range of their socioeconomic realities. Five girls lived in neighborhoods in which less than 10 percent of the population lives below the poverty level; eight girls lived in neighborhoods in which between 11 and 20 percent of the population lives below the poverty level; four girls lived in neighborhoods in which between 21 and 30 percent of the population lives below the poverty level; four girls lived in neighborhoods in which between 31 and 40 percent of the population lives below the poverty level; and five of the girls lived in neighborhoods in which more than 40 percent of the population lives below the poverty level (see appendix for an easy reference of each participant's information).

## Reflexivity and Situated Knowledge

My own experiences growing up both in a mediated environment and in New York City have shaped my understandings of the experiences of the participants in my study. I grew up in a multiracial, lower middle-class community in Jamaica, Queens, and went to New York City public schools. Although I did not grow up in an era of girl power media, I did grow up in the 1970s and 1980s, a time in which, as Douglas notes, representations of women, and girls to a lesser extent, were beginning to shift.[85] My generation is before the age of the Internet and just on the cusp of MTV, yet I was fully immersed in television culture, coming home after school each day to do my homework while watching my favorite cartoons, then soap operas, and, as a teen, music videos.

Feminist researchers often "consider personal experiences to be a valuable asset for feminist research."[86] Indeed, my own experiences informed my questions and my interpretations. At the same time, I was ever cognizant that while we share some experiences of social location—as females, as New Yorkers, as audiences—there are others in which we are greatly divergent: age and education level, in all cases, as well as race, immigrant status, sexuality, and class in some cases. Even within our shared locations there was no assumption of universality; rather the participants' experience has been historically located and contextualized. Throughout the process I reflected on my *a priori* assumptions and the ongoing positioning of the lives of participants beside my theoretical conclusions in order to limit what Lather terms "theoretical imposition."[87]

Although I am familiar with both the geopolitical and mediated environments in which the girls I interviewed have grown up, my reflexive stance also helped me to recognize the "locations of multiple and hybrid identities" from which my participants spoke and from which I theorize.[88] Moreover, reflexivity recognizes knowledge as a social product.[89] As producer of this text, I recognize the structure of power rooted in the research process. Power is always imbalanced in an interview situation but especially when the interviewer is an adult and the participant is a child or an adolescent.[90] My research relationships were not only imbalanced based on age (and therefore educational experience) but also, in many cases, were challenging due to differences in socioeconomic class status and race between my participants and myself. As a White, middle-class, adult academic, I have significantly more social, cultural, and political capital than the majority of the participants in this study. Participants may be more cautious about sharing their thoughts and feelings if they imagine that they are being judged on their answers or if they believe that they can get the answer "wrong." I was aware of this power dynamic throughout the research process and made an effort to establish openness with participants so that they spoke honestly and did not just give me answers they thought I wanted to hear.

Yet, I am not under the illusion that reflexivity and data checking alleviates all miscommunication or misinterpretation or that even in the cases in which I share a race and class background with a participant that I have captured her "reality." Instead, I recognize that each of the girls has expressed a "local and specific"[91] understanding of herself and of gender identity. Since the self (of both researcher and participant) is always partial and shifting, I have created what Donna Haraway calls "situated knowledges," rather than truths about girls in girl power media culture.[92]

## Situating Participants

As I listened to girls name their experiences and define gender identity, I was attentive to how these experiences were vocalized within three cultural realms: (1) a mediated culture that encodes certain meanings in texts, (2) a discursive culture in which specific patriarchal articulations of gender are diffused into the ideological framework that organizes institutions and power relations, and (3) a physical culture in which girls are still faced with violence, discrimination, and economic injustice.

The girls in this study reflect the diverse racial, socioeconomic backgrounds, and living conditions of New York City residents. New York City consists of five boroughs, and although Manhattan often serves as a synecdoche for the whole city, this borough is only home to a little more than 20 percent of the more than half of a million ten- to nineteen-year-old young people in New York City. The remainder of New York City's children live in Brooklyn, Queens, the Bronx, and Staten Island.[93] In addition, the socioeconomic status of New York City inhabitants varies greatly, even within one borough. In 1999, 42,638 families in Manhattan had an annual income of $200,000 or more, while another 39,756 families lived below the poverty level. Living conditions also vary greatly. While a majority of residents live in large apartment buildings, there are children in all five boroughs who grow up in single-family residences or two-family homes. A diverse population for this study provided a range of experiences still within the boundaries of New York City. Having diversity—in race, ethnicity, social class, and region—allowed for a greater understanding of how social location and individual experience contribute to girls' understandings of girl power media culture.[94]

Although there is a dearth of statistical data on girls in New York, a report commissioned by Girls Incorporated of New York City indicates that "girls and young women in New York City show an alarming rate of emotional distress" and in 1997 "nearly one-fourth of high school girls reported having seriously considered suicide."[95] The cause of the emotional distress is far-reaching and includes girls' victimization both in and out of schools and families; "Girls in New York City are three times more likely to be reported victims of sexual abuse than males" and girls report violence and harassment as a major issue in their lives.[96] Nationally, one-third of girls ages thirteen to seventeen are concerned about being forced to do something sexual.[97] In New York City, where vocational and technical education is still largely segregated by gender, and "male and female rates of taking technology courses and advanced placement tests are disparate," girls may also believe that there are barriers to their future "career choice, opportunity, and earning potential."[98]

## THE PARTICIPANTS[99]

Below I will introduce readers to the focus group sites and offer more insight into the girls who participated in the study. Three Girl Scout Troops and four high schools served as the sites for this study. I call the Girl Scout troops: Community Troop, Gardens Troop, and Towne Troop;[100] and the high schools: Monument Academy, Victory High School, Excel High School, and Bridge School.

The *Community Troop* met on Sunday mornings at a Chinese community center in an East Asian neighborhood in Queens. All of the girls in this troop defined themselves as Asian, Chinese, Taiwanese, Chinese-American, or a combination of the former. Nearly half of the participants reported that they speak a combination of "Chinese" or Mandarin and English at home, while another 40 percent reported that they spoke only "Chinese" or Mandarin in their homes. The girls were from middle- to upper-income families; nearly three-quarters of the girls lived in neighborhoods in which the median household income was higher than the New York State median household income and in which fewer than 10 percent of the population lived in a family with incomes below the poverty line. In addition, over half of the girls attended schools in which fewer than 20 percent of students were eligible for the free lunch program.[101] I conducted four individual interviews with the girls from this site: Grace, Helen, Diana, and Fiona.[102]

The *Gardens Troop* of thirteen- and fourteen-year-old girls met in a church basement in a wealthy Brooklyn neighborhood. Although the troop met in a wealthy neighborhood, none of the seven girls lived locally and they represented a range of racial groups and socio-economic classes. Two of these girls were White, four were African-American, and one was Latina; four attended Catholic high schools, two attended public high schools, and one attended an independent high school. All of the participants spoke English at home. Three of the girls had at least one parent who was in a high-paying white-collar position; all of the girls lived in neighborhoods in which between 20 and 38 percent of residents lived below the poverty level and all but two girls lived in zip codes in which the median household income was below the New York State median. I conducted in-depth interviews with two of the girls from this site: Aiyisha and Jenna.

Finally, the *Towne Troop* also met in a church basement and consisted of seven girls, ages twelve to fourteen. Of this group, four reported that they were White, and three reported that they were of mixed Latino and European American heritage. The girls, from a small Northern Queens neighborhood, all spoke English at home and six attended the same public junior high school. These girls lived in a squarely middle-class community. The median household income was just slightly above the state median and the percentage of households below the poverty line was slightly below the state average. The girls' parents had job titles—construction, locksmith, secretary, librarian, and mechanic—that also place them in the middle class. Of all the girls in the study, the girls from this troop were least interested in the project as evidenced both by the small return of requests to further participate in the study through individual interviews as well as by the lack of concentration in the group discussion. Due to the seeming lack of interest, as well as my determination that I was going to focus on girls over fifteen, I did not conduct individual interviews with any of the Towne Troop girls, though data from their focus group is included in the book.

*Monument Academy* is an alternative high school located on Manhattan's West Side. Housed in a former office building, Monument serves 300 students mostly from upper Manhattan's Puerto Rican and Dominican communities. Monument felt like the small alternative school that it is. Students called teachers by their first names, they knew what television shows the teachers watch after-school, and grading occurred through portfolio assessment rather than testing. Although my connection, a teacher at Monument, had mentioned the project to ten girls who said they would come to the after-school focus group, only three Senior girls actually met with me on the specified day. Two of the three girls were Dominican and the third was Puerto-Rican. All three were from working poor families who lived in Manhattan and Bronx neighborhoods in which the poverty level was two or more times above the state average and the school they attended reported that 71 percent of all students were eligible for the free lunch program. All three girls lived with single mothers, two of whom provided home health assistance and the third who was a school aide. From this site, I met with Isa and Juana in individual interviews.

It was a local anomaly that nearly all students from *Victory High School*, located in the impoverished South Bronx, graduated secondary school and attended college. Students who did not come to school in their strictly enforced uniform were sent home or given after-school suspensions. The participants from Victory were a mix of African-American[103] girls as well as girls who were from (or whose parents were from) English- and Spanish-speaking Caribbean countries. A third of the girls spoke Spanish in their homes, while the remainder spoke English. At Victory, half of all students were eligible to receive free lunch and all but two of the girls lived in neighborhoods in which 41 percent or more of the households earned incomes below the poverty level. Five of the girls lived with single mothers or female guardians who did not work out of the home and one girl lived with a single mother who was a home health aide. The remaining seven girls lived in either one- or two-parent families in which at least one person was reported as having a job in the blue-collar sector, although five of these seven girls lived in a community with a median annual household income of below $23,000. Because this school was more accommodating than any of the other groups, and because the administration at the school felt it was a benefit to the girls to participate and encouraged me to keep coming back to the school to meet more girls, I conducted individual interviews with nine girls from Victory: Paola, Yasmine, Bahijah, Stacey, Lili, Michelle, Quianna, Brianna, and Nikke.

At *Excel High School*, one of New York City's top-ranking high schools, I met with eleven ethnically diverse girls from high-income neighborhoods in Queens. This group, from a magnet school that draws top students from all over the borough, was the most ethnically diverse group in my study; the participants consisted of three Caucasian girls, two Korean-American girls, two Chinese-American girls, one Indian-American girl, one Afghan-American girl, one African-American girl, and one Caribbean-American girl. Although these eleven girls came from nine different zip codes, more than 80 percent of the population in all of their communities boasted incomes above the poverty level. I conducted in-depth interviews with Leila, Colleen, Tasha, Razia, and Gillian.

My school group from *Bridge School*, a private school in Brooklyn at which tuition is nearly $30,000 per year, five girls were White and one was Japanese-Brazilian. All of the girls had parents who hold management-level or professional positions and all lived in upper middle-class neighborhoods in Brooklyn. None of the girls lived in a neighborhood with a poverty level over 24 percent. I met with four of the girls from this group for in-depth interviews: Sierra, Ellie, Adrienne, and Meg.

As I have explored in this chapter, one of the missing elements in the study of girls, media, and identity is research that combines an analysis of the cultural with the social. While scholars might articulate their own interpretations of media addressed to girls, their analyses do not explore the complex relationship between media culture and girls' interpretation and use of media. Couldry suggests that we must "decentre media research from the study of media texts or production structures…and redirect it onto the study of the open range of practices focused directly or indirectly on media."[104] From this perspective, media analysis is incomplete without directed attention to everyday life and the interaction of media discourses with other cultural discourses encountered and negotiated by audiences. This book focuses on the intersection of the cultural and the social, exploring how girls weave media experiences with "real life" experiences to form gendered identities.

CHAPTER 3

# Wanna Get Dirrty? Determining Authentic Sexual Subjectivity

> THEA: Look at *The Apprentice*. It's like men versus women and the women used the fact that sex sells. They used what they knew and they won. They won every challenge. Those women are doing awesome and they are just really great businesswomen in addition to everything else. They are intelligent and they are kicking the men's asses and these are the kinds of women that we can look up to that we see on TV. You know what I mean? If we accept what is here now, we'll be able to know how to change it. Like, once these women impress Donald Trump and they get into power, they're in a position to change how things are run. (Thea, seventeen years old, White)

> MEG: OK. Sex sells. It's a given but it doesn't mean that women should continue doing that. Think about it, if women weren't OK with objectifi . . . of, of putting themselves out there like that, it wouldn't be so normal. They're not using their brains. Well, I guess you can say they're using their brains to sell things 'cause they know that sex sells so they use that but . . . Why can't you use your brain and come up with some other great way to sell things? You think, Thea, that if we sort of, like, accept it, we might be able to change it, but at the same time, it could get a lot worse. (Meg, seventeen years old, Caucasian)

Coming of age in girl power media culture, girls receive a series of discordant messages about female sexuality. Female sexuality is something to be guarded; girls are taught not to come home pregnant and to protect themselves from sexual predators. Female sexuality is something to be used; as Thea describes earlier, it is a powerful commodity available as exchange for economic, cultural, social, and emotional capital. Female sexuality is also a political issue; as Meg intimates, girls learn that institutions, corporations, advertisers, and producers may try to conflate girls and women with their bodies, seeing them only as objects rather than as humans, and that girls may or may not be complicit in this equation. This chapter turns its focus to pop music and female performers' public displays of sexuality. By doing so, it explores how the girls in this study work to make sense of girl power media's incongruous messages about sexuality. The girls' discussions of sexual imagery raise several important questions about sexuality in the era of girl power: How do girl audiences determine who is a sexual subject and who is a sexual object in a contradictory mediascape? Does objectification result strictly from control by others or is it linked, in part, to the specific visual imagery of sexuality and sexiness? How do girl audiences make sense of a woman who presents herself as in control of sexual encounters yet maintains a sexual image that is rooted in a stereotypically male-coded fantasy?

## Conflicting Messages: Sexual Power or Sexual Victimization?

In her 2008 video for "Diva," Beyonce Knowles symbolically lights female mannequins with heavy makeup on fire and in the lyrics to "Single Ladies (Put a Ring on It)," she tells an ex-boyfriend, "I put gloss on my lips, a man on my hips...I could care less what you think. I need no permission." The Pussycat Dolls, a burlesque troupe turned pop music phenomenon, writhe around, midriffs exposed, in the video for "Don't Cha" singing, "Don't cha wish your girlfriend was hot like me? Don't cha wish your girlfriend was a freak like me?" while their founder, Robin Antin, tells reporters, "It's always about female empowerment for me."[1] And, in her 2008 chart-topping song, "I Kissed a Girl" Katy Perry, who is out as a heterosexual, sings, "Just wanna try you on" and celebrates her exploration by calling her female partner an "experimental game." Yet, in these same texts, beside the declarations of female sexual agency we are presented with images and narratives that position women as objects of male pleasure. Beyonce's strong stance that her desire is permissible is met with the contradictory line repeated over and over again in the song's chorus: "If you like it, then you shoulda have put a ring on it." With one small two-letter word, Beyonce positions herself as much an object as the mannequin she burns, to be taken at will by the man to whom she sings, and conflates her body (or at the very least her finger) with her self. As for the empowered Pussycat Dolls, their reality show "Search for the Next Doll," claims to teach contestants to have confidence. On one episode Antin, the group's founder, came up with an activity for girls to "show off their confidence"; the challenge was for each contestant to don burlesque attire and dance around for an audience in a glass cage. And, consider the chorus for Katy Perry's song whose other lyrics suggest a sexual agent who wants to experiment with lesbian desire. She sings, "I kissed a girl just to try it. I hope my boyfriend won't mind it." Moreover, as one feminist blogger writes of the music video, which ends with Perry curled up in bed next to her boyfriend,

> We have faux homosexuality that plays into the male gaze with a video full of women in fishnets and underwear, gyrating and having giggly pillow fights, all while not actually kissing each other. The absence of any kissing, while nice because that's one less titillation for the Male Gaze, drives the point home that this song and dance is really just about a male fantasy having nothing to do with the desires of women.[2]

Aapola, Gonick, and Harris argue that despite the new focus on female sexual agency in girl power, "young women are encouraged to relate to their bodies as objects that exist for the use and aesthetic pleasure of others."[3] Likewise, in her semiotic analysis of *Seventeen* magazine, Durham found that sexuality is presented as spectacle for male pleasure and as available for purchase through consumption of market commodities.[4] Ariel Levy notes that this understanding of sexuality is problematic because we come to equate sexuality with sexiness.[5] The message is that sexuality is not a personal experience, not something one cultivates internally, and not something one might seek to honor and celebrate inwardly. Rather, female sexuality becomes conflated with male pleasure, not female pleasure. Tolman, who has studied girls' sexual desires extensively, finds that girls often say that sexual encounters "just happened" because they are "under systematic pressure not to feel, know, or act on their sexual desire."[6] She argues that teen girls are barraged with images of female sexuality but rarely see images of females wanting or enjoying sexual acts.

As we can hear in the conversation between Thea and Meg, which begins this chapter, the girls in this study are often aware of the conflicting discourses they encounter and they struggle to make sense of female sexuality, objectification, and agency in girl power media culture. This struggle is nowhere more clear than in the story of Gillian, a seventeen-year-old Caucasian student from Excel, who tells about watching an awards show several years ago. She explains that a music awards show that was hosted by comedian Chris Rock provoked her thoughts about sexuality:

> The Beastie Boys, one of the guys, came up and it was recently after there was a big rape at one of the concerts somewhere. He was talking about women's equality and how women should not be treated like that. He took time in accepting the award to make that speech and at the same time Lil' Kim wore a dress where, like, her breast was out and she had a shell over the nipple, and Chris Rock came out and said "Well, there would be a lot less raping if Lil' Kim would put her breast away," or something like that.

The member of The Beastie Boys, an all-White, all-male rap group, told audiences that women should not be made into objects and should not be treated as objects, but as human beings who deserve equality and dignity; African-American comedian Chris Rock told audiences that women should not expect to be treated with dignity or respect if they continue to objectify themselves (a la Lil' Kim who wears clothing that encourages a male gaze); Lil' Kim, an African-American rapper, did not have a voice in this narrative except in her style—which communicated either a message of "sexuality as power" (i.e., my choice, my body, my clothes, my power), a message of complicity (i.e., I accept this role as object in exchange for money and/or fame), or a message of exploitation (i.e., I have no control over my image. I am a pawn of the music industry). Gillian is not sure who to listen to and who makes the most sense. Add to the mix the contradictory feminist messages Gillian hears about choice/agency and about sexual objectification, and her confusion becomes palpable:

> So then it's like, well according to the Beastie Boys guy she should be able to wear whatever she wants and guys shouldn't look at her and they shouldn't make comments. But at the same time, you're putting yourself at risk. Is Chris Rock right?... But at the same time, she's allowed to do what she wants to do. If you really want to be a feminist, you can't really make the statement that other people are dressing skanky. They should be able to wear what they want to wear.... But, maybe she shouldn't dress like that. She's giving women a bad name, and then she's just asking to be mistreated. And again, it's like this whole split and I don't really know which side I'm on. It's kinda hard. I don't know if I'm being very clear.

Gillian's confusion is understandable in a girl power media culture that offers a complex discourse about sexuality and then attempts to simplify it with the message that sexuality is power. And, to whom is Gillian to listen? Who should she believe? Does she trust the White man who says women should be treated with respect, the African-American man who suggests women should respect themselves, the African-American—woman who seemingly has no voice in this discussion, or the "feminists" who provide her with another set of conflicting discourses?

## SEXUALITY IN FEMINISM

The "sex wars" of feminism's second wave debated the role of sex in the liberation of women and many of these conversations continue today. One side argues that sexualization of the female body is synonymous with objectification and exploitation; in their view, media texts position women as perpetually sexually available,[7] consumable by the male gaze,[8] and victims in heterosexual encounters.[9] A woman's subjectivity—her whole being, her agency, her intellect, and her desire—is reduced to her body and turned into an object to be consumed by men.

While they share a concern over violence against women and their bodies, sex-positive feminists argue that women should honor, rather than repress, their own sexual desire and pleasure as a key to ending their gender oppression.[10] For sex-positive feminists, media texts that depict women embracing sexual desire and playing with sexuality may be powerful because they challenge traditional representations of women as passive objects rather than active subjects in the heterosexual encounter. Third-wave feminists have tended to reject anti-sex or "victim feminism," in favor of a sex-positive feminist agenda.[11] Baumgardner and Richards explain that for third wave feminists, being opposed to the sexual exploitation of women does not mean being opposed to female sexuality.[12] Riordan elaborates, "While many third wave feminists focus on asserting one's sexuality, it is not necessarily for the male gaze. It is often for a girl gaze, one that allows girls to be both subject and object."[13] These feminists argue that being an agent in the sexual encounter, or in the creation of one's own public display of sexuality, can be liberatory because it challenges normative gender roles that prescribe repression and containment of sexual desire for women.

As a commodified social movement, girl power media culture takes the third-wave desire for power through sexuality and combines it with the capitalist "sex sells" imperative to produce a discourse in which sexuality equals power over men, as well as large revenues for sex-positive performers and those who profit from their public display of sexuality. Gill argues that sexual imagery in girl power is novel and can be read as a backlash in direct response to second-wave feminism, "putting women back in their place—and, simultaneously as a reassurance for men threatened by girls' increasingly good [educational] performance…and women's success in the workplace."[14] While these images of sexual power offer a different narrative to girls—one that stresses desire, self-determination, and sexual agency—this narrative is missing a complex understanding of exactly which women are entitled to sexual agency and power, the anxieties that revolve around positioning the body as an instrument of power, and the social, psychological, and economic requirements of this revised body narrative. Gill identifies this as a narrative that is used to construct the "neoliberal feminine subject" and elaborates:

> What this shift entails is a move from an *external male judging gaze to a self-policing narcissistic gaze.* I would argue that it represents a higher or deeper form of exploitation than objectification—one in which

> the objectifying male gaze is internalized to form a new disciplinary regime. This representational practice offers women the promise of power by becoming an object of desire. It endows women with the status of active subjecthood so that they can then "choose" to become sex objects because this suits their "liberated" interests. In this way, sexual objectification can be presented not as something done to women by some men, but as the freely chosen wish of active, confident, assertive female subjects.[15]

Indeed, as the girls in this study explore the layered meanings in the public displays of female sexuality in girl power, Gill's argument gains even more traction.

## Pop Music and Female Sexuality

Although Frith and McRobbie painted a picture of women as subordinated to men in the world of rock (they "dress up and sing what they are told"[16]), more recent studies have described a music scene in which women's voices are powerful and resistive to patriarchal oppression. Pop stars from the 1980s (Cyndi Lauper and Madonna, for example) have been praised for their ability to speak to female audiences in a language they relate to and with a rhetorical stance that defies the containment of female voice, desire, and rebellion.[17] Whiteley argues that some artists from this era challenged dominant ideologies about gender by playing with traditional codes of femininity.[18] Madonna, in particular, has been seen as a site on which the binary nature of gender and sexuality are challenged.[19]

Contemporary music (video, lyrics, and performance) has also been positioned, by some, as a challenge to hegemonic femininity. Rana Emerson argues that videos in which Black women R&B and hip-hop performers articulate self-determination provide a space in which new, powerful images of "Black womanhood" are produced.[20] In these videos, women are able to demonstrate autonomy over sexual expression and sexual objectification. Writing about a different genre, Gayle Wald highlights the music and performance of Gwen Stefani to argue that female-penned and -performed pop-rock music can offer an image of "transgressive femininity" by adopting an ironic stance and image in relation to the notion of "girl."[21] As did Whiteley, Wald argues that as these performers play with the markers of "girl" and "feminine," they work to challenge traditional ideologies and to express both rage and pleasure.[22]

Still, Lemish raises the concern over the conflicting messages encoded in these musical texts. In her analysis of the Spice Girls and ethnographic study of the group's Israeli fans, Lemish finds that the group promotes a model of girlhood that is independent of men but has lyrical content that largely centers on heterosexual relationships and offers girls no models for what to do with their (sexual) freedom. Further, she concludes that although girl power rhetoric helps girls think less traditionally about female success and of acceptable female sexuality, it perpetuates the beauty myth. These girls considered the Spice Girls' message to be a statement of strength, self-confidence, and agency, and used this message to understand their own oppressive experiences at school and to console themselves as victims of this oppression. However, they also found that being a feminist agent was only possible if one was conventionally attractive. Thus, Lemish argues that the Spice Girls' girl power reifies the importance of looks and beauty in female identity even while it produces an oppositional femininity.[23] Likewise, Kristen Schilt found that while the "angry women" of 1990s pop-rock addressed patriarchy, sexual abuse, and female desire, they perpetuated traditional imagery of female beauty and sexuality.[24] This chapter takes up the questions Lemish and Schilt pose about how girls understand the complex messages they encounter in pop music in the era of girl power.

## "Nobody's Squirting Champagne on Me": Girl Power's Sexual Agent

In a 2004 interview in *Jane* magazine, twenty-four-year-old Irish-Latina American pop singer Christina Aguilera explains her position on the role of sexuality in her music:

> The message I try to convey is to be a strong female and not to be afraid of the flack that goes along with that. If I make a video where I am flirting with being sexually provocative, it can be seen in two different ways. To me, that is my expression of being very much in the power position. I've never backed down to a man in my videos. Nobody's squirting champagne on me.[25]

The other way the sexual image could be seen, according to Aguilera, is as a "total slut."[26] Aguilera's conceptualization of being in the "power position" rather than being the "total slut" reflects discourses of sexuality in girl power media culture that situate women as agents in equal heterosexual exchange and establish sex as a tool that women can use in their enactment of "girl power."

Many of the girls in this study echoed Aguilera's position that being comfortable in her sexuality is an important quality for a woman. While Jenna, a White fourteen-year-old from Brooklyn, recognizes that girl power media culture operates within a larger sexist culture so that "a lot of people think [that] if you're more open about yourself then you're a whore or whatever," she believes that being comfortable in your sexuality is "a very strong thing, a good thing." She says, "to be aware of your sexuality and be comfortable with it, you know, like 'this is my body, this is who I am.' I think it's good, and it's strong."

Ellie, a Caucasian sixteen-year-old, agrees that understanding the self as a sexual being makes a woman strong. She cautions, however, that "there is a fine line between acknowledging that you are a sexual person and being comfortable with your sexuality, on the one hand, and doing what someone tells you that you should be doing like doing seductive moves and wearing lots of mascara." Her sophisticated awareness of the distinction between sexuality and sexiness reflects her understanding of the contradictory nature of girl power media.

Brianna, a seventeen-year-old Panamanian-Jamaican teen from the Bronx, suggests that Missy Elliot fits this description because she appears to be focused on her artistry rather than on her sexuality. Brianna explains that "[y]ou don't have to come with a mini skirt and show your skin to be considered sexy. You can wear a hat to the side or a v-neck shirt, some tight jeans, and sneakers and still look sexy. It's just the way you carry yourself." For Brianna, Missy embodies this genuine sexual identity because she is not one of those people "thinking their voice can get heard by what they're wearing." Instead, Brianna, says, "[I]f you can make your voice heard through who you are and what you're saying then that speaks a lot and so that says more about your character and that you have powerful words." Though Brianna identifies a woman's stance, or the way she positions herself, as the core of her sexuality, she still uses consumer goods associated with stereotypical sexiness—tight jeans and a shirt that has a "V" pointing to cleavage—to describe the attire for a performer who is connected to herself as a sexual being.

Along with many of their peers, these girls share the belief that strong women "own their sexuality." Unlike Brianna, Jenna's understanding of a woman who is connected to her own sexual self is not dependent on consumer goods or spectacle:

> I would say that when you own your sexuality, you know who you are, like you understand your person, you understand what's inside of you. This is all psychological, like inside of you, like in your subconscious, you know the essence of you, like you're a woman, you're a strong woman, and you're proud of every part of your body, and you're proud of your ideas, and you believe in anything and everything that comes out of your mouth and you believe completely in what you say, and so you have opinions. Your opinions belong to you and you believe in them, and they come from your own thoughts and it's just like, not even like your sexuality, like it's who you are, you're being, you're so in tune with it, and it's just like you know yourself through and through like a book that you've read like five times, you know everything, anything, you know.

It is women who own their sexuality that are icons of girl power. The girl power demonstrated by these celebrities is derived from their sexual power, an internal knowledge of themselves as sexual beings, and an active agentic subject position in relation to their sexuality. It is these women who appear able to resist the culture industry's pull to exploit and objectify women's bodies that the girls respect. But, how do girls identify sexual ownership?

## Consistency versus Change: Talking about Public Sexual Display in Pop Music

For many of the girls, the mark of a sexually comfortable woman is consistency rather than change because consistency suggests a natural oneness with sexuality rather than a constructed, false sexuality. Change, on the other hand, which often occurs in the direction of a less overt sexual persona to one that is more overtly sexual, is seen by the girls as fake and as the manufacture of a culture industry rather that as an authentic shift in sexual persona.

Shakira, a Columbian-born, bilingual pop-rock, singer-songwriter, has been consistent in portraying the image of a multicultural, sexy, rock artist who is serious about her craft since she released her first English-language album in 2001. For seventeen-year-old Juana, a Hispanic/Dominican girl from the Bronx, Shakira's consistency is evidence that "she's kind of like her own person." While Juana astutely observes that in the world of music "[y]ou have to compete...and, if you're a woman in that industry, you have to be kind of appealing in some way, and that's basically being attractive to men," she also believes that Shakira's "tough...but at the same time sexy and feminine" vibe is somewhat genuine. In part because she has read and seen less about Shakira in the celebrity gossip mediascape, Juana perceives Shakira to have a lack of interest in making sure she is photographed by the paparazzi. This communicates an authenticity to Juana because Shakira appears to be uninterested in publicizing her sexual exploits or herself, in general.

In addition, it is Shakira's inclusion of cultural identity in her performance and in her presentation of self that suggests authenticity to Juana. Juana speaks of Shakira's sense of style and the belly dancing she does in performances and videos, as well as her ability to be successful in both the Spanish- and English-speaking markets, as evidence of her strong connection to her Latina heritage.[27] Juana explains, "She's...how can I say it...she has like her culture, like she shows her culture in everything she does...She still has the Latin in her." Juana identifies with this commitment to one's native culture as she immigrated to the United States from the Dominican Republic when she was seven, just ten years before our interview. She laughs freely about her old hairstyles and the fact that many of her teachers and classmates had difficulty understanding her when she spoke. At the same time, Juana has a deep sense that she is Dominican. It is this same sense of self and of cultural identity that she senses from Shakira. Shakira's sexual image is genuine to Juana because it is consistent (in terms of staying true to her heritage and in maintaining the same style over the years) and appears to be produced in private rather than in the public eye.

On the other hand, according to Juana, Mariah Carey, another artist whose music Juana enjoys, is not authentic in the presentation of her sexual identity. Unlike Shakira, whose image has been consistent,

Mariah Carey's has changed dramatically over the years. In the 1980s, Mariah Carey, a biracial teen of Irish and African-American descent, was discovered by record executive Tommy Mottola. Her first album, filled with strong pop ballads, was released in 1990 by Sony Records, the company for whom Mottola worked. Three years and two albums later, Mottola and Carey married in a highly publicized wedding and she declared to the press that she was living a "fairy tale."[28] However, when the two split in 1998, Carey revealed that Mottola had been very controlling. While she had wanted to perform a more youthful style of music that had links to her African-American heritage and to dress in a style that reflected her youthful sexuality, Mottola maintained control over her image and insisted that she remain more an elegant balladeer than a sexy soul singer.[29] According to one interview, Carey revealed:

> "When I was a kid I felt like a misfit and an outcast because of my [biracial] heritage and the way people made me feel about it," the native New Yorker said, referring to the days when she could walk on neither side of her family and feel completely comfortable. "In my music—in the days when I was being told what to do, if you know what I mean—I was told to push all of that even further down, and it tore me up."[30]

After the duo divorced, Mariah did indeed begin to dress more scantily and to make music that had roots in hip-hop and soul. In 2001, just months before her first movie was to be released, Carey was admitted to a hospital, and then a psychiatric facility, after suffering a public "emotional and physical breakdown" in which she posted diary entries about exhaustion on her website and nearly stripped on a live MTV show.[31]

When Juana thinks of Mariah Carey, she first reflects on her vocal talent. Juana admits, however, to being influenced by the negative publicity Mariah has received, especially by the news that she was in a "mental institution." This breakdown, as well as her lack of image consistency, is evidence, to Juana, of Mariah's lack of connection to herself. Mariah's video for the 2001 release, "Loverboy," solidified Juana's feeling that Mariah is not true to herself. In the video, Mariah raises the flags to indicate the start of a race at a racetrack on a summer day. She is filmed in various skimpy outfits including short shorts and belly-revealing tank tops. It is not the tiny tanks and revealing shorts that irk Juana, rather it is her sense that Mariah is inauthentic in this overt display of sexual identity. She explains, "Like, you can wear clothes like that and it look good, but on her it just didn't fit, like the way, the kind of person she is." Juana explains the disconnect between Mariah's previously conservative image and her newer sexually liberal image: "For some reason, maybe because I already had an image of her, of like being more reserved, and then when I saw her in the video, it kind of skeeved me out."[32]

What this disconnect indicates to Juana is that, unlike Shakira who is sexy but does not "show too much" and who does not appear overly interested in public displays of sexuality, Mariah is going out of her way by "trying to be sexy. She's trying to keep up with all the other artists." Although Juana does not mention all the "other artists" with whom Mariah tries to "keep up," we can assume she is talking about other female popular artists in girl power media culture who use sexual imagery as a central facet of their celebrity identity.

Moreover, although Juana does not mention cultural heritage in her discussion of Mariah Carey, given the significance it plays for her in identifying Shakira's authenticity, one might speculate that Mariah's shift in sound, from pop to hip-hop–infused R&B, might also be a cause for Juana's skepticism. Despite the fact that Mariah has publicly claimed that she initially marketed her music to a White/pop audience rather Black/hip-hop audience due to pressure from her record label/husband, Juana might see Mariah as fickle and sales-driven unlike Shakira who has woven her Latina heritage into her performance even as she crossed over to an English-speaking audience.

Razia also feels that Mariah Carey has been inconsistent in her sexual styling and has been driven to be more sexually explicit in her dress due to her interest in increasing sales profits:

> There was a point in time when I loved her. She used to wear [pant] suits and she was married and she had that beautiful look, and then all of a sudden I don't know what happened. All of a sudden she's in that song like "Butterfly" and she's like hardly, she's just in a slip. . . . I don't think that's cool, she's so like, eewwwww, she sells her body. I don't like it. I have no idea [why she changed]. Maybe because of her divorce and her husband didn't let her wear what she wanted to wear. I think maybe it was that, or just the fact that she needed more

fame and she wanted to get up there, just like all the other girls, they want to get up there so they have to sell themselves, and I don't think that's cool.[33]

In the end, the defining line is that Mariah has constructed her sexual identity too publicly for Juana and Razia's taste. Shakira seems like she's "just being herself"; but with Mariah, the mediated, open shift in sexual identity has made her seem inauthentic. The difference, Juana says, is that for "some people [sexuality] just comes out naturally, and then others have to really, really work hard at it in order to attract attention."

This desire for consistency was repeated by many of the girls. In the following focus group transcript, the girls from Victory discuss Lil' Kim, a rap artist best known for her eccentric and outstandingly sparse outfits. After listening to the girls argue that some female celebrities just dress in a sexual way "to get famous" or to make money, and others dress in a similar way because they "just like it," I asked the girls how they can discern the difference between the two reasons for sexual dress:

EZ: How can you tell if somebody likes it or she's just doing it 'cause she knows it will make her money?
STACEY: Depending on what they did in the past.
PAOLA: Like, Lil' Kim did it since the first time she came out.
QUIANNA: True.
PAOLA: She's like that.
BRIANNA: I mean, if you been doing it from day one, then everybody knows already you love to do that, but if you just...you go from wearing...
STACEY: From being conservative to being skimpy and then you go back to being conservative.
BRIANNA: Exactly. Instead of having just a bra and panties on [from the beginning]. Then it's an issue.

In an interview, Helen, a sixteen-year-old Chinese girl, who taught herself how to play the guitar, uses the same criteria to determine the authenticity of singer-songwriter Michelle Branch's sexual image. As she discusses the drastic shift in the sexual imagery of Michelle Branch, as well as the shift in her music style from a more folksy sound to a pop-inspired one, Helen explains her suspicions about the lack of authenticity in Branch's new sexual persona:

> Well, I used to like Michelle Branch, but, like, did you see her on *Maxim* magazine? She was wearing shorts and everything. 'Cause, like, when she first came out I thought she was really cool, like she just, for a while she was like those country-ish singers. I'm like "Wow, that's really cool." 'Cause she would just go out there with only a guitar and no amplifier. She would just sing; I'm like that's really talented of her. Then, after a while like they transformed her into like this…'ho of Hollywood. They dress her up in like those miniskirts with those shirts and I'm like "This is not her." When her third album came out it was totally different. It used to be her only and her guitar and I thought "This is really real; this is music." The one that just came out, it sounded like a Britney Spears album and I was like "This is not her."

In Helen's eyes Michelle Branch was "really real" because she was not molded by "them." In her sparse musical approach and her casual style, Branch offered Helen a model of authenticity in a mediated market bursting with constructed images. As with Juana's perception of Mariah Carey, it was the public manufacturing of sexual imagery that led Helen to believe that Michelle Branch was not being herself. When the girls do not witness an artist's manufacture (i.e., when it has happened before the artist is in the public spotlight), they assume, as the focus group from Victory suggests, that her sexual persona is authentic and self-produced rather than constructed within a profit-driven industry.

Helen explains that Branch even stopped playing her guitar, the instrument that was so central to her early identity as an artist, at live performances and replaced the instrument with "shake and dance." On MTV's *Diary*, Branch revealed some of the struggle that she had with her image handlers confirming Helen's own belief that it was "they" who were constructing the new Michelle Branch rather than Branch herself. Helen explains that on the MTV program, Branch discusses how she had wanted to bring her old "beat up" guitar on stage when she performed, but "they" wanted her to have a newer, slicker-looking instrument. Of note, Helen has a limited view of Branch's manufactured persona, not considering that the innocent, rootsy style first appropriated by Branch may also have been a marketing tool.

In the case of Juana, Helen, and the girls from Victory High School, the sense that the changes they see are manufactured by the culture industry or by an artist who seeks financial gain, rather than by an individual who is coming into her own sexual identity, are the central defining factors in who "owns her sexuality" and who is sexually exploited. For these girls, as for many of the participants in this study, lack of consistency in image was a determining factor in assessing the authenticity of an artist's public sexual persona and the ability of an artist to control her own image. While the girls seem aware of the patriarchal, capitalist use of women's bodies for profit, their exchanges imply that the girls think that becoming a pop star happens as an authentic, and one-time, act of self-creation and industry/audience discovery. They appear not to think of the culture industry as manufacturing celebrity or of molding an artist's image to fit into the pop genre but rather as corrupting authentic artists only after they have been incorporated into its industrial fold. Nor do these girls think of identity as a process but as a presentation of one's true self. There is no room in this model for messy contradictions or negotiations of identity and sexuality. These girls do not suggest that it is possible that the celebrity who started her career dressing in stereotypically sexy attire may have done so intentionally to gain fame and fortune from the start or may have been under the control of powerful managers, video directors, and record labels who determined her image. They present identity and image construction as binary—one is either true to her identity and owns her sexuality or she does not.

Yet, while the public manufacture of sexual identity seems to be the prevailing factor the girls use in determining who is a sexual subject and who is a sexual object, the case of Christina Aguilera demonstrates that a strong public relations campaign which includes repeated assurance from the artist that she is in control of her sexual image can override many of the girls' dominant beliefs about sexual subjectivity and how media industries and image production operate. In magazine interviews, on her website, and on MTV and VH1 programs, Christina Aguilera has repeatedly created a narrative that supports the notion that she is an active subject in determining the sexual imagery she portrays.[34]

### XTINA: "DOING HER OWN THING"

Christina Aguilera's public narrative begins in the suburbs of Pittsburgh where, as a child, she and her mother were physically and emotionally abused by her father. Driven to succeed despite her abusive childhood, Aguilera's vocal talent flourished. Though she was victim to peers taunts after she lost a *Star Search* competition at age nine, Aguilera was hired to be a regular cast member on Disney's *New Mickey Mouse Club* show when she was twelve. Aguilera flew back and forth from Pittsburgh to Orlando to shoot the show during school breaks. As a small-time celebrity, Aguilera again faced her classmates' taunts and felt isolated.[35] In 1998, at the age of sixteen, Aguilera, still an unknown, was selected to sing "Reflection," the only single from Disney's *Mulan* (1998) soundtrack. As a Mouseketeer and a key performer on the soundtrack for a Disney children's movie, Aguilera's image was marked by innocence and youth.

At seventeen, with a deal from RCA music, Aguilera recorded a self-titled album. The hit single, "Genie in a Bottle" was described as an "infectious, near-sultry" tune that "finds Aguilera offering sweet rewards if she's rubbed the right way."[36] Yet, says the same reporter, "there's nothing particularly sexual in her offer, which suggests more adolescent heat than adult fire."[37] Another reporter called her look "wholesomely sexy."[38]

When Aguilera released *Stripped*, her sophomore English-language album,[39] in 2002, she proclaimed its title was indicative of her intent to "strip" down and introduce the world to the "real" Aguilera.[40] Much as Mariah Carey had done after her split from Mottola, Aguilera characterized *Stripped* as a mark of freedom from industry control. Her official website detailed this independence:

> "I felt trapped," she admits. "I was under the thumb of people who were mostly interested in keeping me doing exactly the same thing. But I'm not blaming anyone." . . . The sixteen new tracks that comprise *Stripped*. . . showcase an unadorned, unfettered and fearlessly outspoken artist who has liberated herself, her soul and her music on an album that is as much a declaration of independence as it is a convincing demonstration of her fierce and original talent. Simply put, this is the real deal.

*Stripped* serves also as a double-entendre for a performer who is not only stripping off her mask, but also stripping off her clothes. On the CD cover, Aguilera, thin and White, and wearing layers of mascara, appears topless, her long bleach-blonde and black hair covering her breasts. In the video for the record's first single, "Dirrty," Aguilera appears in chaps worn over a bikini. Shortly after the release of her album she appeared nude, or seminude, in *Rolling Stone*, *Maxim*, and *Blender.* And, with a new tattoo on her neck, she gave herself the nickname "Xtina" that suggested an X-rated version of the former Christina.

On this album, Aguilera positioned herself as a survivor. Not only did she confront her father about his abuse on "I'm OK," but in a lead-in for a song entitled "Fighter," Aguilera also refused to be victim to someone who wronged her. Taking a survivor's stance, Aguilera said, "After all you put me through, you'd think I'd despise you. But in the end, I want to thank you 'cause you made me that much stronger."

Aguilera was also public about her fighting stance against the critique, by fans and media alike, of her sexier, edgier look. Aguilera declared, "That's just me growing up and being a girl and exploring all facets of that" and in response to feminists who might argue that she is being objectified by men or objectifying herself, she retorted, "[A] lot of women who criticize other women for not being afraid of their sexuality are actually just afraid of their own."[41]

Moreover, she was vocal about her struggle to convince MTV to air her video for "Can't Hold Us Down," a song about the sexual double standard that celebrates men who have multiple sex partners while encouraging women to be chaste. The song's lyrics promote gender equality, unity, and feminist social change. In this song, Aguilera tells her listeners that there is a female common experience. She says we all encounter men who "don't respect [our] worth" and who think "all women should be seen not heard." The chorus calls on girls to do something about it: "shout louder" and "let them know we're gonna stand our ground."

The song's video begins with Aguilera and guest rapper Lil' Kim walking down an urban street wearing short shorts and bikini tops. After Aguilera's bottom is grabbed by a young man on the street, she confronts him with the pro-women lyrics. At one point in the video Aguilera is holding a hose between her legs and "squirting down boys."[42] It was her intention, she says, to convey an "expression of women having power over the boys."[43] According to Aguilera, when the video was rejected from rotation on MTV because it was too risqué, she "wrote a letter to the board of MTV." She told Esther Haynes of *Jane* magazine: "I gave 10 examples of other videos—like Lil' Jon, for example, in the Usher video, he's doing that [*she simulates masturbation*] with a bottle of champagne. Okay, I don't see that being banned whatsoever. It's like let the women finally be on top for a minute."[44] Aguilera's public relations campaign revolves around the narrative of a survivor: an abused child who is rejected by peers but prevails and gets recognized by the music industry. This previously manipulated girl is finally able to be herself—a highly sexually playful and empowered woman—on her sophomore release. In this narrative, Aguilera wears her sexuality as a badge of power; she controls her image in ways that she has never been able to before (having been the victim of an abuser, jealous peers, and manipulative record executives).

Aguilera's neoliberal narrative of choice is widely distributed across various media and the girls in my study overwhelmingly trust its veracity. While other performers who have moved from being sexually reserved to sexually expressive are often held in suspicion as pawns of an industry that seeks to exploit them or as industry-driven celebrities who are selling their bodies for fame and money, Aguilera is successful at creating an image that it is she who controls her sexual persona and that she made the shift to a more sexual image for the sheer pleasure it brings to her rather than because the near-pornographic images that she creates are financially lucrative.

Lili, a seventeen-year-old Dominican student at Victory, sums up her impression of Aguilera: "She doesn't do it to get famous. She just do it 'cause she likes it." Lili's classmates agree with her and draw on Aguilera's narrative to prove their point:

STACEY: I think she is different because back then they wanted a little innocent teeny bopper, a little pop tart thing, but she comes out and says . . .

MICHELLE: That wasn't who she was.

KRISTALY: That was who the people wanted her to be.

LILI: She was doing what people wanted. Now she's doing what *she* wants.

Several of the girls at the Bridge School, a prep school where students learn media criticism, also take Aguilera's story at face value and see Aguilera as a celebrity who has been able to operate on her own terms within the music industry:

> THEA: She really seems to enjoy it.
>
> ADRIENNE: I was watching this special on her. It was on VH1 or something and she said the first years of her career she was like more conservative, like blonde, little, pop type of person, and like that's what her label wanted her to be like...and then afterwards like "Dirrty" and...
>
> THEA: She's being herself.

Amber, a thirteen-year-old African-American member of the Gardens Girl Scout Troop, also trusts that Aguilera gets to operate outside of the reigns of the culture industry. Although Amber thinks that the way Aguilera dresses is inappropriate, she likes Aguilera's music and respects her as an independent woman who chooses to dress the way she does: "She took a lot of stuff to get where she was. So the way how she covers her little bootie, that's like, that's disgusting, but it's not like people telling her what to do. It's her doing the things herself. She's doing her own thing. She's not a puppet." Many of the girls not only believe that Aguilera enjoys being overtly sexual and suggestive and that she manufactures her sexual image for her own pleasure rather than because of an industrial imperative or the internalization of mythic sexuality, they also accept her assertion that her sexuality is a signifier of her power.

Jenna explains how the song "Dirrty," in which Aguilera announces that she is ready to "get dirty" and identifies what she likes and what she "needs" to "get off," proves her connection to her own sexual identity and her comfort with being a sexual person. Jenna posits, "'I want to get Dirrty' or whatever that song was, she's like really close with her sexuality...I love that song. She's strong. I think she's really strong." Seventeen-year-old Colleen, who identifies as Caucasian/Irish, explains that while Aguilera's style may generate questions such as, "If people look up to you, why are you gonna wear that?" her lyrics in "Can't Hold Us Down" about "the double standard" demonstrate that her overt sexuality is "also sending this message of, like, confidence and encouraging girls to have more confidence and be less insecure."

Sixteen-year-old Sierra, a White girl from the Bridge School, draws on the video images of Aguilera being in "control of the [sexual] situation" to argue that, in Aguilera's videos, "the women are seducing men as opposed to just being toys to them." Sierra contrasts the "sexuality as power" imagery with "a lot of the rapper videos where there's one huge rapper guy and thirty women all over him." In "Dirrty," she explains, "Christina [was] drawing attention to herself or whatever and she was saying I'm proud of my sexuality, let's go have sex. A lot of these rap videos and pop [videos], it's just like a guy thing. Like 'I get all these 'ho's and they love me.' And it's just a different position to put women in." Notably, the girls in this study did not seem to find it ironic that Aguilera's image, although perhaps one of resistance against the music industry and against the representation of female sexual agency, is not one of resistance against "the pop orthodoxy"[45] of what it looks like to be sexy despite her lyrical claim that "[w]e are beautiful no matter what they say." In this sense, Aguilera's public display reifies the cultural myth that sexiness is "directly correlated with the privileged body: a slender, voluptuous, youthful and Caucasian female figure."[46] This demonstrates, once again, the complex, layered messages girls receive about sexuality in girl power media and the confusion they experience as they work to make sense of what they see.

The veracity of Christina Aguilera's sexual image was contested by only a few girls. Simone reminded her troop mates during our focus group that Aguilera has "people who dress her" and Ellie, who sees Aguilera as more of a commodity, suggests that the artist, as the product of the culture industry, may be experiencing false consciousness if she believes that she truly enjoys being a sexual object:

> She's been under a major record label since she hit puberty, so I mean, since like fifteen, so, like, I think that's... people have been telling her what to do with her body since she was young enough to have anything to do with her body in the first place. You know, so who knows what's going on in her life.

The case of Aguilera is significant because most of the girls in this study believed that she is an artist who enjoys and is in control of her public sexual image. While they generally use an unscientific litmus test with consistency as a marker for sexual subjectivity, in the case of Aguilera they accept the story she has told repeatedly in various media texts and trust that she is able to operate outside of industry control. More importantly, in the case of Aguilera, the girls generally accept, without questioning its credibility or implications, that the artist's soft-core pornographic representations are images of female sexual power.

## An Unwilling Sex Symbol: Problematizing Authenticity

The measures that the girls use to determine sexual subjectivity and authenticity of a sexual persona are problematic on several counts, not least of which is that these criteria potentially falter in the face of a well-crafted public relations campaign. In addition, the test creates a binary ruling: one is either an authentic sexual subject and true to her own sexual identity or she is an inauthentic pawn of a culture industry that objectifies her. The complexity of sexual identity and the public crafting of sexual persona are obscured by this simplistic assessment of authenticity. What this dualistic measure overlooks are complicated questions: Is "sexual subjectification," or the shift from passive, victim-ridden objectification to active, self-inflicting objectification more pernicious as Gill suggests?[47] Can an artist choose to make herself an object for a reason other than money and fame? Can a woman take pleasure in positioning herself as object? (Possibilities of this might include pleasure in being submissive, pleasure in creating an ironic submissive stance in response to a previous abusive relationship, pleasure in the money that comes from putting oneself in this position, or pleasure in knowing the paradox between her appearance creating the imagery of a woman lacking power and the reality of her actions creating gains in her personal cultural and economic capital.) Does pleasure in the construction of a sexual image inevitably determine one's position as sexual subject? Does the act of making oneself an object for money and fame position a woman as a subject/agent in her own image production? How do lyrics and public declarations of "sexuality as power" work against, and with, visual images of stereotypically objectified sexuality?

The complicated nature of these questions about the relationship of power, sexuality, and public sexual image becomes clear in my exchanges with Sierra about Fiona Apple, her favorite singer-songwriter.

Fiona Apple is known as being an eccentric artist who demands control over her songwriting.[48] Her first album, *Tidal* (1996) included the single, "Criminal," a song about a woman who has cheated on a male lover and hurt him simply because she has the power to do so. In "Criminal" Apple declares that she's a "bad girl" because she's "been careless with a delicate man" and broken him "just because she can."

In the song's video, Apple was cast as a "Lolita-ish suburban party girl"[49] who "rolled around nearly naked" in a sea of male and female bodies with whom, it was implied, she was "a bad, bad girl."[50] As Sierra worked to explain how she determined an artist's sexual subjectivity, she offered Apple's role in the "Criminal" video as an example:

> I mean, I think like a lot of people who are celebrities just like the attention and they use sex because they like sex. I mean, some people are just oversexed and they want to strip for people and that makes them happy and it's not objectifying themselves. It's like, hey, we don't like clothes. It's like Fiona Apple in her "Criminal" video. She's not the person who is being forced by people to strip. She just felt like being half naked in that video.

Moreover, Sierra understood Apple's sexual role in the video in much the same way as she understood Aguilera's role in her "Can't Hold Us Down" video. She explained that "the whole song was about her using guys" so that she is "really in control of the situation." Sierra, who defines herself as bisexual and as a feminist, tries to reconcile these images of "sexuality as power" against what she has learned about female objectification. She says:

> Even though it is sexual and like "guys should love me" and it's about bringing attention to themselves, and using the typical sex appeal, I don't know, it's just...it's not like a situation where they're being taken [against] their will, you know, being raped, which is also a very common thing. You know it's something that they want. Their sexuality is something that they're proud of.

At the Bridge School focus group, and Sierra's individual interview, where these exchanges took place, Sierra paints Fiona Apple as an agent who controls her own sexual image. She connects the lyrics of "Criminal," written by Apple, with the video directed by Mark

Romanek, to determine that Apple took pleasure in the sexual image she portrayed in her video, felt proud of the sexual image she portrayed, and was demonstrating a sense of power in her sexual presentation.

Approximately a month after our last meeting, however, Sierra sent an email with the following message, which references an article she found on the Internet about Fiona Apple:

> ::sigh:: As much as i've tried to convince myself that Fiona isn't a sex symbol, she says it herself in a recent interview:
>
> ... 'Criminal' is one video in particular that Apple has issues with. It is no secret that she strongly dislikes the video, which is overtly sexual. She is resentful that the people around her at the time convinced her that it would be a good way to get attention in the industry. The video made her an unwilling sex symbol, which she does not feel she can live up to. "Underwear plus good lighting equals sex symbol," she quips. She is flattered that people might find her attractive, but at the same time, the guarded singer is uncomfortable with opening herself up for public scrutiny. She admits, "as smart as I think I am, I'm still going to be hurt if somebody says something mean about me." For the most part, Apple has tolerated her public image. "The only one that matters, I know what he thinks," she says with a smile referring to her boyfriend. (From www. thebookla.com)
>
> We all know sex sells and Fiona sells better with sex. A simple connection of course. Of course i adore her.

Ending her thoughts on Apple with the declarations: "A simple connection" and "Of course i adore her," Sierra overlooks the real complexity of sexual subjectivity in the era of girl power. What makes this even less of a "simple connection" is that Apple publicly shares with the press and therefore her fans that she was raped by a stranger at the age of twelve.[51] Though I do not know whether Sierra was aware of Apple's history as a rape survivor, Apple's appearance, as a Lolita-type sexualized teen in the video for "Criminal," goes beyond the simple "sex sells" adage. It raises questions about what it means for Apple to be giving up control of her sexual image and what it means for her to be in the position of victimizer (she "breaks the boy just because [she] can"), rather than the sexual victim.

Girl audiences in girl power media culture are repeatedly reminded, in lyrics and visual representations, that their sexuality is a powerful tool and that they can, in this era, have control over their desire, sexuality, and sexual representation. Yet the images girls see are public ones, coordinated by various image handlers, coded in the myths about sexuality that Durham has identified—linked to a specific beauty culture and produced as spectacle for a male gaze. Sierra discovers that what she thought was emblematic of the "sexuality as power" motif was actually a painfully wrong choice by an artist who, in retrospect, feels she was objectified and exploited.

In addition, Sierra does not comment on Apple's statement that her boyfriend, not she, is the "only one that matters." This comment is in direct contrast to the notion of "owned" sexuality that, as Ellie explains, describes women who have an inner sense of sexual oneness, women who are "really, sort of, in touch with themselves and [who] really just understand themselves." Apple's very image is confusing. She is reputed to be in control of her art and appears in "Criminal" as a girl who has willingly engaged in sexual acts. Yet, Apple has also been violated in the flesh and in her image production. As Sierra tries to make sense of the complex, contradictory image she falls back on music industry language that "sex sells" and on the simplistic girl power discourse that sexual expression is powerful.

In her analysis of identity and image constructions of women in hip-hop, Imani Perry asks why women who appear to be "linguistic proponents of women's power [and] subjectivity" through feminist lyrics continue to "participate in creating . . . conflicting visual textual representations" in their videos.[52] In attempting to answer her own question, Perry asserts that we are "conflicted beings" who "want to be considered attractive even though we understand how our attractiveness is racialized, gendered, and classed in our society, and how the designation often affirms structures of power and domination."[53] In addition, she argues that conflict may arise between artists and the "record companies, stylists [and] video directors" when the former may (or may not) own their lyrics but often do not maintain authority over their images.[54]

In the answer to her significant question, Perry lays the groundwork for a deeper understanding of the relationship of public figures to their sexual image. However, she creates a dualism between lyrics and visual image when both have become increasingly complicated. In girl power media culture, *feminist* visual images and lyrics are shrink-wrapped with *feminine* visual images and lyrics. What results is conflict that rests not simply in our psyches nor in ownership of lyrics versus image but, as Gillian's discussion of Lil' Kim demonstrates, in a series of contradictory discourses that artists and audiences alike weave in and out of as they create and make meaning of the "sexuality as power" motif. Girls' discussions, which shift back and forth between acknowledging women's lack of power within a culture industry and accepting the neoliberal version of female sexuality that suggests women are free agents acting on their own behalf, demonstrate the confusion they are experiencing as they work to make sense of these images. Ultimately, rooted in individual power, power over men, and a politics of choice, girl power pop music does not encourage the girls in this study to consider the need to change norms of beauty and sexuality or to complexly question the position of women in the culture industry.

CHAPTER 4

# The Clothed Body: Girls' Social and Emotional Experiences of Style

> I get scared of passing through the student lounge. It's like a fashion show. Like everybody just looks at you. Like you could see eyes burning you. Every little step you do. Everything you do. That's why I don't pass through there anymore. (Juana, seventeen years old, Hispanic/Dominican)

> When I was in the fifth grade I used to feel a little bit left out because I wore *Reebok* sneakers. The first time I got *Nike* sneakers was in the sixth grade and I felt so happy. All the other kids were wearing *Sean John* shirts and *Seven* jeans. They're name brands and when you walk it looks nice because somebody is going to know the value of your outfit. (Razia, seventeen years old, Afghan)

> I'm starting to change my whole wardrobe. I [was] a tomboy but now I really want to go overboard. Like, I really wanna wear like heels and a little button down shirt, you know, nice slacks. I'm from the Bronx; all the girls wear jeans and sneakers and that's not me. I wanna look more presentable, more...you know...sophisticated. That's me." (Paola, seventeen years old, Honduran)

ON MEDIALOOKBOOK.COM WEB SURFERS CAN SEARCH BY CHARACTER, actor, or episode to find the fashions worn in *Gossip Girl*, a teen drama about wealthy New York City prep-schoolers. On the "fabsugar (have, want, need)" blog, links are provided to buy the clothes worn on the show. Writing about one of the show's main characters the blog says:

> Blair Waldorf had an exceptional wardrobe, one of them being a delicate white eyelet dress she wore to a fundraiser brunch at a posh hotel. Like a true rich girl, she donned pearl bracelets, a girlie headband and just to spice things up, a pair of sexy patterned tights. Sticking with the innocent-but-sexy motif, she wore black patent Mary Janes on her feet. Do you love her ensemble as much as I do? Get the look below...and don't forget to watch the show next week then check back here for more fabulous outfits!

*Cosmopolitan* magazine's website also offers "style selections from the latest episodes" featuring pictures from *Gossip Girl* along with prices for each article of clothing and links to purchase the goods. It seems there is an endless loop of promotion involving *Gossip Girl*, advertisers, clothing manufacturers, clothing retailers, popular magazines, and web pages. This is not unique to *Gossip Girl*; hyper-consumptive behavior, and the promotion of such behavior, is a central feature of the late capitalist era in which girl power emerged.

Style has been linked to girl power discourse through media texts that feature autonomous, vocal, and sassy teen girls who are clothed in the latest trends as well as through the conflation of the terms "girl power" and "purchasing power" in fashion trade publications and the popular press.[1] Moreover, companies have used girl power discourse and imagery to code their products as empowering. Jane cosmetics was a corporate "power partner" in the Health and Human Services Girl Power Campaign launched during the Clinton presidency; Nike ran the "Let Me Play" ad featuring young girls asking to be allowed to participate in athletics in order to increase their self-esteem and reduce the risks of unwanted pregnancy and depression; and an ad in Dove's "Campaign for Real Beauty" showed a young girl facing the onslaught of exploitative images of women and suggested that mothers talk to their daughters "before the beauty industry does," but failed to mention, of course, that parent company Unilever is brand owner of several beauty products as well as the Slim-Fast diet product. Pomerantz also identifies music videos, reality TV makeover shows, and the tabloid culture that focuses on young female celebrities as mediated locations of the girl power discourse and girls' style consumption.[2] Indeed, as discussed in the introduction, some feminists question whether girl power ever moves beyond style. They suggest that girl power media culture may simply be a stylish cloak for mass-marketed girls' commodities and clothes rather than a cultural moment infused with social critique and offering non-normative narratives of femininity.

While the body has been foreground in many studies of women and girls, the main foci of such studies have been on weight, dieting, body shape, eating, and body dissatisfaction disorders[3] as well as on the relationship between sexuality, representation, and the female body.[4] A few recent studies have turned their attention to the body in clothes.[5] As we can hear in the quotes from Juana, Razia, and Paola, that begin this chapter, just like the naked body, the dressed body represents a site on which gender, emotion, and self are narrated[6] and on which identity is visible, surveilled by outsiders, and enacted upon by its owner.[7] To dress oneself is to clothe and to conceal; creating a style is, at once, a performance of the self and a way to disguise the self from onlookers.

## Style as Communicating Identity/Style as a Technique of Social Order

If style is a "way that the human values, structures, and assumptions in a given society are aesthetically expressed and received," then the practice of producing, selecting, and dressing oneself in a particular style is a means through which members of a culture create a narrative of self and perform identity.[8] Clothing the body becomes a way to name oneself, mark oneself, disguise oneself, and engage in dialogue with multiple and conflicting social discourses. Yet perhaps because of its association with the feminine or with triviality, fashion has been largely under-theorized.[9]

Drawing on Barthes, Cultural Studies scholars have made some inroads into analyzing the role of clothing and style as communication by exploring the ways that subcultural groups (and the individuals who identify with those subcultures) have appropriated various cultural symbols to distort the power of commodities and produce new, counter-hegemonic and collective identities.[10] Extending this analysis, girls' sartorial play has been theorized as an ideological incursion against normative femininity. McRobbie has argued that teen girls may develop alternative paradigms of style to claim independence from the structures they feel imposed upon them by school authorities and by social class status.[11] More recently Heilman posited that girls gain "power and meaning through commodification"[12] and Pomerantz, acknowledging that style is entwined with "constructions of girlhood in the marketplace," lists the potentials of style to "signal belonging, desire, cultural and lifestyle affiliations, individuality, image, and personal taste."[13] These analyses bring light to the ways in which fashion and style are used as tools to produce and reproduce malleable gender identities.

From a more critical perspective, such acts may be seen not only as hyperbolic fantasies about girls' style play "dismantl[ing] the ideological apparatus," as Lisa Lewis has suggested, but also as acts of self-regulation.[14] Driscoll theorizes the relationship between girls and style as a complex one wrought with tension between agency and complicity. Using a Foucauldian analysis she argues that while girls do articulate their identities through fashion, it is also important to recognize them as willing subjects to the cultural sanctions and regulations that organize style. According to Foucault, power operates in such a way that individuals are not forced to behave within ideological boundaries, nor forbidden to resist them, but are rather led to manage themselves. Girls are indeed agentic; they not only use dress to engage in identity projects, they actively participate in self-surveillance and regulate their acts of style.[15] As Skeggs has suggested in her study of British working-class girls, given this self-regulation, the body draped in style, while a site of pleasure, can also be a "site of anxiety, regulation, and surveillance."[16] As a marker of class, race, and gender, the clothed body becomes a site on which girls can demonstrate their knowledge of fashion, and design identities to perform; it also becomes a site on which they have to "prove themselves [and their class position] through every object, every aesthetic display, every appearance."[17] Style is a cultural practice through which girls are not only objects of surveillance but through which girls are subjects, policing themselves and negotiating social locations and relationships. Style play, then, is not only the enactment of individual taste, but also a mechanism through which social difference, power, and economic inequalities are sustained.

## PHOEBE AND MISSY[18]: "I'M GONNA DO MY OWN THING, WHATEVER. THAT'S IT."

Early in my study I was surprised that one of the characters who was repeatedly named as a strong and independent woman was Phoebe Buffay (Lisa Kudrow) from *Friends*. As the program's female comic relief, the Phoebe character has been described as a "birdbrain," and as "the ditsiest [sic] blonde to be seen on television since Goldie Hawn in the '60s."[19] With a cocked head and ever-changing unprofessional career, Phoebe never struck me as anything but distracting and, frankly, annoying. While she was not usually the direct butt of jokes, she was "the blonde" of the show's cast; unlike Rachel (Jennifer Aniston) and Monica (Courtney Cox), the other women on the show, Phoebe was rarely serious and often appeared unintelligent. Phoebe lacked the ambition we saw from Monica, who throughout the show was working toward becoming a noted New York City chef, and from Rachel, who fulfilled her dream of working in the fashion world when she landed a job as an assistant buyer at Bloomingdale's and later in the executive offices at Ralph Lauren. Phoebe, on the other hand, was a masseuse who also worked as a telemarketer, a guitar teacher, a Salvation Army donations collector, an extra on a soap opera, and a temporary office assistant. On occasion Phoebe also performed the mediocre songs she wrote at the café where she and her friends gathered. Phoebe is the female Friend who seemed least connected to the other two women on the show. For the majority of the series, she did not live with any of the other Friends and she often seemed to be a source of laughter for the Friends rather than a source of comfort or companionship.

Phoebe's unconventional career choices and her seeming lack of connection with her peer group could be seen as character flaws. Moreover, if second-wave feminists focused their struggles on, among other things, equality in pay and job opportunities, and the right to be treated with dignity, Phoebe could be seen as a character without feminist sensibilities; she appears to accept the role of the vacuous blonde and is content in low-paying, feminized jobs. Yet, Phoebe was seen by many of the teen participants in this study as a strong and independent woman who does indeed have a feminist, or at least oppositional, approach to life. It is Phoebe's very lack of desire to be respected by the outside world or to take a conventional job that positions her as someone who embodies the feminist values of independence and selfhood to which participants were drawn.[20]

Specifically, girls frequently noted Phoebe's anti-normative style as the core of her unconventionality and self-determination. Jenna describes Phoebe as wearing "really wacky clothes" that have "bunches of fabric sewn together in odd patterns and shapes and sizes" or "weird animal prints." Colleen remarks that Phoebe is also noted for wearing her "hair in a weird style where everything is twisted up or like she's got hair poofing out on different sides." In direct contrast are Monica and Rachel who embody a more typical femininity. Not only are both of these characters often involved with men, but they also both appear to spend more time on their appearance; they wear the latest fashions and their hair is always coiffed. Moreover, the actresses who play Monica and Rachel are high-profile tabloid celebrities who are often noted for their hair, clothing, and choice of mates.[21] The girls who view Phoebe as a strong, independent woman, understand her peers' situatedness in beauty culture to be linked directly to a female gender identity that is concerned with normative success such as male approval and career achievement. Suzie, a fourteen-year-old White girl, for example, contrasts Phoebe with Rachel who is "always thinking about herself and what she can do to get a better boyfriend. She's like, 'Oh, I gotta do my hair so I can get a boyfriend' or 'so I can do well on this interview' or whatever." Likewise, Razia, a seventeen-year-old Afghan-American living in Queens, explains, "Both of the other two girls focus on their looks sometimes [but Phoebe is] always wearing these gramma dresses, her hair . . . she just doesn't care. She's just doing whatever she feels like." Phoebe's attire constructs her as a free spirit who does not concern herself with "dressing for success" in either social or professional realms.

Several girls contrasted Phoebe's style with what is typically expected of a woman and what they know is expected of them as girls. Jenna articulates very clearly why Phoebe's anti-normative style is appealing to herself and her peers:

> Most people enjoy wacky characters because in life there is a certain way that you have to act—society's way. Like with the wearing things there is always like this certain kind of conformity that people feel the

> need, you know.... There are certain fashions, certain trends that you feel the need or you want to follow and, like Phoebe, she just doesn't care what people think and she just does what she wants whenever she wants.

And Razia illustrates how this unique style makes Phoebe a strong woman:

> It's like she goes in her own world and she'll wear what she wants. I look at her and I'll be like I don't think anybody would ever wear that. I like that character though. She could care less what she's wearing, what she's saying and what she's doing. So, when you have that in you, you make yourself happy. That makes her strong.

Though the girls in this study are growing up in a girl power era informed by third-wave feminism, in which femininity is celebrated, accentuated, and consciously performed, they recall the language of second-wave feminists when they establish Phoebe's style as a commitment to an authentic self rather then one whose femininity is mandated by her dress. Second-wave feminists distrusted fashion and considered it a patriarchal tool that had to be resisted. They extended the "personal as political" discourse to fashion and conflated the rejection of mainstream fashion with the rejection of enforced stereotypical femininity.[22] Phoebe represents to these girls, not a dumb blonde, but a woman whose style articulates, "I'm gonna do my own thing, whatever. That's it." (Colleen). It is Phoebe's control over her own style and her refusal to use clothing in the performance of a normative femininity that resonates with the girls in my study.

Another woman that was repeatedly touted by participants as a strong and independent woman based on her unique, somewhat comical, atypically feminine style was rapper Missy Elliott. Missy, whose first video, for the 1997 song "Rain," featured her with spiky hair and dressed in a garbage bag, kept up the penchant for unusual outfits when she appeared in a 1999 video wearing a space-age jumpsuit and showed up at the 2003 MTV Video Music Awards in green and yellow plaid knickers and a hat topped with a yellow pom-pom. Missy is respected by critics and fans alike for her nonconforming sound and style. Although some women vocalists in the hip-hop have succeeded in resisting sexual exploitation by creating "public displays of physical and sexual freedom [that]...challenge male notions of female sexuality and pleasure,"[23] bell hooks argues that industry-supported, popular female hip-hop artists have often used their bodies in ways that fulfill male fantasy rather than ways that demonstrate sexual agency.[24] In her analysis of contemporary music videos, Imani Perry demonstrates how the "visual image of Black women in hip-hop has rapidly deteriorated into one of widespread sexual objectification and degradation" so even female performers who vocalize an oppositional, nonobjectified stance in their lyrics are depicted visually as sexual objects.[25] Missy, however, represents a Black woman who has succeeded in the culture industry without adopting the feminine styling and formulaic musical approach of her peers.

Many of the girls in this study are drawn to Missy's style and appreciate that she challenges the gendered and raced categories established by the media industry. Brianna idolizes Missy because she believes the artist is "creative; like she comes up with her own style. She tries something new, different." African-American Quianna, an eighteen-year-old senior in high school, explains that Missy's style is "flamboyant, like she's just like out there and she does what she wants, she wears what she wants, and you can tell that's her sense of style." Gillian explains, "[Missy Elliot's] style is so different, just her beats...they're so weird....In one song, she played it backwards, I mean, who does that? And she always wears cool clothes; she came one year to the Grammy's in a suit with razors on it, which is kind of weird but again, it's different." Isa, an eighteen-year-old Hispanic girl who attends Monument Academy, feels she can sense Missy's authentic self-presentation in the artist's choice to continue wearing clothing atypical for women despite the fact that she has faced rumors about being gay.[26]

Missy's antiauthoritative stance could be interpreted as an example of pseudo-individualization or the appropriation of a counternormative persona for industrial profit.[27] Harris argues that in girl power culture girls' appreciation of style choices as powerful acts may be seen as a conflation of "making a choice at the mall" with "making a difference in the world."[28] However, this counter-hegemonic character, while certainly a commodity, is attractive to the girls because they are aware that female performers in the culture industry must fight consciously if they do not want to be objectified and they rarely see women who are able to resist the norms of femininity and society while still succeeding. Moreover, Missy supports her acts of style with lyrics that demand attention to the sexualization of young women. In "Wake-Up," a song urging Black youth to stop violence and illegal hustling, Missy admonishes, "if you gotta keep yah clothes on, it's alright." These lyrics speak to the girls in this study who respect Missy's ability to get her records sold without having to sell her body, and her suggestion that other girls growing up in the inner city can also succeed without selling their bodies. Unlike Phoebe, whose "wackiness" precludes a quest for success, Missy is strong to the girls precisely because she can be successful even as she refuses to follow the trends of the culture industry. Missy's success as a hip-hop artist, in conjunction with her position as an icon of feminist resistance (at least in the girls' eyes), is symbolic of girl power media cultures' conflicting, yet interwoven, discourses of the market and feminist politics.

This discussion demonstrates the pleasure girls experience in observing the fashion choices of a television character and a rapper who use style to play with identity and resist normative roles. This consideration of style as powerful is similar to that expressed by teens who, in previous studies, have felt empowered by their *own* involvement in the production and appropriation of styles that provided alternatives to the authority of school and industry.[29] However, the girls in this study rarely talk about using fashion and style as tools of power in their *own* lives. Rather, they often communicate a feeling of powerlessness and fear when it comes to their sartorial acts.

## Where Is the Fun? "I Might as Well Just Wear What They Wear"

At Victory, a public high school in the impoverished South Bronx, all students are required to wear uniforms to school. Most of the participants who attend this school live in neighborhoods in which nearly half of the households earn incomes below the poverty level.[30] Uniforms are intended to discourage clothing-based competition and discrimination as well as to encourage students to take themselves seriously. However, three to four times a year the school allows students to "dress down" and wear "street clothes" to school. The girls at Victory explained how such days can be "fun because you see other people and you feel good in what you're wearing" (Nikke, sixteen years old, Black-Nigerian), but are also fear-inducing days in which competition is rife. Yasmine explains, "It kind of is [stressful] because you are worrying about what everyone is going to think. Like, do I look nice and are these pants gonna look phat on me?[31] How is everyone going to react? Is she going to be wearing the same thing I'm wearing?" Her classmate, Paola admits, "I feel if I do wear [a style different than everyone else] then they're gonna start talking about it, you know what I'm sayin'? Even though I care less . . . I'll feel like I'm like an outcast." Bloustien also found that the girls in her study used style to volley for status within their peer group. For the girls in Bloustien's project, it was knowledge of fashion and the presentation of their bodies that was at the core of their positions within peer groups.[32] At Victory, however, as at the other sites in my study, socioeconomic status consistently emerged as the central factor in determining who was able to fully enjoy playing with style. Though they never see themselves as gatekeepers, girls from middle- and lower-income communities frequently feel that they are surveilled by classmates and worry that they will lose status if they are not dressed according to an unspoken code. Juana, who worries that she is exposing something "too deep" in her analysis of the social relations surrounding fashion at her school explains, "[I]n our environment it's not about sexy or skin that much . . . now it's like they look at the way you dress more like they judge your economic background on the way you dress." Although most of the girls do not express their anxieties about status as a socioeconomic class issue, we can hear in their discussion that losing social status is not solely about losing "cool points" but also about performing a classed identity.

As the girls speak about their experiences, it becomes clear that class and status are determined by clothing brand, cost of the clothing (regardless of its brand), and where clothing is purchased. Sixteen-year-old, Caribbean-American Stacey discusses how on dress-down day at Victory there is "probably a lot of discrimination because people like to come out and show that they have money. 'Cause you're wearing uniforms all year and when dress down days come, people like to show off that they have name brands." But class status is equally, if not more, prevalent at nonuniformed schools. Jenna grew tired of her classmates asking, "Why are you wearing that? Where did you buy that? How much did you pay for that?" and came to the decision, "I might as well just wear what they wear and spare all the grief." Suzie took a similar approach when she was "criticized" for her sneakers; she explains, of her more recent purchase, "I bought them at Payless just because I wanted the better price. I didn't want to have to spend $120 when I could get them for a cheaper price at Payless. Now no one makes fun of me anymore and they don't even know I bought them at Payless 'cause they're a brand name so they assume I bought them at some place like Modell's or Foot Locker." Suzie is not alone in concern over the point of purchase and being associated with a store that not only charges less for its shoes but also announces its intentions to do so in its name. Razia, whose quote about the anxiety she experiences over brand names, insists, "You will not catch me dead in Payless Shoes; you will not catch me dead in any of those. All of my sneakers are name brands... mostly I like name brand stuff."

In their study of young Asian and White women in the United Kingdom, Malson et al. noted that many girls proudly identified as "bargain girls" in celebration of their deal-finding skills in the marketplace.[33] Likewise, Skeggs' participants, though seeking to disidentify with working-class culture, did not want to be associated with middle-class "dispositions" and a sense of entitlement.[34] However, unlike the girls and young women from these other studies, who eschewed the styles and skills of their peers in upper social classes, the middle- and working-class girls in my study worked hard to avoid being associated with any class that would need to bargain shop and they certainly do identify with the sense that consumer-citizens are entitled to buy name brands and trendy styles. As Beattie discusses, it is important when translating British cultural theory to U.S. class politics to take into account that class in the United States is understood as temporary.[35] While "respectability" has been central to the "development of the notion of Englishness,"[36] it is the myth of equality and upward social mobility that has been central to the development of the notion of American-ness. This myth engenders the girls in this study with the belief that they can rise up out of the environment into which they were born and that this can be done, in part, through the consumption of style.

In addition, the girls at two of the high schools and those attending Girl Scout troops are participating in institutional settings designed with the mission of helping youth to elevate their educational, political, and social status (beyond that of their parents and many of their community members). With its uniform, Victory also imparts the "dress for success" myth so that the students are encouraged to equate appearance and style with the possibility of social class and status elevation. It is within these discourses—the social myths of equality and upward mobility that they learn at home and at school, as well as the girl power discourse of choice and power through style—that girls construct their identities and experience style locally.

The middle-class and working-class girls in my study fear that they are always in jeopardy of being judged, losing their social status, and not distancing themselves far enough from less entitled peers. Though they value style as a means of expression, and rejection of authority (and thus admire television characters and pop stars who use style to create alternative images of femininity and self), many of the girls in this study identify a great deal of regulatory pressure not to deviate from strict styles in their local cultures. The pressure they experience belies their love of fashion and shopping because they feel locked into style boundaries, based on socioeconomic coding. It is this mechanism that exerts regulatory pressure on girls and creates what Skeggs calls the "emotional politics of class," a visceral experience of inequality.[37] Girls may *wish* to use clothes to create symbolic economies of style but their classed performances often turn clothing into a disguise or a uniform that protects their standing but hides their sense of who they are or who they want to be.

## "I Don't Care How You Dress, I Don't Care How You Look": The Bridge School and Rhetoric of Choice

The girls at the Bridge School, a costly independent school in a wealthy neighborhood, dismiss the notion that social class is a factor in how girls in their school make style decisions. According to seventeen-year-old Meg, a Caucasian girl from a wealthy Brooklyn neighborhood, the Bridge School, is "a lot more laid back than other schools," and while there is peer pressure to conform to social norms, there is also room for experimentation in style. Moreover, each of these girls uses a rhetoric of choice to argue that she personally feels no anxiety about style.

Using the language of girl power, which values individual choice and personal agency, Adrienne, a sixteen-year-old Japanese-Brazilian girl who attends the Bridge School, says that the school's small size and progressive philosophies lead people to "just do their own thing and it's OK." She explains that social class and brands are not something people "worry" about because although "there's people who are really rich and people who are on scholarship...everyone just gets along." Meg agrees that their school preaches a nonconformist philosophy to the students but she says, "[I]t's like everyone's going to conform to some degree and it's your own choice on how much you are a conformist." She explains, "You've got some preppy people, you've got some people that are 'Oh, I'm really punk,' you've got some people who are like 'I'm really sad I'm really Emo.'" However, describing herself Meg says, "I don't care how you dress. I don't care how you look...I just want to feel comfortable, like, I don't care what I'm wearing." Similarly, Ellie claims that while there is some talk of style and competition around clothing at school, worrying about her looks is not important to her so that she just does not have "enough of a vested interest to be truly upset about any of it." Sierra says of her own style play,

> I tried to be the goth girl, I tried to be a preppy girl, and I tried to be this really eccentric girl. Now I don't tend to dress up and don't tend to care as much what people think. I really have great friends and I'm okay with who they are and they're okay with who I am and I don't really need to be something to be their friend which I'm more comfortable with because I'm not trying to live up to something that they think I am, so...it's where I fit in: being me.

This discussion suggests that this group of wealthier girls may not have to concern themselves with the indignity of always feeling that their worth is being judged by others. Moreover, they may speak of style as a nonissue because they do not necessarily feel that they must use style to promote their social class image. Indeed, recent scholarship has suggested that conspicuous consumption, or the act of making wealth visible through the acquisition and display of consumer goods, is not a universal act but one used more often by those who seek "to fend off the negative perception that [they are] poor."[38] Of her own research participants, Bloustein noticed that "the girls who could least afford the expensive fashionable labels wanted them and bought or attained them in some way."[39] Living in wealthy neighborhoods, attending an expensive school, and having parents in professional, high-income-generating careers, visible consumption may seem less important for these girls because their status is already solidified in the upper tier and they already have a level of social power within the system that their low-income and middle peers are struggling to attain.

Yet, the girls' complete denial that style is an issue at the Bridge School also indicates that there is more to uncover in this story. While there have been relatively few studies of girls in private schools, abundant research establishes that girls' performance of style—to position oneself socially, to fashion the body as desirable or near-perfect, to differentiate oneself from the norm—occurs across classes; though how they communicate about this performance may be distinct.[40]

## Style: Regulating Race or Opening Space for Hybrid Identities?

Inseparable, though distinct, from social class, race becomes a factor in who gets to play with fashion and in what ways. Girls—both girls of color and White girls—who attend schools with diverse student bodies often speak about feeling locked into certain styles based on racial codes. They express frustration that they are expected to wear racially coded styles and have been received poorly when they have crossed these raced style boundaries. Juana, who describes herself as Hispanic/Dominican, explains how she feels boxed in by some of the racially coded styles:

> For a Spanish girl mostly they stereotype you like you wear tight jeans and like you wear like very short shirts and its like Hispanics wear that and like Black girls wear like, they always wear their hair in braids and it happens all the time. I don't like it personally 'cause it's like I do wear tight jeans but if one day I want to come in with my hair braided, right away they are gonna say "Oh, you're trying to act like a Black girl." Right away you get judged for that. Sometimes you don't even want to hear it. That's why you just do what you can do.

Suzie, who identifies as Caucasian, and attends a school that in her estimation is two-thirds Black and Latino, feels like she cannot play much with fashion either. In her experience, White girls who try to dress in the contemporary hip-hop style can never quite succeed because "[e]ven if [White people] do try to dress like Beyonce, or try to dress like someone in publicity, they are still gonna make fun of you because you are White. No matter what, you are gonna be White to them and you're not gonna measure up to the expectations of being like Beyonce and stuff." Both Juana and Suzie seek to play with fashion by adopting styles they have seen in media and in their communities. While neither expresses a desire to be seen as a different race, both learn that people assume they are trying to pass as something else by coding themselves through style.

Cultural theorists have suggested that we are moving toward a hybridization of culture in which young people engage in a bricolage of cultural production by drawing on elements from their own and other races to piece together nonessentialist identities.[41] In such a global, commercial world, the essentialist notions of nation and race have emerged as arbitrary so that "the mythified unity of an imaginary community based on 'race' has evaporated."[42] Using the example of Blackness and hip-hop, Gilroy argues that youth cultures may contain "an inherent challenge to the logic of racial, national, and ethnic essentialism" because they are organized around age and generation, and are therefore hybrid by nature.[43] He imagines this hybridization of culture to allow for the creation of more organic identities that are produced in the cobbling together of cultural discourses and practices that resist traditional notions of fixed, unshifting identity.

In this age of the hybrid identity, Juana and Suzie want to adorn themselves with styles that represent multiple sides of their identities as fans of hip-hop and as arbiters of taste. But rather than acting as a conduit for the crossing of ethnic and/or racial borderlands, style becomes a way in which racial identity is policed. The peers who police Juana's style feel more comfortable when her identity is fixed and nameable; they do not want her to abandon her Hispanic identity for a more popular hip-hop culture with roots in the African-American community. Rather than resist this regulation, Juana submits because she fears losing friends and social status. In Suzie's case it is the students who are part of the African-American community who she believes want to stake a claim on what has now become a commercialized culture. Although Suzie may simply want to mimic the celebrities she admires, her actions are read against a history of envy, desire, hatred, and racism in which the "right to representation" comes under contest.[44]

Afghan-American Razia also has difficulty playing with her multiple styles. Where Malson et al. and Dwyer found that some of the young people they studied felt ease in shifting between British or "White" styles one day and "ethnic" styles the next, Razia would not dare wear her ethnic clothes outside.[45] Her parents are Afghan and she has spent time living in Pakistan, but in the United States she risks ostracization by peers if her dress is too un-American and risks getting in trouble with her family if her style is too American. At home she wears a Punjabi, which she describes as "loose" and "comfortable," but she insists she "would never go out in one." Yet to go out, she must be careful not to be too revealing because it will anger her father. Razia, at least at this moment in her life, does not seem to experience the "new ethnicity" of hybridity in the pleasurable way that the theorists imagined it to be. Rather than fun, flexibility, or fluidity, Razia feels stress because she is constantly having to negotiate "the rules" of those around her. Though she embraces a girl power discourse of individual choice, and seeks to be a woman in control of her career, her finances, and who she marries, Razia does not feel the ability to enact individual power in relation to her dress.

Other girls of color expressed feeling that their ability to play with style, and explore new approaches to fashion, is limited by the retail workers who stare and follow them around stores when they try to browse. Indeed, Hollows suggests that the "emphasis on freedom to play with lifestyles often neglects very basic questions about access to opportunities to consume."[46] The girls from Victory, who attend school on the edge of Manhattan's wealthy Upper West Side, and right near a new high-end mall, describe numerous experiences of discrimination during shopping excursions. Juana laments: "You walk into the place and you just feel like you don't belong there. You walk in and you just walk right back out 'cause you can see the people who work there look you up and down like, 'what are you doing here?' or else they just think you are a thief right away."

Although they do not specify to what exactly they attribute the reactions they receive, as they discuss their experiences, it becomes clear that they feel they are stereotyped based on a combination of age, class, and race. Juana feels that the retail workers are making the assessment that "you can't afford this store" based on a quick look at her.

These types of experiences may limit girls' ability to experiment with style because even if they want to try new brands and approaches to fashion, mimic their favorite celebrities, or challenge gender or racial norms, they may begin to feel as Juana does that "there are some places that we don't even dare to go." While studies demonstrate that "new hybridized subjectivities can be constituted" through these radical practices of subverting national and racial boundaries,[47] such studies do not always account for the young people who feel they cannot or who are not willing to transgress the system of surveillance that monitors and regulates the cultural borderlands.

When we explore the emotional responses that the girls in my study experience to their attempts at border crossings, we begin to understand that, while possible, border crossings are difficult and threatening. Attempts may not always be filled with the joy that cultural theorists feel when hearing about them. Indeed, the girls in this study who attend racially diverse schools and have attempted to cross racial boundaries in their style have been received with anger and skepticism. Rather than articulating new hybridized identities, or enacting the choice discourse they encounter in girl power media culture, these girls narrate selves that are regulated by peer surveillance.

## Rejecting the Margins: Girls Who Go Mainstream with Style

There were a small number of girls who did discuss the way in which style play was a pleasurable experience. Notably, these girls were not playing with subcultural style nor were they embracing the wacky counter-normative dress inspired by the Phoebe Buffay character and Missy Elliot. Rather, these girls experience the joy of fashion play as a powerful act not because it is outside of the mainstream but precisely because it is *in* the mainstream.

Paola, the seventeen-year-old Honduran girl, whose voice begins this chapter, explains that she is "trying" things out and experimenting with clothes so that she can change her image from a "tomboy," and a stereotypical jeans-clad Bronx-girl, to something "sophisticated," and "unexpected." Paola wants to look "nice," but she also wants to upset the norms in her dress. She wants to be "that little sassy girl with a bit of a boy in her 'cause I'm kind of rough." Borrowing style from popular magazines, and mixing with her own Bronx roughness, happily puts Paola outside of the realms of her local culture. She explains that her style can be described as

> [u]nexpected because nobody would expect me to do a style like that 'cause all the girls here wear pants and sweats. I'm bein' like, the way I'll dress I'll fit in if I go to Manhattan, you know Manhattan, I'll fit in there, you know what I'm sayin'? So that's what I'm tryin' to say, basically. I fit in over there more than I fit in over here.

Paola experiences her stylistic changes as pleasurable and also as a means of communicating (and perhaps initiating) her intention to be more "Manhattan," her code for sophisticated and successful.

Lili, another student from Victory, is less experimental but sees the work of fashion as something that "feels good." Lili, who is Dominican and lives in a working-class Bronx community, is very meticulous about her outfits when she leaves the house and on two occasions describes dressing up, and the acquisition of goods she wants, as something she might regret were she to die before satisfying her desires:

> Every time I go out, I don't like to wear the same thing; I like buying different things all the time and I'm very materialistic that way. I'm very concerned with how I'm gonna go outside. And I know that's not really good, but it's, the way I see it. That's how I'm happy and if I didn't get to enjoy it, and then I die, it will be like I didn't live up to what I wanted.

Even though Lili talks about buying things as an immediate satisfaction, and something she might miss out on if she died "tomorrow," like Paola, she describes her style as something that helps to set her up for the future. For these girls, cloaking themselves in a specific style creates an opportunity to explore a public persona and how people react to this image. She articulates

> The reason I think that I'm so much like this is because I think especially when you are in high school, you keep thinking that you are already gonna get out of high school. You already tryin' to find somebody. You don't want to get old without being with somebody. So I see that as that person needs to see how I handle myself. If I go outside not caring how I look, I'm sure I'm gonna find someone just like that. But, if I'm sure of myself, they gonna look at me the same way.

Like Lili and Paola, seventeen-year-old Tasha, who is Black and Guyanese, is actively using style to play with identity. Tasha explains that she did not really fit in with the other Black girls at her junior high school because it "was like really ghetto . . . and I would hang out with some people; they'd always be like 'Why are you so White? Why are you trying to be White?' " She says that she is different, not only in her musical tastes, but because she refuses to wear the "uniform" she associates with girls of her race. Trying to break into the music industry, Tasha has put extensions in her hair, wears clothes that "look good" to her, and sports blue-colored contacts in her eyes.

Paola, Lili, and Tasha talk about using style play to help them prepare for the future: find a suitable mate, situate them in a respected community position, launch a singing career. As working- and middle-class girls of color, being outside of the mainstream is not a goal but a reality. Living in the margins, these girls may play with fashion and style as a means to move closer to the center. Miller has suggested that for oppressed people, playing with style may be more about "gaining access to resources than [about] using acts of consumption as some kind of 'resistance.' "[48] Tasha, Lili, and Paola's acts of style could be interpreted as both a vehicle for access and also as resistance to racial codes, class stratification, and a social system that limits their upward mobility while promising the myth of a meritocracy. But significantly they choose to resist and fight for access by acquiring middle-class, mainstream styles rather than the alternative styles typically associated with resistance.

Yet these discursive acts are never undertaken without acts within competing discourses. These girls are able to experiment with dress and experience the joy of fashion play but they are still operating within a system of self-regulation. Thus while style may become a practice through which girls play with identity and publicly challenge their social location, it is also an act that fortifies their social, economic, and cultural power. Paola will not wear her new look to school for fear that she will be the victim of "a group of girls [who] huddle and like be in a corner and just watch anybody pass and say something about whatever they wearing" and Tasha feels ostracized because the very core of her racial identity is questioned. She rejects the essentialism of "Blackness" and "Afrocentric style" but is unable to create a "multicultural 'mix and match' ";[49] rather her style is limited by being definitively un-Black.

## Conclusion

Between 2006 and 2007 a debate emerged in the *European Journal of Women's Studies* that highlights current debates about how to theorize relationships between style, gender, power, and identity in girls' lives. Duits and van Zoonen, two Dutch feminists, published an article exploring how talk about Muslim girls' use of headscarves and White girls' adoption of new "porno-chic" styles reflects the current imposition of moral debates about decency, religion, ethnic identification, and femininity on girls' bodies.[50] In such a culture, they argue, girls' bodies are "entities that can be objectified, classified, and disciplined, and that do not need listening to."[51] The authors suggest that by shifting perspective, and giving girls the freedom to voice their own deliberate sartorial acts, feminist scholars might refocus the discussion from one of morality to one of agency, choice, and communication that evokes political and cultural values.

In a critical response, Gill argued that rather than bringing new light to girls' dress, the call to explore choice and agency actually "remains trapped in precisely the individualizing, neoliberal paradigm that requires our trenchant critique."[52] She questions how listening to girls speak about what they wear, why they wear it, and what they hope to communicate through their style will advance scholarship when it cannot account for the real social and cultural manifestations of ideology. She claims that girls living in girl power media culture cannot be critically engaged because they are already subjects of the cultural ideology. Thus, they celebrate girl power and highlight its freedoms rather than note how it oppresses and objectifies them.

Duits and van Zoonen rightly call for the inclusion of girls' voices into scholarly discussions of their bodies, clothes, and roles in society. Further, I agree with their rebuttal that the inclusion of girls' voices does not suggest that scholarship start and end with the reporting of girls' choices and intentions. Yet, along with Gill, these authors miss a crucial element to the discussion: when asked to talk about acts of style, what emerges is not a celebratory dialogue about choice and agency but a pained one about surveillance and restraint. Indeed, girls *feel* the impact of the neoliberal discourse in which their lives are enmeshed.

Gill argues that the "model of choice eschews psychological complexity by refusing to address how power works in and through subjects...by structuring our sense of self, by constructing particular kinds of subjectivity."[53] While girls certainly may not have the language to articulate all of the ways in which their bodies are observed and regulated, nor the roots, and the political ramifications, of such discipline, they are happy to discuss the social and emotional experiences of self-construction in neoliberalism.

Adding girls' voices and choices to the discussion of their relationship with style does not necessarily lead to a passing over of power or psychological complexity. While the girls in this study express admiration for characters such as Phoebe, and celebrities such as Missy Elliot, who use style as a subversive tool to play with identity and to offer alternative versions of femininity, they are also keenly aware of the socioeconomic and racial classificatory systems that limit their own transactions with style. The inability or refusal to participate in style play may be a sign of struggle to stay afloat in the commodified world and to perform the upward social mobility that is expected of them. While girls are active in selecting clothes, combining accoutrements, and performing narrative of self through style, an experience of pleasure and power does not always result from the act; often it is pain and fear that dominate. Girl power media culture may make promises of gaining power through style but for many of the girls in this study these promises are mitigated by real relations of power that are enforced not only by a culture industry but also by their local peer culture. It is, in fact, the discourse of choice, of individual power, that leads to such intense monitoring. Thus, the girls in this study feel a cultural discordance between the girl power discourse of style as a source of power and the reality of their own, often disempowered, experiences.

CHAPTER 5

# "I Don't Know What I'm Going to Do When It Happens": Independence, Motherhood, Careers, and Imagining the Future

> I want to be somebody who can actually get up and say, yeah, I got a job. A person who can actually pay bills, even though bills is like the worst thing, but you could be proud of yourself. You know, "This is my house. This is my phone," you know. You don't gotta share with anybody. Like you could just look at your mother, and your mother could look at you, and she could just say "You really make me proud" and that would be something nice because you did so much because even through a lot of downs you still bring yourself up. (Paola, seventeen years old, Honduran)

> I want to be in advertising...and I wanna have at least three children...and I want to live in a Brooklyn brownstone. And whenever I have my children, until they're old enough to take care of themselves, I'm gonna take off work...I want to be able to be home for them and like, you know, make them after school snacks and make sure they do their homework and everything and, until the older ones are old enough to bring the younger ones to school and make sure they get back safely...and I figure once they're old

> enough, I'm probably gonna get a part-time job doing what I did, and make sure I'm still home in time, or a little bit before or after that, to make sure that they're okay and that they've finished all their homework. (Jenna, fourteen years old, White)

When I started this project I did not intend to have a chapter that explored mothering and motherhood. As far as I know, none of the girls in this study were pregnant nor were any planning to start a family in the near future. Yet, when I began to ask the girls to discuss what strength and power looked like in women's lives, talk of mothers surfaced repeatedly. Specifically, the talk revolved around (real and fictional) mothers' independence—both their financial autonomy as well as their social and professional self-determination. Not surprisingly, issues of mothering also emerged when girls were asked to imagine their own futures. In discussions about their own mothers, celebrity mothers, mother characters on television, and the mothers they hoped to become, the girls drew on neoliberal girl power media discourse as they identified mothers' strength and power. Across race and class differences in social experience and in media preference, girls spoke about mothering (and the power associated with strong mothers) as an individualistic achievement rather than a collective enterprise. In their talk, girls constructed independence as power that emerges from the choice-making of individual women and did not address social and systemic issues surrounding childcare, state support, or corporate reform. The investment in individualism that pervades their discussions of mothers, aunts, and celebrities demonstrates the ways in which they have come to use the discourse of girl power as a means to accept the lack of meaningful state- or corporate support available in the postindustrialist service economy and to see this lack of support as choice rather than as the only option available to them.[1]

This chapter explores the ways in which the girls lauded mothers' self-sufficiency that emerged and flourished in isolation from other women, men, and/or community, as well as women's ability to create a satisfying work-family balance. While social location determined the specific dimensions of independent mothers, there was across race and class distinction the experience of cultural discordance between the mediated discourse of choice and power alongside the realities they have witnessed in the lives of women around them. Further, trapped in a neoliberal discourse that extols independent agents, and spurns collective movements of change, the girls flounder in girl power discourse—struggling to imagine individual solutions to the balancing of work and family as they dream about their futures.

## Media Moms: Representations of Mothers and Motherhood

Living in American media culture, specifically in a postfeminist girl power media culture, these girls are growing up in a discursive environment that values individualism over collectivity. Although there is surprisingly little written about representations of mothers, feminist scholars of media generally agree that two models of motherhood exist in postfeminist media: "good" mothers are valued power brokers who negotiate social systems by summoning their personal resiliency and "bad" mothers are women in the inner city who are (unworthy) dependents surviving off of the welfare system.

The widely circulated image of the welfare mother became a news media icon in the late 1980s and continued throughout the 1990s when the girls in this study were growing up and beginning to forge a self-image. The "welfare queen" stereotype positioned inner-city women of color as too lazy to work, as baby machines who reproduced simply to get an increase in welfare benefits, and as drug-dependent, irresponsible, mothers.[2] Consistent with the American "ideology of a culture of poverty," the representation of the mother dependent on state assistance focuses on the individual deficits of poor people, and women in particular as the "chief culprits," rather than on the structural deficiencies of the country's hierarchical class system in which poor people, a disproportionate number of whom are people of color, receive unequal education, social opportunities, and discrimination in the workplace.[3]

The image of the "bad welfare mother" who failed was promulgated in opposition to the successful, middle-class "new mom" who was seen in both news and entertainment media. Susan Douglas and Meredith Michaels demonstrate how:

> As media obsessions about the status of the family and the state of motherhood dominated the national stage in the 1980s and '90s

> [when a record number of women were working in the paid labor force], African American mothers and other women of color became the scapegoats onto whom white culture projected its own fears about mothers "abandoning" the home, losing their "maternal instinct," and neglecting their kids.[4]

They argue that as middle-class mothers solidified their positions in the professional world of work outside the home, they had to redefine the role of the mother. Johnston and Swanson demonstrate that contemporary women's magazines consistently offered women mixed messages about the roles and responsibilities of mothers; alternately suggesting that women who had a public-professional life were powerful but selfish while their counterparts, the stay-at-home moms, were selfless, overinvolved soccer moms who had failed to make a mark outside of the domestic sphere.[5] If these white, middle-class women were unsure whether they were spending enough time with their children, whether they were too lenient, whether they were too child-centered, or not child-centered enough, at least they could remember that they were not like the welfare mother—who was the quintessential "bad mother."

The "new mom" put women in an even tighter double bind. Going beyond the 1970s superwoman in which the working woman was expected to "bring home the bacon, fry it up in a pan, and never, never let you forget you're a man,"[6] "new momism" also requires that women never, never let themselves forget they are mothers. New moms are now expected to have high-status jobs, maintain sexy exteriors for their husbands, *and* also act as matriarchal martyrs who dote over their children.[7] Like the welfare mother, however, the "new mom" is still solely responsible for her own success or failure. Representations of mothers who fail to achieve success are not premised on structural inequities or social barriers, but rather on lack of "individual resiliency" and inability "to change and adapt to a volatile educational and labour market."[8] Mothers whose children do not achieve traditional markers of success, mothers who receive public assistance or support from family members, and mothers who cannot juggle all that "new momism" demands of them, appear to fail in this media culture because they seemingly can*not* "do."

Bonnie Dow who has analyzed representations of feminism on primetime television argues that the central question for postfeminism revolves around the integration of family life and work life.[9] Representations of "new moms" in postfeminist media have tended to exaggerate the ease with which women create harmony between their work and family lives, overlook the discrimination women experience in the workforce, and ignore the domestic labor women endure as primary caregivers and household maintainers.[10] As such, female characters who struggle to balance work and family, or fail at doing so, are portrayed as having made bad decisions rather than as victims of an oppressive system.[11] Dow notes that much of the postfeminist family television programming (as opposed to shows set in the workplace) refers to the mother characters working but rarely show the mothers' workplaces (although they do show the fathers' workplaces),[12] and Kaplan argues that mothers in postfeminist movies may have careers but focus most of their energies on mothering.[13] Positioning the home as the mother's primary location and nurturing as her primary vocation reifies motherhood as women's leading role.

A more recent sub-story within the tale of the "new mom" is the popular media feature about mothers who choose to leave the professional world to raise their children.[14] The myth that women are opting out of work outside the home in increasing numbers has been circulated in various forms since the end of World War II and its latest incarnation in a 2003 Sunday *New York Times* article was quickly replicated in major TV and print media. Like its antithetical story of women who choose to delay motherhood in order to assure unencumbered career development,[15] the story of the "opt-out revolution" is one rooted in neoliberalism. The most current version of this story is constructed around a postfeminist rhetoric of choice and individual responsibility, which overlooks the possibility that reforms in government and corporate aid, structure and mandates, as well as reforms in social philosophies about mothering, might create new ways in which women could participate in public/professional worlds and still provide adequate maternal care.[16]

Stories about "bad" mothers, "new moms," and those who opt out are all steeped in a trope of individual choice, leaving the girls in this study with the image of mothers as isolated agents whose strength, power, and success has been achieved without support from community, state, partners, or children. Despite what they know to be true about communal and supported childcare in their own lives, the girls' talk about mothers reifies this image. Moreover, raised with these images, many girls believe that the struggle encountered by women, in their quest to be active and successful in both family life and the paid labor force, is a result of individual failure rather than a result of the lack of progressive childcare policies, continuing sexist division of labor in the household, and wage inequities that make integration of these disparate spheres a difficult endeavor.

## BAD MOTHERS MAKE GOOD

When asked for examples of strong, independent women on television, the girls in this study—across their racial and class differences—frequently identified mothers who were unmarried and not in parenting relationships. As single mothers, these women fall perfectly into the myth of the isolated agent who operates outside of structural realities. At the same time, the single mother is always already a bad mother. She has failed at one of the primary responsibilities of traditional mothering: the creation and maintenance of a nuclear family. Further, if the labor of care is a mother's central duty,[17] then the single mother is seemingly remiss for not providing enough nurturance to keep her coparent happy and present. It is perhaps their starting point as bad mother that leads girls to revere single mothers for their ability to succeed as nurturers who provide care and direction for their children. The lower-income, inner-city girls in this study were particularly drawn to single mothers who demonstrated resilience in the face of economic hardship.

One such television mother, whose status as strong mother made her a topic of conversation in my focus group at Victory High School, was Nikki Parker—the lead character of UPN sitcom *The Parkers*. Played by voluptuous, full-figured Mo'nique Imes, Nikki Parker is a mother with a history. Her story, which first aired on *Moesha*, from which *The Parkers* spun off, is one of an African-American woman who elects to continue her education eighteen years after dropping out of high school to be a teenage wife and mother. The sitcom's humor revolves around the mother-daughter conflict that arises as Nikki enrolls in the same junior college as her daughter, Kim. While Nikki is a comedic character whose big personality invades her daughter's space and creates discomfort with a professor for whom she pines (and eventually marries), to the girls at Victory, what shines through are Nikki's survival skills and her ability to make good on a bad decision. Kristaly, a seventeen-year-old Latina, sums up Nikki's appeal in a slang phrase that needs no explanation: "No matter what she did, she was up on her school work and still trying to 'do her.'" Michelle explains in greater detail: "She's strong in that she had a child, dropped out of school, and then, now continuing to go back to school with the child, she lives by herself, she got divorced, and didn't let that bother her, she was strong enough to carry on and keep going and provide for her daughter."

Classmate Quianna agrees that Nikki is a likeable, resilient character: "I like the fact that she messed up when she was young, and she had a child and then she went back to college and then got back on track. And she's living with her and her daughter and she's getting everything situated together and that's what I like about her."

Another mother celebrated for her ability to transform from "bad mother" to "new mom" was Lorelai Gilmore of the *Gilmore Girls*. Although Lorelai does not attend school with her daughter, Rory, their situation is quite similar to that of Nikki and Kim Parker. Like Nikki, Lorelai had her daughter when she was very young (sixteen years old) and, as in *The Parkers*, the *Gilmore Girls* chronicles a mother and daughter growing up together. Living in the small Connecticut town of Lorelai's youth, the Gilmore girls have a close relationship talking openly about education, love, and Lorelai's wealthy parents. While Rory attends school, Lorelai begins to date and manage a new career. Unlike Nikki, Lorelai is a daughter to parents so wealthy that they are a part of Connecticut "society." Because she felt that her parents were controlling, Lorelai chose to raise Rory without their financial support and only finally accepted her parents' help with private schooling for Rory when it was determined that the public school she attended would not be challenging enough for the bright high schooler.

As the Victory girls value Nikki's ability to rebound from early mistakes and to achieve success with little or no help, Juana, of Monument Academy, says of Lorelai,

> I think she's very powerful for being able to raise her child. She's a single mom, raising her child alone, being able to give her a good education, give her a good life, and then she's like setting up her own business, like it was her lifelong dream and she was achieving it on her own basically without any help from anybody.... She decided, instead of relying on her parents' wealth, she decided to go around and raise her child and live by herself and she did a very good job. I admire her because she never depended on her parents' money although she had the opportunity. But she did her own stuff and she raised her own child in that way to be independent and to depend on herself only.

It does not matter to Juana that Lorelai *could* fall back on her parents' wealth, nor that she eventually did; it is the fact that she chose to struggle on her own, to live without financial and emotional support from those who could provide, that makes Lorelai independent.

The girls' interpretations of Nikki and Lorelai are based on their own experiences. Just as they discuss the bravery and power of the television moms, so, too, do they honor their own mothers—often single—who are surviving cheating or abusive husbands, poverty, the welfare system, and children with consumerist desire.

## "She Had Only Herself": Inner-City Girls Make Sense of Strength

The overwhelming sense that the inner-city girls of color have that independence is defined by resiliency is not surprising given what many of the women in their lives have experienced. It was not uncommon to hear girls' pride as they spoke about their own mothers' struggles and successes. For example, Stacey's mother who survived a rough marriage to a drug-addicted husband is powerful to her daughter because "[s]he's been through a lot—pregnancy at a young age, dealing with my father, divorce, raising two kids on her own, and taking the responsibility of my ten-year-old cousin—and it's really surprising to see her still standing, still working strong." And Michelle, who lauded Nikki for her independence, remarks that her mother raised four children without a husband and "she did it working by herself and doing it by herself and not depending on her mother, nobody. She only had herself."

Nancy Lopez documents that many Dominican, West Indian, and Haitian-American girls, most of whom grow up in female-headed households, learn that being independent means not relying on men for emotional or financial support.[18] Niobe Way found that the urban teens of color that she interviewed expressed pride in their mothers' ability to remain strong through the difficult experiences of poverty and to survive economic and emotional hardships without the support of fathers or other community members.[19] My own inquiry reflects these findings; girls construct independence as living without support from fathers/husbands, parents, churches, communities, or government aid. The language they use as they discuss the mothers of television and real life belies their sense that it is not just men without whom their mothers are able to function, it is community in general. At the same time, research in these communities suggests that single mothers do *not* raise their children in isolation. Independence may be a misnomer for the experiences of low-income women of color who have varying levels of community, family, and institutional support as they maintain successful families without the input of fathers.

Oyewumi explains that female community networks serve as important support for women in people of color communities. "Nonexclusive" mothering has historically been significant in African-American, Mexican-American, and Caribbean communities.[20] Collins calls the women who help to raise a family of children "other-mothers" and explains that the role of these women has been to assist biological mothers with parenting responsibilities.[21] Cauce et al. discuss how for young African-American mothers support is often found in churches or informal networks that organize to provide assistance. The community is important for established families as well; "African American women realize that the survival of the community's children depends on people willing to raise them" often alongside the children's biological mothers.[22] On several Caribbean islands there is a unique term, *macoumere*, which is a special friendship among women that "encapsulates a particular kind of relationship among women that is founded on trust and an expectation of mutual support—material and otherwise—particularly with regard to the raising of children."[23] This support from a community of women extends to New York City–based Caribbean families where "godmothers, aunts, grandmothers, and mothers" all serve as the "nodes in the women-centered webs of emotional support" whom young women can turn to in times of need.[24]

While some of the girls spoke about their experiences being raised by aunts, grandmothers, and foster mothers, these "other-mothers" were spoken about as stand-ins for biological mothers (either permanent or temporary) and praised for their own independence and personal strength rather than as a community network surrounding single biological mothers. When biological mothers were praised for their independence, none of the girls of color spoke about extended family, church, institutional, state, or community support that may have helped their families. Although I do not know how much public assistance or any informal support these particular families receive, I do know that many live in public housing and that in the Bronx, where many of the girls in this study reside, just over 10 percent of the population receives public assistance income and a greater number receives food stamps, social security, or disability payments.[25] In addition, some girls mentioned that their mothers had been in drug rehabilitation programs, attended career-training programs, and received treatment for depression. We can conclude that while the girls employ a neoliberal discourse of independence, many of their mothers did not, and do not, operate completely in isolation of community and institutional support networks.

In addition, within biological families, female children are expected to help support families by contributing to household organization and child rearing of siblings. Dodson and Lopez found that girls in low-income families were commonly asked to care for younger children (siblings, nieces, nephews, cousins) and that often "older daughters are considered 'second' or 'little momma' to younger siblings and are responsible for watching, disciplining, and nurturing them."[26] Female children are also responsible for household chores and for providing emotional support to parents who struggle financially and in personal relationships.[27] Indeed, although the girls in my study spoke about their mothers as fiercely independent, in other contexts they spoke about their own contributions to helping to maintain functional families. The girls talked about caring for siblings when parents were away or unable, participating in household chores, and in some cases, offering emotional stability when parents were in crisis.

Bahijah, a seventeen-year-old Black girl from the Bronx, whose mother stays at home to raise her seven children, explains that helping her mother with her younger siblings or with the household chores takes up most of her free time. When Bahijah talks about her experience helping with her youngest sister, who at the time of the study was three, she even uses the language of a mother—stating that *she*, rather than her mother, "had" her youngest sister:

> I remember having my sister, I had to take care of her a lot, because my mother would be stressed out. She was kind of old—she was thirty-five—and she already had six, so when she had my sister I kinda took it upon myself to take care of her whenever she cried. Like in the middle of the night, I would get up and give her her bottle; I would take her out like in the middle of the night in her stroller and push her up and down the street for her to sleep.

Paola, whose mother was clinically depressed, served as a surrogate parent for her siblings. Moving between the past and the present tense, it is difficult for both Paola, and readers, to know whether she is still acting as a "little momma": "She was going through depression. It was real bad. Sometimes the way she acts scared me, so I kind of took over. I take care of them. You know, sometimes I feel like they are my children 'cause I was with them for the longest. I honestly could say that I never really had a regular childhood." Why—if girls participate in family work, see female relatives participating in support positions, and likely see their mothers receive at least some assistance from churches, the state, and other community networks—do they maintain a definition of a strong woman as one who depends on no one but herself?

Anita Harris argues that this discursive construction of the independent woman reflects the materialist reality of an era in which young women are expected to achieve these successes without significant state- or community support. She posits that while education in the girl power era appears to create new opportunities for girls—and in many low-income, single-mother communities, women are expected to be primary wage earners—the deindustrialized, service-focused labor market as currently structured cannot accommodate all of the educated young women.[28] Young women's "choices are delimited by their lack of resources on the one hand and the diminishing youth job market on the other."[29] Moreover, the lack of institutionalized support for childcare, a weak policy on family leave, wage inequities, and the continuation of the "second shift" of housework, lead girls to use a neoliberal language of self-reliance.

Another reason they adopt the language of independence is because they are caught between what Harris calls the "can do" girl and the "at risk" girl. Where Harris positions the "can do" girl in opposition to the "at risk" girl, noting that these are raced and classed identifiers, the girls in this study straddle both monikers.[30] In their local environment they see men and women, including their mothers, who have "failed" to achieve the American Dream, have "failed" to achieve the new momist ideal, and have taken help from others, including their daughters. In this, and because they live in inner-city neighborhoods, they are "at risk." At the same time, they repeatedly encounter the message of a neoliberal, postfeminist girl power media culture, which stresses that they will, as Paola says at the beginning of this chapter, "become somebody." At the epicenter of these interweaving, conflicting discourses, the inner-city girls of color in this study forge an understanding of what it means to be a strong and independent woman in girl power media culture.

As they make sense of what it means to be a strong woman, they struggle between what they know to be strong—the resilience of their own mothers who have survived poverty and single motherhood with the support of public assistance, their families, and their own daughters—and what girl power discourse suggests is strong: mothers who survive with no support, whose independence connotes fiscal and emotional autonomy. These girls are engaged in an ongoing struggle to deny the image of the parasitic "welfare queen," while simultaneously struggling to become the "can do" girl. The discourse of individualism suggests that failure to achieve is due to personal inadequacies and reminds young women that "they must take personal responsibility for success or failure because the choices appear to be all before them."[31]

The intention here is not to suggest that mothers who receive government benefits should be grateful to receive what they are entitled nor that daughters should discount the work that their mothers do to raise them (including the work of creating community and fighting for existing services/benefits). Rather, the discrepancy between the discourse of independence and the reality of interdependence is significant because it not only highlights a sense of cultural discordance that may be experienced by the girls in this study, it also reifies a socioeconomic system that continues to make cuts to social welfare as well as a sociopolitical sensibility that views change as arising from individual acts rather than collective struggle.

While their middle-class peers encounter a different set of discursive constructions, they come to the same conclusion: to be a strong woman means to function independently rather than interdependently. Personal achievement is highly valued; collective struggle and community support are often overlooked.

## ABLE TO DO EVERYTHING FOR YOURSELF: MIDDLE-CLASS GIRLS MAKE SENSE OF STRENGTH

Although they less frequently invoke mothers in their discussion of strong women, a pattern emerged in which the middle-class girls, primarily raised in two-parent households, cited celebrity moms who are raising children without men or other partners, and female relatives who have broken from the norm and chosen less traditional work-family balancing acts as strong, independent women.

In their discussions of television-viewing habits, the lower-income girls generally focused on family-oriented programming such as *Everybody Loves Raymond*, *Reba*, *Gilmore Girls*, *The Parkers*, and *Sister Sister*, while the middle-class girls more commonly spoke about their appreciation of programming that emphasized friendship relationships (*Real World*, *Road Rules*, *Friends*, *Sex and the City*, *The OC*, *Will & Grace*) or professional lives (*CSI*, *American Idol*, *The Apprentice*, *Las Vegas*) rather than familial relationships. The women on the shows that the middle-class girls watch are either younger than typical middle-class mothers (as in the case of *The OC*, *Real World*, and *Road Rules*), do not raise children (as in the case of Grace from *Will & Grace*, the four female leads on *Sex and the City* until the fifth of six seasons, all of the friends on *Friends* until the ninth of ten seasons) or have children but are not depicted as the jugglers they need to be in order to be working mothers today (as in the case of the contestants on *American*

*Idol* who can seemingly leave their children while they go live on television for three months). Further distancing the image of motherhood from what these girls know in their own lives is the image of the successful mother in celebrity-profiling where mothers are portrayed as glamorous, sexy, and very often adoptive parents.[32] The middle-class girls are much less likely to focus on motherhood, especially independent motherhood, as a demonstration of strength for several reasons: most of them have not been raised by single mothers, their mothers have had access to higher education, childcare, health care, and other institutions of social capital; motherhood is not the determining factor of maturity in their communities;[33] and in much of the television programming with which they engage, women are childless.

Despite their less routine references to mothers, it became evident that a paradigm existed in which these girls praise those who they believe have chosen to raise children without men and emphasize the ability of these women to live outside of normative gender roles while successfully raising children, maintaining careers, and pursuing personal interests. Unlike the inner-city girls, whose own mothers were similar to the television mothers they found strong, the middle-class girls identified strong women who were decidedly *unlike* their own mothers. Many of these girls view their mothers as more traditional and less willing to live outside the norms of gendered social order than they themselves hope to be. Gillian, for example, who describes her mother as a loving parent, and as a feminist, hopes to be more financially independent than her mother. Although her mother has a job she loves, it is low-paying, and the family relies primarily on the steep income generated by her father. Gillian says of her future, "I'll choose a job I do like, but I really think I'd be contributing a lot more to the income. My mother really isn't a big part of it, it's really my father. So I'd like to think it'll be more of an equal thing." Similarly, although more about social than financial independence, Sierra intends to live a life that is different from that of her mother. Sierra's mother, now a teacher, had her first kiss in her senior year of high school, stayed home for her first year of college, and hopes Sierra will have a religious and family-oriented life. Her mother recently had a difficult time upon learning that Sierra is bisexual and has a girlfriend. Sierra says that "[s]he's obsessed with me having children and this perfect family which is not what I really want. If I have children, I'd rather adopt, because the population is a big deal to me, and I don't see marriage as such a big deal." Moreover, family is not central to Sierra's image of her future. Although her mother is supportive of her interest in biology, she often suggests that Sierra consider being a doctor—which would enable her to have a family rather than do field research, which would make family life and children more difficult.

Colleen's mother is also able to balance a career as a lawyer, wife, and parent, but Colleen hopes to differ from her mother as she gets older because Colleen is not certain she wants "the three kids and the house." Instead, Colleen explains, she might live similarly to her Aunt Jeanne, who is also a lawyer. Aunt Jeanne's lifestyle represents a nontraditional future that is more in tune with one that Colleen imagines:

> She got arrested for protesting the Viet Nam war and.... She and her partner adopted a child and they're just like totally breaking the stereotype. They're two lesbians who have an African-American child and she did this like fourteen years ago, so she's like ahead of everyone, but she just did what she wanted. She didn't care. She's really successful also, she's a lawyer, too, but it took her awhile. First she had her life, and she had like all her like passions, I guess, and then she pursued her career.

Like Colleen's aunt, Ellie's aunt is a parent and a professional. Still, with children and a medical career, Ellie's aunt has been able to devote time and energy to personal interests: she followed the Grateful Dead on tour as an adult, continues to educate herself on alternative medicine, and actively supports reproductive rights. Ellie takes pride in the fact that her aunt did "not wear a bra until she was 35 and became a doctor" and that her aunt now "knows a lot of people very high up in the fight for abortion rights."

Few of the girls feel that their own mothers successfully manage their roles as wife, parent, professional or laborer, and engaged citizen. Warner argues that American women have a difficult time achieving the perfection expected of mothers when there is little institutional or policy support for mothers who work in the paid labor force.[34] Where motherhood has traditionally been held as the symbol of maturity in inner-city communities, this symbol is no longer salient for middle- and upper-class girls who encounter a repeated admonishment that they delay motherhood in order to build successful careers or delay career goals to be full-time mothers.[35] In her study of upper middle-class girls, Amira Proweller found that women's new social roles as dictated by increased participation in the workforce, without a decrease in domestic responsibility, often led girls to imagine a future that involved delaying their entry into the workforce so they could devote themselves to childcare. She explains that for many of these wealthy girls, "[f]rom what they have seen of their mother's struggles to balance family and work, they gather early on that these two roles are not complementary as has traditionally been the case for men and that family responsibilities can interrupt women's labor-force participation."[36] Similarly, Colleen and Ellie praise their aunts who delayed career development for motherhood and selfhood. And Adrienne, who resents her mother for moving the family across country three times as she established a medical career, vows to delay childbearing until she is "well established." However, not all girls in this study felt the same way. Sierra and Jenna, whose quotes begin this chapter, want to take the other route and delay motherhood for work. Still, they do not see the role of professional and parent as compatible.

Not surprisingly, then, the mothers in media, both fictional and real-life celebrity moms, who were lauded by the girls were noted for their ability to successfully juggle the work-family balance and to do so without partners. These women are able to support children, work in high-profile jobs, and, in some cases, to spend energy and time on other personal passions.

Razia, who has been watching *General Hospital* religiously for years, thinks of character Alexis Davis when asked about strong women. For Razia, who dreams of making her own decisions, independence entails "[n]ot being married anytime soon. Fulfilling your education so you don't have to hear your husband saying 'you're dependent on me so now you're stuck with me, deal with it'. . . being able to go out for yourself, work for yourself, be sufficient all by yourself." Alexis fulfilled this definition, at the time of the interview, because she was both a practicing lawyer and a caring mother. Compared to some of the other female characters on the show, Razia feels that Alexis "is more of a role model for girls, saying, 'I'm a lawyer. I've done this on my own. I don't need anybody's help. I don't need a man in my life.'"

For Sierra, it is not characters but un-partnered celebrity mothers who demonstrate a powerful female identity. The celebrity mother is a representation of a woman who can balance her public image and private life, proving to the world that she is capable as a mother and a celebrity. As with the mothers described by the inner-city girls, the women Sierra describes are seemingly successful without the support of men or community. Angelina Jolie, a film actress, who at the time of the interviews had adopted one child on her own, and Jodie Foster, an unmarried actress who gave birth to two sons whose father(s) she has never publicly identified, stand out to Sierra because they are able to "take care of their public lives and their families." She further elaborates on how mothers who operate without men are strong in her eyes: "There's a lot more spotlight on women who are really in control of their careers and are really successful. I just see a lot of that, like how Angelina Jolie ditched her boyfriend and has her little son now and is really in control of her life."

For Sierra and Razia, both raised in heterosexual, two-parent households, the balance of family and career is epitomized not in two- or multi-parent families in which men and women, two women, or women and community work together to organize family time and work time, but in a single motherhood that does not acknowledge the resources—social, cultural, and economic—required to achieve this balance. Razia does not appear to question how the Alexis character can have a thriving legal practice and also raise her child with only the help (at the time of the interviews) of a part-time, high school–aged babysitter. Neither does Sierra mention baby Maddox's childcare when she speaks of Angelina Jolie's mothering, despite Sierra knowing that Jolie spends long hours on movie sets and traveling to refugee camps as a UN goodwill ambassador. Although in Sierra's eyes Jolie and Foster "take care of their public lives and families," she does not indicate awareness of how their child rearing may be supported by a community of caregivers and how the management of their "public lives" is certainly supported by a team of professionals.

Where the inner-city girls of color in my study focus on financial independence, resilience, and child rearing without support when they speak about the strength demonstrated by women, the middle-class girls speak about the successes involved in balancing work, family, and social interests. Each of these discourses reflects the larger cultural and media worlds they inhabit, yet common to both groups was an understanding of strength as demonstrated through individual achievement. In neither group was the concept of collective or community work noted as a significant source of strength; instead both groups of girls spoke about the power demonstrated by women who do not receive assistance; women who, as Razia says, can be "sufficient all by [themselves]."

In listening to the ways in which these girls speak about celebrity mothers who balance work and family life, we can hear the neoliberal discourse of girl power deeply embedded in their belief in choice. Moreover, what they do not speak about—particularly childcare costs and time commitments—indicates that choice becomes an empty marker because it is void of material reality. In this discussion it is clear how girl power media texts serve not simply as shared culture forms through which to discuss gender but serve also to produce and reify the sense that one need not question the concept of choice nor who really has it and when.

## "I Don't Know What I'm Going to Do When It Happens": Imagining the Future

When asked to imagine their own futures, most of the girls—both those from impoverished families, and those from the middle class—described being married and having children after getting a higher education and starting a career. In the following section I use two girls' dreams of the future to argue that the myth of the individual organizes the girls' visions so that as they imagine how they will live their lives as professionals, wives, and mothers, they focus on questions of personal choice rather than social structural realities.

While coming from distinct backgrounds, Gillian and Aiyisha have been raised in a culture infused with the same neoliberal message about choice. They have learned that in a postfeminist society, girls have the power to orchestrate their own life directions. According to this discourse, played out in popular images of fictional characters and media celebrities, girls have learned they may do anything. In the words of the 2005 American Girls/Girls, Inc. fund-raising bracelet, girls have learned the "I can" message. The first-person singular pronoun illuminates the discursive emphasis on individual achievement as well as its lack of emphasis on collective, structural change. While coming from divergent backgrounds, the girls not only share the experience of growing up within girl power media culture, they also share the experience of not seeing the girl power discourse reflected in the lives of adult women they know. While they are told that life will be different for their generation, they have a difficult time imagining what a grown up "girl power" might look like when there is a cultural discordance between what they hear and what they know.

Gillian and Aiyisha are honest about their confusion as to how they will handle the work-family balance as they get older. Both aware of the socioeconomic realities of being working mothers, Gillian and Aiyisha come from radically different backgrounds. Gillian, a seventeen-year-old, white girl who lives in a house in Queens, grew up in a wealthy community where only 3 percent of the population live below the poverty line.[37] Her father, an attorney, brings home the substantial part of the family's income. Her mother, who stayed home to take care of the four children until they were all in elementary school, is now employed only because she enjoys the day care center where she works. Gillian is aware that should something happen to destroy her parents' solid marriage, her mother would be unable to support herself. Thirteen-year-old, African-American, Aiyisha, on the other hand, was raised in a housing project in Brooklyn. She and her single mother share a one-bedroom apartment, sometimes with her aunt and uncle. After graduating from high school, Aiyisha's mother worked in a correctional facility and went to community college. She relies on support from Aiyisha's aunt to pay reduced tuition for Catholic school and to help keep Aiyisha in trendy clothes.

Gillian dreams of a career in music. Although she does not play an instrument she hopes to work as a record executive, or behind the scenes at her favorite television station, MTV. Although she plans to have children as well as a career, Gillian is confused as to how she can succeed at both. While the discourse of choice is pervasive in her talk of her career aspirations, she is also aware of the economic and professional realities faced by women:

> It's kind of hard because I know some women who just like. . . . There's this teacher at school who scheduled her C-Section and took exactly 30 days off and then she came back to work, and it's like, it's hard,

you want to be with your little baby, you want to play with it, and hang out with it, and you need to have influence over it. If you have a nanny raising your kid it's different, there's a lot of feelings that I had toward my mother when I was younger, they might feel toward the nanny instead, so it's like you're depriving yourself from that relationship. But then again if you do want to stay in that position, like "I'm a woman who makes money," you almost can't stay home with your baby, other people in your profession are like "oh, there goes another one going home to the baby." It's a hard decision to make. I don't know what I'm going to do when it happens. I guess I'll wait 'til it happens.

Gillian is similar to the girls in Proweller's study, whose "realistic appraisals of the future are framed by the structural barriers that they foresee pressing down on their lives."[38] Gillian is further confused by the mixed messages she receives from her mother and from Oprah. While Oprah "talks about working women and being in the workplace and always being equal to your male counterpart… [and] encourages having a child and going right back to work. Don't stay home with the kid, don't put yourself in that situation," Gillian's mother says that if "you love your child…at the end of the day, you want to be at home with your kid." Her mother, a huge fan of the talk show queen, also reminds Gillian that Oprah has never had children and therefore has "never had to make that decision so she can say 'Oh, it's easy, just go back to work,' whereas if she had a child, she might think differently."

Although Gillian is aware of the mixed messages women receive about being professional and powerful, her own discussion of them is steeped in the discourse of choice. She presents this disconnect as a "decision" that individual women must make for themselves to either advance professionally or to have a bonding experience with their newborn. In addition, Gillian's dream husband does not appear to be in the running for the position of primary or equal caregiver. It is clear from her comments on her teacher that Gillian understands the double bind faced by women but she is unable to articulate the dilemma outside the neoliberal framework of the girl power discourse; she views her teacher's choices as personal decisions not as choices framed by a lack of progressive social policy regarding maternity leave, childcare, and career advancement.

Like Gillian, Aiyisha works to imagine a future in which she can fulfill all of her dreams: that she will be married, have children, have a college education, and be in a career rather than a job. She wants all these things in part because they fulfill the American Dream and in part because she has seen how she and her mother have struggled because her mother did not follow the normative path of this fantasy. At thirteen, Aiyisha dreams of becoming a fashion-designing doctor. In her ideal scenario she will deliver babies and then give her fashions to the parents as gifts for their infants. In addition to these professional plans, Aiyisha plans to be a wife and a mother. Her own mother raised her without a father and Aiyisha says that she wants the experience of her children to be different from her own experience and the experiences of most of her classmates—whom she calls "sex babies" because they were conceived out of wedlock and raised without fathers in their lives. In addition, she wants to be a strong, financially independent woman like the mother on the animated *The Proud Family.* She explains, "Trudy, the wife, she's a veterinarian and she brings home the money. The father, Oscar, his business is gonna go straight downtown cause he's not making any money and she's paying all the bills and everything for the house. *She's* taking care of everybody, not the father." As Aiyisha discusses her dreams, however, they keep shrinking as she confronts the social and economic realities of being a working mother. Aiyisha starts her imagining by telling me that she hopes to "become a doctor like Cliff Huxtable on *The Cosby Show*" because "delivering babies sounds fun, then I can make them little clothes 'cause I'm gonna be a fashion designer, too." As far as family goes, Aiyisha dreams, "I'm gonna have a husband...and I'm gonna have one child and adopt a child. I'm gonna adopt like three children."

Shortly after these declarative statements, Aiyisha's future projections begin to unravel. The first things to go in her dream future are her children, followed shortly by her husband:

> I'm gonna have a job. Me and my husband's gonna have a job. That's why I don't think I'm gonna have children cause I'm not gonna see them until never. I'm gonna be just like Cliff Huxtable on the show because he always working. I'll be coming home at like 2:00 [in the morning] and then I'm gonna have to go to a hospital everyday and

> I'm never gonna have time with my family so I think I'm gonna actually live alone and have a boyfriend.[39]

When I ask about the inconsistency in her imaginings, Aiyisha tells me, "If I'm a doctor then I will never have time to see my family. I would like be gone every 5, 10 seconds" yet she finishes the same sentence with a word about how she will be able to support her family in style: "but I'll still be making money so they can still be going to school and wearing everything I have." Understandably, thirteen-year-olds do not have articulate, well-formed plans for the future. At the same time, Aiyisha's struggle raises the specter of cultural discordance. Privy to the same girl power discourse as Gillian, Aiyisha cannot quite reconcile the messages she hears about what her future can look like and the reality of what she has seen both on television and in her own life. Aiyisha, like Gillian, already anticipates a double bind in which she will not have enough resources to raise children and peak professionally. Situated within a postfeminist media culture in which "patriarchy is gone and has been replaced by choice,"[40] neither girl sees strategic solutions beyond personal choice in which one part of the dream must be sacrificed; they certainly do not consider changes in social policy or equally shared parenting responsibilities.

For Gillian and Aiyisha being a strong woman in the girl power era, which demands an individualistic power and an independence, rather than interdependence, seems almost impossible to achieve. Moreover, as they attempt to carve out dreams of professional and domestic lives, they articulate the "choice" discourses of postfeminist girl power that continually repositions them as unencumbered agents who operate outside of social structural imperatives. Thus, their attention is continually askew; it is turned inward rather than toward collective change.

If these girls struggle to imagine a womanhood that is as liberating as those of the women they see in girl power media culture, do they articulate any resistance to the economic, social, and political constraints they see their mothers experiencing or believe they themselves will experience? The following chapter explores the ways in which girls articulate resistance to gender oppression and how they understand the oppositional acts, vocalizations, and images practiced by female celebrities and characters in girl power media culture.

CHAPTER 6

# "If Feminism Is Believing that Women Are Humans, Then I Am a Feminist": Girls Define Feminism and Feminist Practice

> Women's issues always lay dormant (rather than active) in my mind simply because I never thought I'd have to actually say that women deserve more respect than they get. If feminism is believing that women are humans (i.e., equal to men), then I am a feminist. But it will always sound strange, because to many [people], feminism is this crazy idea spearheaded by hairy hippie women who are all probably lesbians and who have petty issues at hand. Maybe it's because people don't really realize that much larger, simpler issues exemplify feminism, like a woman's inability to (easily) get a big position at a firm—there's always gonna be some big strong man who will naturally and more easily take the position she's been working so hard to get. (email from Leila, seventeen years old, Guyanese)

IN FACT, Leila, herself, was one of those people to whom feminism sounded strange. When she was in her early teens, she imagined that feminists were all "lesbians like Ani DiFranco and Paula Cole,"[1] who did not shave their armpits and always "focused on petty things" that they would "magnify" out of proportion. Although she admits to never having listened to Ani DiFranco's lyrics, or knowing specifically what issues feminists exaggerated, Leila had formed a stereotypical opinion about feminism. We can hear in her voice a struggle to figure out whether feminism is a word to which she wants to attach her identity.

A few weeks later, Leila emailed me again. This time she felt that her encounters with a male classmate had helped her to come to some kind of understanding of why people identify with feminism. In class Leila read *A Doll's House*, a play that explores nineteenth-century gender roles through a story about Torvald and Nora—a husband and wife whose marriage is ultimately destroyed by Torvald's inability to treat his wife as an adult rather than a "doll."[2] In Leila's class, a male student had sided with Torvald and "couldn't see past [the husband's] perspective, and it was so crazy. And the worst part was that [the male student] thought he was some sort of genius who was saying profound words." Leila is beginning to come to a feminist consciousness, aware that gender politics may not be as "dormant" as she first felt. She writes: "I remember I told you that I associated feminism with women who had hairy armpits and were butch—it's just so hard to stray from that stereotype unless you've been in a situation that challenged you or your values..." In this case, the situation that challenged Leila was her classmate's inability to recognize the paternalism with which Torvald treats Nora.

Leila's feminist awakening occurred during the course of the research; for many of the girls in this study, however, feminism, the concept, though not necessarily the word, was a position with which they already identified. Faced with discriminatory attitudes and actions that challenge their belief in equality and justice, many of the girls in this research recognize some need for a visible feminist presence in the public sphere. Yet, how do girls in an era of girl power media define feminism? In a media culture that normalizes female "power," who is feminist? Is feminism, in girl power media culture, still a movement for social change or has it become, as Goldman et al. suggest, "a manipulatable set of semiotic markers—confidence and attitude—which bear meanings of individual freedom and independence associated with feminism?"[3]

This chapter begins with a discussion of the participants' experiences of gender discrimination in order to situate their understanding and awareness of unequal power relations. While the girls in this study do not employ the term oppression, many believe that they receive unfair or discriminatory treatment by parents, teachers, and peers. Because they are aware of these practices, many of these girls identify with feminism. The chapter continues with a discussion of recent literature on young women and feminist politics in order to position the girls in this study in relation to others in this nascent field of study. Finally, the chapter moves to exploring the three versions of feminism imagined by the girls in this study and examines the limitations and possibilities of these feminist imaginings.

## Experiences of Gender Discrimination

In ethnographic studies, teen girls consistently express that they see an inequality in how their sexuality is discussed and imagined in relation to that of their male peers.[4] Often girls feel a palpable sense that there is a double standard about what constitutes promiscuous behavior. Not surprisingly, the girls in my study share this awareness. They bemoan the fact that girls who dress in certain ways or date more than one boy are, as Colleen explains, considered "sluts, skanks, whores and whatever" whereas boys who "get with a lot of girls" are "not labeled anything." Brianna states succinctly, "If a man has a lot of girls, he's considered a man, but if a woman has a lot of men, she's considered a 'ho.'"

Many of the Black and Latino girls in this study, who live in communities in which the rates of teen pregnancy have been highly publicized, also experience a double standard when it comes to responsibility for pregnancy. In their eyes, their mothers unfairly hold them responsible for protecting themselves from the predatory behavior of boys and from pregnancy. Nikke, a recent immigrant from Nigeria, says that her mother puts a lot of pressure on her not to get pregnant and to "know when to say no to a guy." The burden of pregnancy has been made clear to Michelle, a sixteen-year-old African-American girl from the Bronx, through her mother's actions:

> My mother, she has two girls and one boy. Me and my sister that's in college now, she was very, very hard on us. Like, we couldn't have a boyfriend, we couldn't go nowhere, but with my brother, his first

> girlfriend was thirteen, and she would spend the night. I feel that boys are treated differently because a lot of mothers, and a lot of people, feel that girls bring the problem home.

And Stacey describes a similar situation in her friends' home where "her mother has a fifteen-year-old son and he gets to date, and she's seventeen now and she can't even have a boy call her house."

Many girls feel that they are unfairly restricted in who they can go out with, and when, in part because of this fear that they will come home pregnant. As with the girls in Lees's study of gendered identity, the girls in my study understand that parents are trying to protect them from sexual predators and dangerous streets, but feel frustrated that they are not trusted more and that their brothers and male peers have more freedom over their time and space.[5] Razia says, "A guy can go out until twelve, one, two in the morning because of a friend's birthday, and I wouldn't be able to do that. I think that you need to set the rules the same... but it doesn't work out that way because 'you're my daughter, because you're my baby girl.'" Similarly, Juana, a Hispanic/Dominican living in Manhattan, says,

> I can't be alone after 6:00pm. I can't be out alone. Like, let's say, for example, I come late from school sometimes... not out alone... like when it gets dark, they don't want me out alone then. I can't go out with my friends as much as I'd like to; I can't go out because they're afraid that whatever little thing could influence you to do stuff. I mean, I understand that but not when you know the type of person that your daughter is. You know? It just gets to me.

But where some girls in previous research have claimed that they personally do not experience gender discrimination other than the "double standard," most of the girls in my study feel that they *have* experienced or seen gender discrimination, or believe they will be victims of sexism as they get older.[6] Many of the girls of color in my study also understand their experiences of discrimination as both gendered and racial and are aware of the interconnected relation within their identities. Listening to the girls discuss their experiences, it becomes clear that sexism occurs at school, at home, and in their communities. Moreover, the girls detect this gender imbalance in both attitude and behavior so that their discussion of gender reflects both an ideological and a material inequity.

Three decades after the passing of Title IX, much of the discussion surrounding sexism is in relation to sports. Interestingly, however, the sexism discussed by the girls is interpersonal, rather than institutional, and therefore not protected by Title IX. Girls describe feeling let down by male peers who are unsupportive of their athletic teams or who make assumptions about them based on their gender. In general, as Suzie states, the girls find that "a lot of guys think girls are weak because they're girls." For Colleen, who lives in a waterfront community in Queens, this discrimination is unspoken but felt. She explains, "In my community we do a lot of sailing 'cause I live by the water...and a lot of the men in the community have sailing races and, like, I've sailed all my life and no one's ever asked me [to race], but if I was a guy they would have asked me." For the girls at Monument High School, the derogatory beliefs about girls and weakness are vocalized loudly. Juana explains how at one basketball game in which the girls' and boys' teams would both play, some kids were discussing which girls on the team would be playing. She heard "a guy yell out 'who cares about which girls are playing? We only coming to see the guys.'" Similarly, Isa became frustrated when the boys in her class did not believe that girls would even be interested in watching a professional basketball game. Her teacher was taking the girls on a trip to a basketball game and there were no extra tickets for the boys. Isa says, "You don't know how much comments I had to take. They were like, 'Oh, those girls probably don't even watch basketball games... they shouldn't even play basketball. Basketball is for guys.'" Isa also had to listen to a boy in her class tell her that "women can't drive" when she announced she was going to get her permit.

At home, some girls find they are tasked with more responsibility for helping to maintain the domestic sphere. Stacey, whose mother is also raising her younger, male cousin, finds that "he doesn't do anything; he throws everything everywhere and I have to clean up after him." Brianna has been doing laundry since elementary school and Razia cooks and cleans and, as many of the girls described in chapter 5, looks after a younger sibling.

Several of the girls also imagine that in the future they will be faced with gender discrimination. Adrienne thinks that she may not get "as good a job as men"; Aiyisha fears that she may eventually have to face a partner who thinks "women are just to have babies and stay home with the children"; and Leila, who says in our first meeting that she has not experienced any discrimination based on her gender, does expect that "job interviews are going to be slightly harder because you're a girl." The girls' expectation that they may face this kind of discrimination in the future speaks to their sense that gender inequity continues to be an issue for women and girls.

Many of the girls of color who discussed experiences of gender discrimination view the discrimination as linked to their particular communities and to either the oppression they feel within their culture or the oppression they feel from those outside of the culture. From Stacey's point of view, the domestic responsibility that is put upon her is linked to her "Caribbean descent." She says,

> A lot of Caribbean people, they put stress on the girls. My mother, she has three brothers, and I think she's the middle child, and no matter what, she had to wash everybody's clothes, had to clean the house before she left to go to school every day. It was always on her. I think that's what she's doing to me. I'm the oldest; I'm the girl, so I have to do everything. So, I guess that's, I think that's mostly for Caribbean people, I'm not sure about anybody else.

Though Stacey sees her mother's insistence that she do work around the house as linked to Caribbean culture, responsibility for family maintenance through housework, childcare, and emotional support is often common to girls in low-income American families regardless of ethnicity.[7]

Just as Stacey believes her ethnic decent is the central factor in her mother's discriminatory practices, Juana, like many Latina teens, feels that the limitations she experiences on her physical mobility, her voice, and her sexuality are all linked to the Latino culture of her Dominican family.[8] Juana explains,

> Especially in our race, 'cause it's more conservative, more close-knit, women just belong to one guy and not being able to... for example, guys get to experience a lot with girls before they enter into marriage. Well, it's looked, it's wrong for women, in their eyes, to do the same thing. Like, [women] can't have sex before they are married.

She experiences this strictness as a limitation on her freedom to move physically, as well as her freedom to be honest about who she is and what she believes: "You can't be as outspoken and as independent as you'd like to be [because] it doesn't look right.... You can't go out as late as a guy; you can't go out alone; you can't just have any type of conversation with people; they just won't allow that. I'm coming from my background, I mean." Given the girls' awareness of gender discrimination in its various forms, and the ways in which it impacts them personally, it should not be surprising that a great number of them identify with feminist ideals.

Though most of the girls in my study would not call themselves feminists in their everyday conversations, when asked to define feminism and then position themselves in relation to the definition they had provided, most of these girls said that they do share these beliefs. Neither an awareness of feminism, nor an inclination to identify with feminist ideals, nor a perspective on feminist strategy, appeared to be either class- or race-based. Girls from all of the socioeconomic classes, ethnic backgrounds, and racial backgrounds said they identified with feminism. As girls spoke about their own belief systems, their role models, media personalities, and media characters, they defined what it means to be a feminist and how a feminist works to achieve equality for women.

## FEMINISM IN THE ERA OF GIRL POWER

Over the past ten years, there has been a small body of empirical research exploring girls' relationships to feminist politics in an era of girl power media culture.[9] The findings of these studies have suggested that, as in this study, while most girls do not consider themselves feminists, many identify with feminist ideals. Several studies suggest that girls and young women believe that feminism is now redundant because feminist goals have already been achieved.[10] Using a language of postfeminism, these girls believe that (at least some level of) gender equality has been achieved and that a feminist movement, therefore, is unnecessary and antiquated. In some cases, feminist achievements have been taken as a given and girls express a sense of entitlement to the freedoms and opportunities afforded them. Melanie, a participant in Jowett's study of young British women, sums up this position as such: "Years and years ago this feminist thing was really big and people did fight for women's rights, and that was good. But we're equal now, so there's not that need."[11]

Interestingly, only one girl in my study expressed the sentiment that feminism was no longer relevant. There are several factors that make feminism a position, if not a term, they still consider relevant. The girls in this study were interviewed in an election year in which Democrat John Kerry was hoping to defeat incumbent Republican George W. Bush. In the previous four years, during the first term of his presidency, Bush had voiced and enacted policies in opposition to sexual freedoms (of gay Americans) and to reproductive freedoms. Living in New York City, a liberal and generally Democratic Party aligned region, it is likely that many of these girls encountered opposition to the president's positions in their homes, schools, communities, and media outlets. Indeed, when the girls discuss feminism, they use the language of rights and focus on the right to vote as well as the right to reproductive and sexual freedoms.

In addition, the girls in this study are high achievers. Although many of them are economically disadvantaged and live in inner-city neighborhoods, these girls attend schools that far surpass most schools in their neighborhoods in terms of test scores and college placement. As such, they live in the borderlands of the "at risk" categorization; they are expected to exceed the class position of many of their neighbors as well as their own parents. Families, teachers, and school administrators put a lot of pressure on these girls to succeed by conquering the class, race, and gender barriers to their parents' success. The act of conquering these barriers, most often articulated through achievement in education and subsequent financial and social independence, often shares the language and practice of liberal feminism.[12]

Finally, many of the girls in this study may identify with feminism because they express having been discriminated against based on their gender. Although the girls do not discuss feminism as a possible strategy for overcoming discrimination, it may be that feminism is not a passé form of resistance to them because it responds to gender inequities, or as Leila puts it, in the beginning of this chapter, because they have been in situations that challenged them or their values.

Chilla Bulbeck also found that girls may distance themselves from feminism as a movement even if they find the concept relevant. She found that the Australian high schoolers she studied associated feminism with a movement that "belonged to the past," a movement that was too "radical," or a movement that had too narrow a focus and was not a "pressing political necessity" for our time.[13] While they were able to identify with feminist values, they did not identify with it as a movement; they were more involved in movements they considered to be pertinent for their generation, such as environmental concerns. Much of the research on contemporary feminism finds that girls do not connect with the concept of a movement because they identify with the feminist ideals of individual change and achievement rather than collective social change.[14] Girls tend to focus on individual solutions for change such as the pursuit of higher education, professional career achievement, and sexual self-determination rather than structural interventions for change.[15] Seen through this lens girl power era feminism revolves around a neoliberal discourse of individual choice and agency, which elides the collective strategies of second-wave feminism. Indeed, many of the girls in this study find the identification with a movement to be too political for their relationship to feminist ideals and, like third-wave feminists, feel that one can live a feminist life or, as I discuss later in this chapter, perform as a feminist, rather than be active in a feminist movement. While feminism in girl power seems, at times, to address the struggles of girls within a culture that does not recognize their abilities, rights, and freedoms, does it fall short in helping girls to envision long-term objectives that would contribute to the end of gender oppression?

## Goals of a Feminist: Rights and Choice

Tasha explains that a feminist is "someone who actually really believes in women's rights." Like Tasha, most of the girls use the concept of rights to define feminism. Specifically, girls talk about women's rights to vote, earn equal pay, have freedom of choice regarding abortion, and have freedom of choice regarding sexual identity. Yasmine, a sixteen-year-old Dominican girl, says that she believes a feminist to be "someone who is for women's rights, who is for women, keep abortion legal and things like that and like, you know, let women vote, and things like that." Razia agrees that equal rights are central to the definition of a feminist. She argues that a feminist is someone "who thinks that even though you have all those [feminine] traits, you have all the rights everybody else has." For both Ellie and Sierra, a women's right to sexual freedom and desire are also key to feminist thinking. Ellie explains that if a woman believes in her equal rights, she need not call herself a feminist, although she should be defined as one: "I think that any woman who doesn't believe in her own mental strength, and her own right to her sexual urges and, you know, her right to choose, her right to vote, has some serious problems, you know? So, yes I would consider myself a feminist, but I would also consider most women a feminist." For all of these girls, rights and/or choice are the central organizing discourses of feminism. The language they use to discuss the rights and choices of women falls squarely into a model of liberal feminism. In the liberal feminist model, like liberalism on which it is based, the individual on whom rights are bestowed is free to make choices and direct her own life outside of the power relations that govern race, class, nationality, sexuality, and other aspects of women's lives.[16]

Within the framework of liberal feminism, however, the girls have divergent views of the role of the feminist. While some girls believe that being a feminist means being vocal about your beliefs on these rights issues, many others feel that a feminist is someone who embodies and enacts feminist values even if she does not work for change. In the later case, she may just "represent" a woman who is strong and empowered, a woman who enacts her choice and her rights rather than one who fights for the maintenance or expansion of such rights. As a representation of strength and power, this woman performs feminism.

## Activist Feminism versus Feminism Performed

As Jenna and Simone, fourteen-year-old girls in the Gardens Girl Scout Troop, discuss whether certain film characters should be labeled feminists, the debate over the role of a feminist can be heard. Early in our discussion of feminism Simone defines a feminist as someone who fights for equal rights for women. She sees the role of the feminist as one that is activist, either in practical action or voice, and distinctly focused on gender. In discussing the character Elle Woods (Reese Witherspoon) from the *Legally Blonde* movie series, Simone and Jenna's positions begin to take form in contrast to one another.

The Elle Woods we meet in the original *Legally Blonde* (2001) is a former sorority president, who appears to be focused on fashion, all things pink, and getting her nails done. When she discovers that her college boyfriend is heading to Harvard Law School and leaving her for someone less "blonde" and more "serious," Elle studies for the LSAT and is admitted to Harvard Law. At Harvard Elle is driven to succeed, initially to impress her former boyfriend. She uses her knowledge of fashion, her sorority skills, and her own common sense to help solve a professor's important legal case. In the sequel, *Legally Blonde 2: Red, White, and Blonde* (2003), Elle learns that her beloved chihuahua's mother is locked in an animal-testing facility. Determined to end animal testing, she heads to Washington to be a congressional intern for a senator who is an alumna of her sorority. On Capitol Hill, Elle finds that the women she works with are not always honest, that her sorority sisters can be mobilized to plan a mass protest, and that with hard work she can successfully pass a bill banning animal testing. To Simone, although Elle is an activist, she is *not* a feminist because she is fighting for the rights of animals rather than for the rights of women. Jenna counters, arguing that "[e]ven if [Elle] isn't fighting for women's causes, she's kind of seen as a feminist because she worked her way to the top. So that makes her—even if she didn't want to be—it does slightly make her a role model and a feminist even though maybe she didn't start out that way."

The distinction between the two definitions of feminism develops further when the girls move on to discussing another female film character. In *Dirty, Pretty Things* (2002), Senay (Audrey Tautou) is a young Muslim Turkish woman illegally working in London and dreaming of going to New York. When immigration officers try to pick her up at work, her boss blackmails her into keeping quiet if she gives him oral sex. When Senay gets the courage, she physically attacks her boss and takes her chances on another path to New York. Jenna calls Senay a feminist because she works hard as a Turkish immigrant, "doing things that nobody should have to do to try and get to America and try to be a citizen and try to lead a good happy life." Since these acts do not fit into Simone's definition of feminism, which requires acting on behalf of women, she begins to question her friend asking, "But how is that being a feminist? You didn't say anything about . . ." Jenna interrupts to clarify her position. She begins by retracting her use of the word, but ends with a renewed conviction that Senay is a feminist:

> I think, in a way, not really a feminist, but she's independent because like maybe she's the image of other immigrant girls, or other immigrants period, doing what they have to do to get to this country... she's alone and she's by herself and she needs to try and find a way to get away from where she is and the situations that she's in so I think that's how.

Jenna's definition positions Senay as a feminist because she serves as the model of a woman who refuses to cower to her abusive boss or be pushed around because she is female and an immigrant.

At my request, Simone states her position one last time and explains why this character, although independent, and perhaps embodying some feminist ideals, is not someone she would consider a feminist: "A feminist [is someone who will] stick up for the rights of other women but when you're independent you only try to stick up for yourself. Like it's sort of like self-preservation in a way. And, like with feminism, being a feminist you're more standing up for other people and other women, not just yourself." This discussion frames the different perspectives on feminism held by the girls in this study: one group of girls, like Simone, believe that "feminist" is a characterization that should only be given to women who are active in their resistance to patriarchy and seek to make change for women collectively, not just to live the role of the empowered woman. For these girls, a feminist is an activist who fights for women's rights with her voice, her body, and/or her time. This definition contends that feminists are women who work for change in women's lives; in this model, feminism is an *activist* identity.

An equal number of girls, like Jenna, believe that to be identified as a feminist a woman simply needs to be independent, strong-willed, empowered, and/or self-sufficient. These girls often imply that the feminist performs her powerful position for others to see and, as such, serves as a role model. These girls imagine feminism as a *performative* identity, rather than as a social change movement. Feminism, then, becomes a cultural identity marked by cultural practices rather than a political movement activated by political practices; it becomes an individual marker rather than a collective strategy.

These dualistic strategies of feminism defined by the girls in this study—*activist feminism* versus *feminism performed*—share a common overriding commitment to a strategy based in a liberal feminist approach or, as Nancy Fraser offers with more complexity, an approach of "affirmative recognition."[17] Fraser's typology of political redress against injustices is useful in situating the girls' understandings of feminism. She argues that the central dilemma over how to correct inequities is that of redistribution versus recognition. Where redistribution feminists believe that the central injustice against women lies in their political and economic inequality, recognition feminists identify "social patterns of representation, interpretation, and communication" as the main injustices against which women should fight.[18] For redistribution feminists the road to equality would begin with a consideration and reorganization of the division of labor, redistribution of wealth, and an equitable role in the democratic process. In contrast, for recognition feminists, the primary remedy would occur in the realm of the cultural or symbolic such as the "revaluing" of cultural identities and/or cultural products of oppressed groups. Recognition feminists believe that the cultural perception of women must change in order for the social position of women to change.

Harris has characterized third-wave feminism as a politics of recognition, which she notes is a marked shift from earlier waves of feminism that focused on a politics of redistribution—especially in regard to political reform and inclusion. She attributes the shift to the following four societal changes: (1) the successes of feminism: because women have made some cracks in the glass ceiling and because they have garnered some significant rights, feminists now feel able to change the focus of their activism; (2) the neoliberal move from collective politics to individual choice and freedoms and from structural change to self-improvement; (3) feminism's awareness of multiple, partial, shifting identities, which calls for a more complex form of resistance; and (4) the acceptance that resistance will be absorbed and cycled through the market as a commodity thus compelling feminist activists to fight for control over the representation of feminist politics and of women more generally.[19]

Recognition itself, according to Fraser, may be typed as either "affirmative" or "transformative." Affirmative remedies, which are nearly universally sought by the women defined as feminist by the girls in this study, are "aimed at correcting inequitable outcomes of social arrangements without disturbing the underlying framework that generates them," while transformative remedies aim to redress inequity through restructuring the framework within which social arrangements are generated.[20] Affirmative recognition, in a feminist political spectrum, emphasizes the cultural revaluation of women through boosting self-esteem and promoting the contributions of women within the existing social structure. In the girls' talk of rights as the goal of feminists, we can hear a liberal feminist commitment to maintaining the established social structure. As the girls name the women they identify as feminist, it is their commitment to a politics of affirmative recognition that prevails. Like the mass of women in the second wave who embraced liberal feminism, these girls seek reform rather than radical change. Unlike their fore-sisters who fought for equal opportunities in education, work, and politics, most of the girls in this study, although they talk of rights, primarily seek change in the cultural realm rather than in the political or social realms.

## Marching, Organizing, Funding, and Speaking Out: Activist Feminist

Seventeen-year-old Meg, who is one of three girls interviewed individually who does not identify as feminist, believes that feminism is imbricated with activism. Although Meg says that she believes that "women should have equal rights and I'm very pro-choice and stuff like that," she does not "picture herself" as a feminist because that is "going a little too far." To Meg a feminist is not just someone who believes in feminist ideals, she is someone who fights for those ideals; someone who uses her voice and her body to work for change. She describes her friend, Georgia, whom she says fits the bill of a feminist:

> Georgia is very much feminist; she desperately wanted to do the [reproductive rights] march in Washington, but she couldn't go because she had like some sort of earth club that she had to deal with because it was almost Earth Day, but she's very feminist. Like, she'll wear revealing shirts sometimes and guys have made comments about her chest and she'll start fighting with them like "Stop treating me like a

> pig. I'm a woman, you should respect my body" and she's a very big feminist.

Georgia may dress in a way that displays her body, a behavior at which second-wave feminists might scoff, but for Meg the determining factors of Georgia's feminism are her voice—which she uses to articulate her values—and her desire to participate in collective action/vocalization to fight for the sociopolitical rights of women.

Unlike Meg, sixteen-year-old Yasmine does consider herself a feminist. She identifies as such because she believes in the right of women to vote and to make their own choices regarding reproduction, but also because "when people make certain stereotypes about girls I voice my opinion because that's not true." She believes that feminists are women who work to make change. For her, Oprah and Missy Elliot are both good examples of celebrities whose actions are part of a feminist identity. Oprah, she posits, is a feminist because she "sets up schools in Africa for girls" and tries to help girls get "out of rough situations." This answer refers, in part, to the Oprah Winfrey Leadership Academy for Girls that began operations in South Africa in 2006. In December of 2003, just months before my first meeting with the girls at Victory, Oprah discussed her visit to South Africa, her Christmas gifts of clothing, school supplies, and sneakers for 50,000 South African children, and her commitment to founding and sustaining a state-of-the-art educational and leadership training boarding school for girls in South Africa on *Oprah in Africa: A Personal Journey, a Global Challenge*, an ABC *Primetime* Special with Diane Sawyer. In addition, in the months preceding our interview, Oprah had aired shows such as "Is Your Child Leading a Double Life?" which offered ways to help your teens stay away from high-risk behaviors and "Suburban Teens: The New Prostitutes" that promised to help parents learn how to protect their daughters. This kind of subject matter, not unusual to the Oprah Winfrey Show, can be seen as educating parents so they can help girls "out of rough situations." In these cases—of the African school and of the programming geared toward girls—Oprah uses her time, money, and/or voice to help less advantaged girls. It is her act of financial and educational redistribution that makes Oprah a feminist in Yasmine's eyes.

Missy Elliot, who uses her voice to actively advocate for change, is also a feminist in Yasmine's eyes:

> She has a song called "She's a Bitch" and it's kind of funny 'cause that's something that like if you walk on the street, and a guy starts to talk to you, that's something he might say, "Oh, she don't want to talk to me" and he might call you a name or something like that. So she basically is saying "Well, I may be that, but look where I'm at and look where you are." She makes being a woman positive.

Here Missy's lyrics are being used to demand a revaluation of women and to reclaim the term "bitch," which has been used as a derogatory word to demean (powerful) women. Missy has been quoted as saying, "A bitch is what they call a woman who knows what she wants.... I'm just taking the term back. If a bitch is what I am for achieving that, then so be it."[21] For Yasmine, who feels "discriminated against as a girl" in her neighborhood where girls are not expected to focus on school work and not expected to achieve success outside of heterosexual relationships, the risk Missy's takes, as she resists the masculine power to name, in her reclamation of "bitch," leads Yasmine to call her a feminist.

Gillian offers the female hosts on the talk show *The View* (1997–present), billed as a "morning chatfest featuring a team of five dynamic women of different ages," as feminists in the public eye. She begins by positioning these hosts as "women in power" because "they're always talking about politics and stuff, and they're pro.-choice and stuff and...they talk about their views on politics." For Gillian, women in power, who discuss important political issues, and who vocalize their belief in women's reproductive freedom, are important because "like the president is always a man, most of the senate is men, like white men, so it's very cool to see [the women's] ideas on something" and "they have an audience watching who are probably influenced by their ideas so everything they say is getting out there." Noting feminist representation in a totally different genre of programming, Gillian also identifies fictional character Jesse (Elizabeth Berkley) from *Saved by the Bell* (1989–1993). On *Saved by the Bell*, a teen comedy set in the halls of a suburban Bayside High School, Jesse is created as the antithesis to her frivolous friend, Kelly (Tiffani Amber Thiessen). Kelly wore "little skirts"; Jesse wore more "professional clothes." Kelly "had more fun";

Jesse always had her "nose in a book." Kelly was also flirtatious and encouraged the male gaze while Jesse was very "pro-woman" talking about "women's issues" and yelling at her boyfriend for his "macho" behavior and his wandering eye.

Diana and Helen, sixteen-year-old Chinese girls in the Community Girl Scout Troop, agree that being vocal about equality is an important marker of feminist practice. Diana believes that her Girl Scout troop leader is a feminist not only because she contributes her time to working with girls but also because she promotes "girl power" by talking regularly to troop members about what they hope to accomplish and achieve as young women. For her troop-mate Helen, who contemplates joining the Reserve Officers Training Corp (ROTC)—the U.S. Armed Services program that trains college students for military service—her gym teacher is someone she would call a feminist. When Helen asked the teacher whether she should consider ROTC in college, her teacher

> [g]ave me these stories about how these people... like the girl would go to ROTC and the guy doesn't and the girl's more mentally strong. Even though the guy is more physically strong, he doesn't have the mentality to continue, but the girl made it through and like she's in the Air Force and stuff, and [the teacher is] telling me: "Don't quit! You can do it!" and stuff and like "You're stronger than any guy."

Both Diana and Helen call these adult figures feminists because their language focuses on strategies of gender recognition where girls are celebrated for their physical power and opportunity to advance professionally. Both the troop leader and the gym teacher use their voices and time to actively help girls to gain self-esteem and to imagine a future in which their "girl power" is valued.

In her study of punk girls, LeBlanc defines resistance as an act of political protest that is defined by "subjective intent": an awareness of oppression, the intent and desire to counter the oppression, and the initiation of conscious action intended to counter oppression.[22] It is this approach to resistance that Meg, Yasmine, Gillian, Diana, and Helen echo as they name the feminist women they know in their lives and see in the media. For these girls, a feminist is an activist who not only represents power and strength but who advocates for change in either: laws and policies impacting women; regulation and exploitation of women's bodies; representations of women; and/or resource distribution. In the case of the Oprah Winfrey Leadership Academy for Girls, an affirmative redistributive feminist remedy, which seeks to rectify injustice through the redistribution of political and economic capital while maintaining the existing social structure, is applied. In the other cases, a feminism that calls for a revaluing of women and a recognition of their power is considered a solution to gender inequality.

## She Fights for Who She Is: Feminism Performed

For fifteen-year-old Taiwanese-American Grace, women who appear physically powerful, like Angelina Jolie in the *Tomb Raider* series (2001, 2003) and the women of *Charlie's Angels* (2000, 2003), are feminist because they demonstrate an ability to fight on par with men and to be the saviors rather than the victims. The *Charlie's Angels* movies (based on the original television show) follow the professional lives of three women (Drew Barrymore, Cameron Diaz, and Lucy Lui) who work for Charlie as undercover agents. Where Grace says that the Angels were feminists because they demonstrated that they could "save the world" and did not back down, a review of the first movie offers this assessment:

> One of the movie's recurring jokes is that the Angels can reduce any man to a state of drooling cretinism, but of course the camera, zooming in from behind Ms. Liu so that you can count the stitches on her very tight jeans, or exploring the bouncing contents of Ms. Barrymore's blue racing jacket, strives to do the same to the audience. But the Angels, in addition to looking great in a variety of elaborate and revealing costumes, are also crack martial artists, fluent speakers of Japanese and steel-nerved bomb defusers.[23]

Grace, who refuses to wear skirts, and prefers to play computer role-playing games than do almost anything else, finds in the Angels a rejection of the weakness associated with traditional femininity, despite the fact that they visually embrace femininity and are sexualized in the cinematic text. Similarly, she identifies Lara Croft (Angelina Jolie), a highly sexualized video game character, come to life on the big screen, as a feminist because Croft uses her physical and intellectual skills to fight off evil. Grace understands feminism to be a demonstration that women are equal to men and capable of succeeding on their own. In her eyes, though the Angels and Croft are sexualized, they perform their feminism by using martial arts, successfully completing missions, and "saving the world."

Notably, the Angels and Croft are not just physical powerhouses; they are also women who are romantically unattached to men. While they may have relationships or sexual encounters, these women maintain an air of independence, of being un-hitched, and of using men to achieve their goals. As with Grace, other girls associate single women, who have never been married and who have successful careers, with feminism. Nikke identifies Condoleezza Rice, then the first female U.S. national security advisor, as a feminist because "she's a member of the Cabinet and usually you don't see people doing that and I think she's like a voice to women telling them 'you could do it.'" What is required for Nikke to name someone a feminist is not necessarily a voice *for* women but a voice *to* women. In other words, Rice is not known for her pro-woman positions, or for fighting gender oppression.[24] From Nikke's perspective, however, a woman need not fight for, or even support policy in, the collective interests of women to be a feminist; she must instead be a woman with power who serves as a role model for girls.

Similarly, Oprah is a feminist to eighteen-year-old African-American Quianna because of the way in which the celebrity represents herself, rather than because she intentionally advocates on behalf of women and girls. Unlike Yasmine, who found evidence of Oprah's feminism in the fact that she builds schools for girls, Quianna sees Oprah as a feminist because she performs the role of independence, strength, and power for African-American women. Although Quianna uses the language of "fight" she does so with the conclusion that the role of the fighter is performative rather than activist: "[Oprah] fights for a lot of things. She fights for who she is; she is an African-American, black woman so it's kind of hard on African-American black women. So that's why I would say she's a feminist because she fights for who she is, she represents herself as a black woman out there." "Fighting for who she is," Oprah "represents herself." It is this representation, this performance of self-determination, that casts Oprah in the role of a feminist.

Sierra, the only girl in this study who has attended "feminist meetings" with other high school and college students, also identifies two talk show hosts as feminists. Although she does not think that a state of equality will be reached for several generations "because there really is still the very patriarchal family and men get better jobs [and] get paid better," she does believe that society is moving toward equality for women because there are now "a lot of women in higher business positions and women are able to be intelligent . . . and make their own decisions." It is these intelligent, autonomous women, who occupy the high positions that Sierra thinks of when she is asked to name feminists in media. Sierra cites two lesbians, Ellen Degeneres and Rosie O'Donnell, as feminists. Conscious that she might be accused of falling into a trap of eclipsing feminism and lesbianism, she explains, "I know the whole lesbian thing comes in, too. But [Ellen's] really . . . and Rosie O'Donnell are both really women who take a stand about being open about their sexuality, and being women. They really have control." Sierra does not look to these two women for their work on securing rights or their other activist work but because they are open about their life choices to live without men (something that Sierra herself is considering) and to live as out lesbians (something that she is also considering).[25] Sierra especially respects their ability to be true to who they are "under the mass companies" that attempt to tame gay and lesbian lifestyles. Once again, these media personalities are identified as feminist because they perform the image of empowered women thus symbolizing women as self-determined and already equal.

If feminism has been a movement for social change, it has always called for a collective struggle against gender injustices. The "sisterhood is powerful" model and the critical antiracist politics of intersecting identities of second-wave feminism called for the kind of collective organization typically considered necessary for social change. More recently third-wave feminists have argued that women may live "feminist lives" rather than participate in activist movements.[26] As they identify feminists in their lives and in the public eye, Grace, Nikke, Quianna, and Sierra are more closely aligned with third-wave feminism than they are with its second wave. For these girls, being a feminist does not necessarily include action or collective struggle. In their articulations, feminism is the performance of an identity. In this model, a feminist need not use her voice, body, time, or money to actively fight for equal rights. Instead, a woman need only appear to possess power, self-determination, and the achievement of equal rights in order to be a feminist.

By performance, I do not mean to suggest that the feminism of these women is inauthentic. Rather, I use the term in a variety of overlapping ways. To perform, on one account, means to accomplish a task or "to do." In this sense the women who perform feminism are simply, as we will see, being feminist. They do not perform an action that makes them feminist; they simply exist as feminist. Building on this I use Judith Butler's conception of performance, which involves ongoing construction of identity through the performance of said identity.[27] For Butler gender is constituted through performance. In other words, it is through the everyday enactment of femininity and masculinity that one's gendered identity is formed. Similarly, in the model of feminism performed, feminist identity is constituted through the everyday enactment of strength and self-determination. Like gender, it is obviously not a natural or given category. Moreover, for the girls who define feminism as performative, it is a category constituted through its own enactment. Just as one becomes a woman by enacting femininity, one becomes a feminist by enacting personal power.

The definition proposed by these girls is deeply rooted in a media culture that emphasizes individual choice and the performance of a feminist identity rather than the practice of feminist politics.[28] Since the 1970s, when television began to incorporate feminist interests into its narratives, it has done so by using visual and rhetorical codes of appearance, career, and lifestyle to mark characters as feminists rather than by exploring characters' political beliefs or acts.[29] Mass media has also created contradictory images of women that suggest women should be "pliant, cute, sexually available to men, thin, blond, poreless, wrinkle-free, and deferential to men" while still being "rebellious, tough, enterprising, and shrewd."[30] Postfeminist television narratives have focused on individual women's struggles for self-actualization and success rather than on collective feminist politics and on the "problems" experienced by individual women rather than on gender oppression and inequity.[31] In the girl power media environment in which the girls in this study live and make sense of gender identity, feminism continues to be represented by codes that signify a certain lifestyle or identity rather than a political stance.

The feminist performed, still within the realms of a politics of "affirmative recognition" that calls for reassigning value to all things feminine, becomes the symbol of change. Rather than actively fighting for recognition as the activist feminist, the feminist performed embodies the desire for the revaluation of women in society and offers an image that is intended to produce change in how women are recognized. The feminist performed works by herself and is focused on her personal achievement. She appears to embody feminist ideals but does not work in concert with feminism as a social movement.

## The Feminist Performed as Change Agent

The feminist performed model, often seen as a product of neoliberal ideology, has been accused of leading girls toward a vision of personal success and achievement and away from a collective critique of oppressive social structures.[32] In recent work feminism performed has been imagined to be intensely individualistic, reducing feminism to individual choice and individual success at the expense of the collectivity required for social change.[33] Indeed, McRobbie suggests that there is an implicit contract by which upwardly mobile girls abandon a critique of gender oppression, and especially of inequalities among women, in exchange for access to, and seeming success in, institutions of masculine power.[34] Seen in this light, feminism becomes an accoutrement, as well as a justification for the recent reduction of social welfare resources, rather than a change agent.[35]

The impacts of this brand of feminism may be seen in two ways. On the one hand, as suggested by several girls' studies theorists the goal of individual women's achievement may serve to quash girls' impulse to respond collectively to the injustice they experience in their daily lives and they expect to experience in their futures.[36] From this view, girls who see women in positions of power will strive to emulate those women. Rather than seeking social/structural change that will put an end to sexist oppression, these girls will celebrate the advances made by individual women and seek their own personal successes rather than collective change. As seen in chapter 5, this celebration of success and choice often conflicts with the realities faced by the girls and the women in their lives. In this case, girls may be confused as to how to approach their futures, how to enter into nontraditional gender roles, or how to balance the work and family lives that many of them dream of for their futures as evidenced by Aiyisha and Gillian, discussed in chapter 5. On the other hand, although many girls use a discourse of individualism to construct their definition of performative feminism, they also appear to imagine the performance of feminism to be a model through which girls, like themselves, are able to imagine taking on roles not traditionally available to them. It is through role modeling that the women who perform feminism may be able to offer a sense of the collective. These women appear, to some of girls in this study, not only to be succeeding for themselves, but also to be demonstrating, through their public presence, that women can be powerful/independent/self-determined. While clearly not a *movement* for social change, performative feminism may be foundational for some girls as they come to consciousness about the inequities they experience and the ways in which they might personally embrace nontraditional gender roles.

Nikke is direct in her assessment of Condoleezza Rice, arguing that she is "a voice to women saying 'you could do it.'" Jenna calls Elle Woods a "role model" and says of Senay: "she's the image of other immigrant girls." Several of the other girls imply that the feminist performed serves as a role model for them. Sierra, for example, who has only recently come out to her parents about her bisexuality, and her relationship with another girl, looks to Rosie O'Donnell and Ellen Degeneres as models of women who have successfully taken "a stand about being open about their sexuality." Grace, who does not wear feminine clothes, and engages in typically masculine role-playing computer games, seeks models in characters who demonstrate their ability to engage in behavior not typically associated with the feminine ("saving the world") and Quianna, an African-American girl who is headed to college away from home, looks to Oprah as a woman who "represents herself as a black woman out there." In this way, girl power feminism finds a home between a movement for social change and an individual success story. While a feminist in girl power media culture fails to challenge existing social structures that maintain social inequities, she becomes the protagonist in a transgressive narrative about gender, femininity, and power.

Although there is no doubt that this model is individualistic, it may not be radically different from the affirmative liberal feminist movement. Framed in a language of rights and choices, liberal feminism embraces the feminist role model because she serves to remind women of the multiple options available to them. The role model does not necessarily work in coalition with other women, or encourage a collective action, but her presence has a collective *sensibility*. She enacts her power not simply for herself but also serves an instructive and liberating role. From this perspective, the feminist performed is not only lauded for her personal achievement, she is also providing girls with a demonstration of how to be powerful/independent/self-determined.

Yet, as McRobbie notes, it is problematic that girl power media culture seems to find only liberal feminism "palatable enough to be taken on board."[37] What happens to radical, or transformative, politics in girl power media culture? Are they erased by the commodification of some feminist values?

Harvey suggests the inevitable focus on the individual in a late capitalist culture, where an ideology of consumption and commodification prevails, puts us at risk of experiencing life vicariously without having to make sense of the structures in which cultures are produced, distributed, or experienced.[38] Likewise, Comaroff and Comaroff have argued that neoliberalism intensifies "the abstraction inherent in capitalism itself," decontextualizing production so that connections between labor, personhood, and consumption become increasingly difficult to identify.[39]

In Harvey's discussion of Disneyland and Epcot Center's "it's a small world after all" mentality he argues, "The general implication is that through the experience of everything from food, to culinary habits, music, television, entertainment, and cinema, it is now possible to experience the world's geography vicariously, as a simulacrum."[40]

In Harvey's example, world-cultures and the experience of travel have been commodified, packaged, and sold back to the public. Visitors to these amusement parks do not need to think of where the food is actually coming from, who has produced the displays, or whether the culture that is being simulated is accurately represented.

If we use this analogy to look at feminism in girl power media culture, we might say that just as people can "experience the Old World for a day without actually having to go there," girl power media culture allows for the experience of feminist power without actually having to go there.[41] As Comaroff and Comaroff explain, identity in neoliberal capitalism becomes linked with what one consumes, and the market takes control of signs once used to demark community, so that class difference is magnified even while class consciousness is undercut.[42] The same may be said about gender identity, difference, and feminist consciousness. Indeed, it may be that in girl power media cultures, girls and women can participate in what Skeggs called "entitlement feminism";[43] they can play with voice, with anger, and with alternatives to femininity, but they may never have to understand the history of feminism, the feminist labor that was involved in creating a place in which the feminist as empowered self is possible, or the continuing material and ideological inequities faced by women and girls.

## NEGOTIATING THE COMPLEX: HOPE FOR TRANSFORMATIVE POLITICS

Colleen and Razia, both students in a social science research class at Excel, a magnet school that attracts the city's top students, and Juana, a Monument student, who identifies as a feminist, think critically about the feminist representations available to them. These girls straddle the divide between imagining a feminist as an activist and as a performative identity, and articulate the ambiguity of contemporary, girl power feminist strategies. Although they do not disagree with the group of girls for whom feminism is a performed identity, they do expose the weakness in this model.

Juana first became aware of feminism when she entered Monument High School. Many of the teachers at the school, she says, are feminists and "feel very strongly about women—like women should be powerful and stuff." Juana, however, struggles to determine what exactly it means to "feel very strongly about women" and how this feeling gets enacted in everyday life. Her struggle illuminates the two conflicting definitions of feminist constructed by the participants. Initially, she argues that the female characters on the television sitcom *Friends* should be considered feminists because they look the part and are "modern" in that they have jobs, "do their own stuff," and are "their own person." However, as she continues to speak, Juana begins to question this definition that revolves around "just being" a strong woman. She considers whether the women from *Charlie's Angels*, who physically defend themselves and "give you that vibe" that they are powerful, are truly feminist. We hear her struggle with the core of feminist identity: "I don't know if they're feminists or . . . they're not really talking about anything like that but they just seem. . . . I don't think, it's not, they're not really like, the theme of the movie wouldn't be that, well probably yeah, but. . . ." Juana questions whether a performance of power by the characters from *Charlie's Angels* and *Friends* makes them feminist when their words and actions do not necessarily advocate power or strength for women. Where Juana cannot complete her own thoughts, Colleen and Razia have the tools to more fully challenge the existing paradigm.

When Colleen considers Susan Sarandon and Angelina Jolie feminists because they are "active in pursuing what they really want," she grapples with this assessment because, she says, "I guess they're not like fighting for women's rights, I guess, exactly per se." She sees Jolie and Sarandon as feminists because they are both politically vocal (Jolie on issues of refugee rights and protections and Sarandon on a range of progressive, left-wing political issues from AIDS awareness to antiwar) and because they are known for taking on strong women's film roles.

Colleen calls herself feminist because she believes in "women's rights like totally" and because of her active use of voice. Colleen describes herself as a feminist because she'll "be like 'excuse me, no' " to correct people who "say something that is demeaning towards females." At the same time she believes that imagining feminism as activist may be an antiquated vision. Struggling to define why the notion of feminist as activist is "old-fashioned" she says, "[Now] it's not as open of a fight as, I guess, it used to be, but, umm, [Jolie and Sarandon] are just like being their own person and being successful and, umm, like, being active and fighting for what they think is right and, just, I don't know. I don't know how to describe it." Later Colleen begins to suggest that the act of performing feminism and enacting the feminist self, rather than being part of a social change movement, is a more contemporary model of feminism. She explains, "Now more people are filling the role of, like, feminist that older women fought for. They fought for this, but now we're, like, filling the role. . . ." Colleen's articulation of this model as a performative one, "filling the role," is similar to that of the third wave espoused by Baumgardner and Richards who write of young feminists as living feminist lives. What distinguishes Colleen's articulation, however, is her awareness of the constructed nature of feminist performance and her implication that there is an intent in feminist performance.

Razia, whose social science research project focuses on women's body image, also expresses an understanding of the constructed nature of the performance of feminism. In doing so she exposes the potential weakness of this model. Razia doubts that most women are truly the empowered women they present themselves to be. As a self-proclaimed feminist with body-image problems and an eating disorder, Razia wonders whether these symbolic feminists are authentically feminist when they do not admit to their own internalized oppression and, in some cases, their complicity in contributing to gender oppression.

Razia calls herself a "hypocritical feminist" because although she "always advocates everything a girl should be able to do," she is still very invested in beauty culture. She spends a lot of time thinking about her weight and her style and says, "I follow the same rules as everybody else." Razia does not think she is alone in this hypocrisy. In fact, she feels that nearly every feminist is hypocritical except for the kind of girl who "wears big baggy jeans and could care less what the whole world thinks about her weight, and she's like maybe fifty pounds overweight and she's like 'I'm happy with myself, I'm gonna do this,'" though she is not even sure that those girls really exist. Oprah, whom she admires both for her own self-representation ("just being there . . . as an African-American woman standing up on a TV show and being probably the richest woman") and for her work with other women (portraying women who survive domestic abuse and "caring for everybody") is equally hypocritical because "[s]he does follow the codes of dressing, of looking good, of wearing this, of wearing that, because she has the money, and losing weight because she wants to and it looks good, but then going against it . . . saying things like 'women have the same rights, the same privileges as any other man.'"

Jennifer Lopez is also a hypocritical feminist in Razia's eyes because she presents herself as a self-determined woman who "does everything" from singing, dancing, and acting to clothing design but she also "uses those standards" and "tells young girls that you have to be beautiful to get somewhere." In fact, according to Razia, she not only uses "those" standards, she also creates them: "She's one of those women who puts the standards for girls that you should be exercising twenty-four/seven to look beautiful, you should wear clothes like this, you should look like this, your face should be clear." On the one hand, Jennifer Lopez, who grew up in the Bronx, demonstrates to Razia that young women from at-risk communities can overcome adversity and become successful in a variety of business realms that are difficult to break into (music, film, fashion). At the same time, she is hypocritical to Razia because her investment in beauty culture (both in her appearance and in her clothing line) demonstrates that she embraces, and encourages girls to embrace, normative gender roles when it suits her purposes.

As these girls negotiate the two dominant definitions of feminism that emerge in girl power discourse, the limitations of the affirmative recognition paradigm emerges. Yasmine and Colleen question how change might occur from a performative feminism when being an empowered woman does not necessarily raise issues of gender inequality or use strategies effective for social change. Razia adds another dimension to the discussion of affirmative recognition suggesting that a "surface reallocation of respect"[44] for women who act powerfully may not be truly transformative because it does not change the normative gender ideologies within which girls are raised. Moving away from a liberal model of feminism toward a poststructuralist model, these girls are beginning to think about the discursive construction of feminism and the ways in which relations of power are reproduced and destabilized by the two models of feminism.[45] Such a politics of poststructuralist, transformative recognition could yield a "project of deconstruction" in which group differentiation and the normative roles for girls and women would be destabilized.[46] But Juana, Razia, and Colleen's awareness of the constructed nature of the feminist performed, and of the fissures in this model, offer hope that a more transformative feminist politics may yet reemerge. Ultimately while the model of affirmative recognition—either as activist feminist or feminist performed—does offer a narrative of resistance against dominant ideological perspectives on femininity, it fails to make girls aware of a range of possible strategies for social change and to change the material realities of girls' lives.

CONCLUSION

# Cultural Discordance: Neoliberal Girl Power Meets Social Reality

All the women who independent
Throw your hands up at me
—"Independent Woman," Destiny's Child, 2000

In 2000, as the first *Charlie's Angels* movie hit theatres, "Independent Woman, Part I" a song from the soundtrack, shot to the top of the charts. The song's R&B flavor, along with its lyrics, which talk to "all the women who [are] independent," address young women as the song's primary audience. The song's video reinforces the address to this particular audience as it begins, and frequently cuts to, the image of the three singers from Destiny's Child sitting at the head of a conference table, while the remaining seats are filled with young women who take notes, as they watch a video training them to be "independent women," and obligingly "throw their hands up" at the appropriate moments. The song might well be girl power's anthem; it calls for young women to embrace self-determination, self-reliance, and a power achieved through displays of financial success and sexual subjectivity. "I buy my own diamonds and I buy my own rings," the song begins, referring to the engagement ring, a symbol of male power that both marks a woman as taken and serves as a representation of the male purchaser's wealth. "Independent Woman" contributes to a rewriting of the feminine script; women are self-sufficient ("I depend on me"), women are not waiting by the phone for men to call ("Only ring your cell-y when I'm feeling lonely"), women are equal in heterosexual exchange ("Always 50/50 in relationships"), women are in control of their sexual desire ("When it's all over please get up and leave"), women are not moving from their parents' home to their husband's home ("The house I live in/I've bought it") and women are not waiting around for a rich husband, they are successful in their own right ("The rock I'm rockin, I've bought it."). The video adds images of the singers breaking the glass ceiling by taking seats at the head of the table, in control of their sexual display, dancing around in gold minidresses and high heels, fighting off a faceless robot-man, and using typically masculine tools (motorcycles and the remote control). The song and video conflate independence with power and, while the lyrics call for women to "throw your hands up at me," this dance move is in recognition and support of the singers' self-affirming testaments rather than in an activist, raised-fist, change-producing stance.

Girl power media culture is both a point of production and a mode of expression that shifts the ways in which we conceptualize femininity. In this new model, some elements of traditional femininity (beauty, care, and sexiness) are retained while others (passivity, weakness, and dependence) are met with a feminist reimagining so that girls are repositioned as active, choice-making agents. In this discourse, even acts of traditional femininity are recoded as empowered: one can "own her sexuality" and use it as a tool or weapon to gain economic or social capital, or she can simply enjoy her own desire (which is coded as a sign of her connection to herself and her resistance to the denial of female sexual longing), and her own desirability (which is coded as a choice to be sexual subject and to be appreciated by the female and male gaze).

Girl power focuses on style as a mark of one's autonomy, on sexual expression as a symbol of one's connection with the self, on independence from men rather than from patriarchal systems and relations of power, and on the individual as independent resister rather than as member of collective social change movement. In this sense, girl power has a home in neoliberalism, which places an emphasis on self-improvement, self-correction, and individual empowerment over social change or state support.

While "Independent Woman" may be an anthem, girl power continues to be ubiquitous in mainstream media addressed to teen girls. Though many of the references in this book refer to media that was popular during the qualitative interviews, the cultural moment that is girl power—a cultural moment in which the promise of feminism has been incorporated into hegemonic cultural production—continues to be diffused through the whole mediascape. While I could elaborate and introduce discussions of more contemporary girl power media texts—television's *Alias* and *Veronica Mars*, pop music's "Stupid Girls," by Pink and "If I Were a Boy," by Beyonce, or advertising's Right Hand Ring campaign—these would become quickly outdated, as well, while girl power will likely continue to be relevant for many more years. Rather than focusing on specific texts, readers should use the media referred to throughout the book as demonstrations of the ways in which feminism's political aims and emancipatory intentions have become accessible through the popularization of rhetoric and images that code characters, pop music stars, and other celebrities as strong and independent. At its core, girl power is a commodification of opposition to traditional femininity. It takes feminist ideas and feminist language, and makes them popular, accessible, and, sometimes, less potent.

It is important to heed Driscoll's missive that popularity and quality are not incompatible and that a text or act might have a popular *and* authentically feminist message.[1] As seen through my discussions with the seventy girls whose voices shape this research, girl power as a popularized feminism does make the oppositional ideology accessible and more functional in part because it does not require a complete rejection of femininity's familiar tropes.[2] Yet, girl power media culture, as a neoliberal commodity cannot address many of the real social concerns of the girls in this study because it is a personal tool, not a tool of social change. Feminism made popular through girl power media becomes a part of the feminine identity constructed by and for the girls as well as a key feature in the construction of their dreams for the future. Rooted in individuality and a politics of choice, girl power feminism does not encourage girls to consider the structural forces that contribute to the need for change, the ongoing oppression of girls and women, or the collective nature of social change movements. Girl power celebrates girls, independence, and feminism performed by bodies of a corporate media culture but does not celebrate a feminist movement for social change at structural levels.

I have provided an analysis of how a diverse group of urban girls understand themselves in girl power media culture and how they speak about living in a patriarchy in which cultural products are infused with both hegemonic ideologies of femininity and resistive ideologies of feminism. Moreover, I have explored girls' interactions with media beside their interactions with peers and family members to better understand the social experience of girls within girl power media culture. This contextualized, multilayered analysis of the intersecting discourses that girls negotiate as they construct narratives of themselves as female has highlighted the disjuncture between girl power discourse and the lack of power that girls really experience. Many of these girls come to recognize strong, powerful, independent women as feminists because they see them as the embodiment of feminist politics. At the same time, although girls adopt this feminist vision of their own lives and futures, this version of feminism may not aid them in actually achieving the futures they seek. The power and choice the girls witness and value in the lives of the women they see on television and in the sphere of pop music, and that they intend to incorporate into their own narratives of self, are not available to them as young women growing up with the race, class, and gender injustices of their everyday, social world.

The girls in this study experience a sense of cultural discordance in girl power media culture where transgressive and commercial girl power cultural discourse collides with the constrained social, political, and economic realities of their lives. Thus, although the girls in this study *do* strive for equality, *do* imagine a multifaceted future as professionals and mothers, and *do* have a vision of femininity that includes sexual desire, power, and agency, they speak about the processes toward these gains as individual journeys and hurdles to jump rather than as social, economic, and cultural inequities that require a collective social movement as well as legal, policy, and regulatory support. And, although the girls *do* adopt girl power rhetoric about choice and individualism, they describe feeling confined in their own style, voice, sexuality, and imaginings of the future.

It would be easy to argue that the girls in this study who feel they have an awareness and connection to a pro-woman, feminist discourse are in a state of "false consciousness." However, cultural discordance better represents their experience. These girls are not fooled into believing that the ideologies of the ruling class are natural and best serve their interests. Rather it is evident in their talk about the ways in which socioeconomic class, race, and gender are used to organize social networks (as discussed in chapter 3), access to space (as discussed in chapter 3), sexual identity (as discussed in chapter 6), and household responsibilities (as discussed in chapter 5), as well as their talk about the construction of sexual personae by a culture industry that objectifies women and manipulates artists and audiences in a quest for sales (see chapter 4), that the girls in this study are politically conscious, socially astute, and aware of how inequities impact their lives. Cultural discordance fits their experience because just as two musical notes that clash produce a discordant, unpleasant sound, girls' investment in a set of conflicting and contradictory cultural discourses leads to an unpleasant experience; a social experience that lacks harmony.

Using a postmodern theoretical perspective, this lack of harmony is no surprise. As discussed in chapter 2, individuals do not have core, unwavering identities but rather are constantly in dialogue with the self, with culture, and with various discourses that may contradict one another. While not surprising, it is certainly elucidating to listen as the girls in this study work through this particular internal debate. What becomes clear is that they have a great deal of difficulty reconciling not only the conflicting discourses of femininity and feminism but also the social realities of their everyday lives. These girls are encouraged by narratives of feminist-femininity and an American-inspired dream of playing the lead role in one of these narratives. Yet, girl power media culture does not offer images of how to work collectively to make these dreams possible nor does it offer suggestions of how to shift social structures so that all girls will have an equal shot at being cast as the leading lady in these productions of womanhood. Girl power may claim to bring together all the "ladies who truly feel me" as Destiny's Child sings in "Independent Woman," but at the end of the day, it reminds girls: "I depend on me."

# Appendix: Participants

| Name | Age | Race/ ethnicity (self-reported) | Affiliation | Borough of residence | School type | Percentage of people in neighborhood below poverty level |
|---|---|---|---|---|---|---|
| Adrienne | 16 | Japanese-Brazilian | Bridge | Brooklyn | Private | 24% |
| Aiyisha | 13 | African-American | Gardens | Brooklyn | Catholic | 23% |
| Amber | 13 | African-American | Gardens | Brooklyn | Catholic | 23% |
| Bahijah | 17 | Black | Victory | Bronx | Public | 45% |
| Brianna | 17 | Panamanian/ Jamaican | Victory | Bronx | Public | 41% |
| Colleen | 17 | Caucasian/ Irish | Excel | Queens | Public | 3% |
| Diana | 16 | Chinese | Community | Queens | Public | 6% |
| Ellie | 16 | Caucasian | Bridge | Brooklyn | Private | 12% |
| Gillian | 17 | Caucasian | Excel | Queens | Public | 3% |
| Grace | 15 | Taiwanese-American | Community | Queens | Public | 6% |
| Helen | 16 | Chinese | Community | Queens | Public | 18% |
| Isa | 18 | Hispanic | Monument | Bronx | Public | 29% |
| Jenna | 14 | White | Gardens | Brooklyn | Catholic | 19% |
| Juana | 17 | Hispanic/ Dominican | Monument | Manhattan | Public | 35% |
| Kristaly | 17 | Latina | Victory | Bronx | Public | 38% |
| Leila | 17 | Guyanese | Excel | Queens | Public | 7% |
| Lili | 17 | Dominican | Victory | Bronx | Public | 43% |
| Meg | 17 | Caucasian | Bridge | Brooklyn | Private | 20% |

| Name | Age | Race/ethnicity (self-reported) | Affiliation | Borough of residence | School type | Percentage of people in neighborhood below poverty level |
|---|---|---|---|---|---|---|
| Michelle | 16 | African American | Victory | Bronx | Public | 48% |
| Nikke | 16 | Black-Nigerian | Victory | Bronx | Public | 21% |
| Paola | 17 | Honduran | Victory | Bronx | Public | 38% |
| Quianna | 18 | African American | Victory | Bronx | Public | 39% |
| Razia | 17 | Afghan | Excel | Queens | Public | 18% |
| Sierra | 17 | White | Bridge | Brooklyn | Private | 12% |
| Simone | 14 | White | Gardens | Brooklyn | Public | 21% |
| Stacey | 16 | Caribbean | Victory | Bronx | Public | 41% |
| Suzie | 14 | White | Towne | Queens | Public | 40% |
| Tasha | 17 | Black | Excel | Queens | Public | 12% |
| Thea | 17 | White | Bridge | Brooklyn | Private | 12% |
| Yasmine | 16 | Dominican | Victory | Bronx | Public | 39% |

# NOTES

## INTRODUCTION A DECADE AFTER SPICE: GIRL POWER MEDIA CULTURE IN THE NEW MILLENNIUM

1. Spice Girls, 1997, 49.
2. Doherty, *Teenagers and Teenpics*; Palladino, *Teenagers*.
3. Palladino, *Teenagers*; Pecora, *The Business of Children's Entertainment*; Schrum, *Some Wore Bobby Sox*.
4. Nash, *American Sweethearts*, 217.
5. Brooke, "Girl Power."
6. Ibid., 18.
7. Munk, "Girl Power!"
8. *Teen People* (1997), *Jump: For Girls Who Dare to Be Real* (1997), *Twist* (1997), *Girl* (1998), *Latin Girl* (1999), *Honey* (1999), *CosmoGirl* (2000), *Teen Vogue* (2000), *ElleGirl* (2001), *marykateandashley* (2001).
9. *Felicity* (1998–2002), *Dawson's Creek* (1998–2003), *Buffy, the Vampire Slayer* (1997–2003), *7th Heaven* (1996–2007), *Moesha* (1996–2001), *Sabrina, the Teenage Witch* (1996–2003), *Charmed* (1998–2006), *Gilmore Girls* (2000–2007).
10. *Daria* (1997–2001), *The Powerpuff Girls* (1998–2005), and *Kim Possible* (2002–2007).
11. *10 Things I Hate about You* (1999), *Dick* (1999), *Mulan* (1998), *Clueless* (1995), *Bring it On* (2000), *She's All That* (1999), *Ghost World* (2001), *Save the Last Dance* (2001), *Mean Girls* (2004), *What a Girl Wants* (2003), *Legally Blonde* (2001), and *Titanic* (1997).
12. Consoli, "Girl Power"; Douglas, *Where the Girls Are*.
13. Aapola, Gonick, and Harris, *Young Femininity*, 19.
14. Throughout this book I use the terms postfeminism and postfeminist as a means to capture the particular discourse about feminism commonly associated with the era following second-wave feminism. I am not in any way implying that feminism is nonexistent, nor that

we are in a moment after its efficacy or viability. Rather, the term postfeminist is used to refer to a cultural moment in which feminism has been declared both as a failure that has made women miserable, as well as such a big success that it is no longer warranted. For further discussion, see Modleski, *Feminism without Women*; Walters, *Material Girls*; Stacey, "Sexism by a Subtler Name" and Probyn, "New Traditionalism and Post-Feminism."

15. For a history of girls' studies, see Mazzarella and Pecora, "Revisiting Girls' Studies" and Driscoll, "Girls Today."
16. Driscoll, *Girls*, 272; McRobbie, *In the Culture Society*, 101.
17. Durham, "The Girling of America."
18. Lamb and Brown, *Packaging Girlhood*, 3.
19. Harris, *Future Girl*.
20. Driscoll, *Girls*.
21. Ibid., 281.
22. Lemish, "Spice World," 20. See also Whiteley, *Women and Popular Music*, 217.
23. Lemish, "Spice World"; Lemish, "Spice Girls' Talk"; and Whiteley, *Women and Popular Music*.
24. Five years earlier, in 1992, a *Buffy* movie was released for the big screen. It is widely agreed that the original cinematic text did not have the same feminist core as the television series.
25. Fudge, "The Buffy Effect."
26. For more on women on television fighting evil, see Inness, ed., *Action Chicks* and Early and Kennedy, eds., *Athena's Daughters*.
27. Durham, "The Girling of America." See also Ono, "To Be a Vampire."
28. Early, "The Female Just Warrior"; Marinucci, "Feminism and the Ethics of Violence"; Pender, "I'm Buffy and You're…History."
29. Helford, "Introduction."
30. Aapola, Gonick, and Harris, *Young Femininity*, 37.
31. Harris, *Future Girl*.
32. Harvey, *A Brief History of Neoliberalism*.
33. Aapola, Gonick, and Harris, *Young Femininity*, 7.
34. Ibid.
35. Durham, "The Girling of America," 30.

## 1 Growls and Whimpers: The Roots of Girl Power Discourse

1. Gonick, "Between 'Girl Power' and 'Reviving Ophelia,'" 5.
2. Pipher, *Reviving Ophelia*.

3. Brown and Gilligan, *Meeting at the Crossroads.*
4. American Association of University Women, *Shortchanging Girls, Shortchanging America.*
5. Orenstein, *School Girls*, xvi.
6. Ibid., xvii.
7. Sadker and Sadker, *Failing at Fairness*, iii.
8. Ibid., 77.
9. Ward and Benjamin, "Women, Girls, and the Unfinished Work of Connection." *School Girls* was also a *New York Times* Notable Book of the Year and received praise from *The Washington Post* and the *Los Angeles Times.*
10. Pipher, *Reviving Ophelia*, 38.
11. Quoted in Gonick, "Between 'Girl Power' and 'Reviving Ophelia,'" 12.
12. Mastronardi, *From the DSM to Ophelia.*
13. Gleick, "Surviving Your Teens."
14. Glennon, *200 Ways to Raise a Girl's Self-Esteem*, 77.
15. Mackoff, *Growing a Girl*, 115.
16. Ibid.
17. Pipher, *Reviving Ophelia*, 38.
18. Ibid., 243.
19. Ibid., 12.
20. Brown and Gilligan, *Meeting at the Crossroads*, 226.
21. Erkut et al., "Diversity in Girls' Experiences," 53.
22. Way, "'Can't You See the Courage, the Strength that I Have.'"
23. Brown, *Raising Their Voices.*
24. While Gonick (in "Between 'Girl Power' and 'Reviving Ophelia'") positions the crisis in girls' lives as occurring concurrently with girl power discourse, studies on the crisis started as early as 1982 and became popular in 1994 while girl power did not become popular until 1997. Thus, I believe that girl power emerged, in part, as a result of the discourse on the crisis.
25. Faludi, *Backlash.*
26. Ibid. Chapter Two.
27. Rogers and Garrett, *Who's Afraid of Women's Studies?* 109.
28. Walters, *Material Girls*, 139.
29. Faludi, *Backlash*, 71.
30. Ibid.
31. Edmondson, "The Demographics of Guilt"; Holcomb, *Not Guilty!*
32. "How Women Have Changed America."
33. Rosch, "Sugar Daddies," 52.
34. Edmondson, "The Demographics of Guilt," 33.

35. Seiter, *Sold Separately.*
36. Douglas and Michaels, *The Mommy Myth*, 270.
37. Mattell purchased The Pleasant Company in 1998.
38. Zaslow, "In the Business of Little Girls," 15.
39. Inness, " 'Anti-Barbies.' "
40. Zaslow, "In the Business of Little Girls."
41. Luker, *Dubious Conceptions.*
42. Ibid., 76.
43. Ibid., 77.
44. Tolman, "Adolescent Girls' Sexuality," 255.
45. Luker, *Dubious Conceptions.*
46. Gonick, "Between 'Girl Power' and 'Reviving Ophelia,' " 5.
47. The term "third wave" feminism may have originally emerged from feminists of color who demanded a feminism that accounted for race and class oppression alongside gender oppression. *The Third Wave: Feminist Perspectives on Race*, an unpublished anthology, which was stymied by the financial troubles of a small feminist press, suggests that the third wave was originally begun as a movement to position antiracism as central to feminist discourse (Henry, *Not My Mother's Sister*, 23). By the mid-1990s, however, the "third wave" was used largely as a term to represent a new generation of feminists (ibid., 24). Where the radical antiracist discussion of late second-wave feminism has disappeared, there remains, in third-wave feminism, an interest in exploring how race informs feminism.
48. Hollows, *Feminism, Femininity, and Popular Culture*, 3.
49. For more on third-wave politics, see Baumgardner and Richards, *Manifesta* and "Feminism and Femininity"; Henry, *Not My Mother's Sister*; and Walker, *To Be Real.*
50. Baumgardner and Richards, *Manifesta*, 136.
51. Morgan, *Sisterhood Is Powerful.* For more about sisterhood see Henry, *Not My Mother's Sister.*
52. hooks, *Ain't I a Woman?*; Lorde, *Sister Outsider* Moraga and Anzaldua, *This Bridge Called My Back.*
53. hooks, *Feminist Theory*; Mohanty, *Feminism without Borders*; Spivak, "Subaltern Studies."
54. Heywood and Drake, *Third Wave Agenda.*
55. Baumgardner and Richards, "Feminism and Femininity," 66.
56. Henry, *Not My Mother's Sister.*
57. Garrison, "U.S. Feminism-Grrrl Style!" 142.
58. Gottlieb and Wald, "Smells Like Teen Spirit"; Kearney, "Don't Need You" Riordan, "Commodified Agents and Empowered Girls"; Schilt, " 'A Little Too Ironic.' "

59. Riordan, "Commodified Agents and Empowered Girls."
60. Rosenberg and Garofalo, "Riot Grrrl."
61. Garrison, "U.S. Feminism-Grrrl Style!"
62. Rosenberg and Garofalo, "Riot Grrrl," 810.
63. Leonard, "Paper Planes."
64. Kearney, "Don't Need You," 149.
65. Ibid., 158.
66. Ibid.
67. Gottlieb and Wald, "Smells Like Teen Spirit," 265.
68. Chideya, "Revolution, Girl Style," 84.
69. Gottlieb and Wald, "Smells Like Teen Spirit."
70. Kearney, "Don't Need You"; Schilt, " 'A Little Too Ironic.' "
71. Kearney, "Don't Need You," 161.
72. Riordan, "Commodified Agents and Empowered Girls," 290.
73. Hebdige, *Subculture.*
74. Cohen, *A Consumer's Republic*; Frank, "*The Conquest of Cool*; Goldman, Heath, and Smith, "Commodity Feminism"; Heath and Potter, *Nation of Rebels*; Hebdige, *Subculture.*
75. Harvey, *The Condition of Postmodernity*, 347.
76. Klein, *No Logo*, 81–82.
77. Goldman, Heath, and Smith, "Commodity Feminism."
78. Riordan, "Commodified Agents and Empowered Girls," 294.
79. Driscoll, *Girls.*

## 2 When Asked to Talk: Qualitative Research with Teen Girls

1. Couldry, *Media Rituals*; Couldry, "Theorizing Media as Practice."
2. Berger and Luckmann, *The Social Construction of Reality*; Goffman, *The Presentation of Self in Everyday Life.*
3. Geertz, *The Interpretation of Cultures*, 49.
4. Althusser, "Ideology and Ideological State Apparatuses," 158.
5. Hall, "The Rediscovery of 'Ideology,' " 75.
6. Ibid., 68.
7. Buckingham and Bragg, *Young People, Sex, and the Media.*
8. Goffman, *The Presentation of Self in Everyday Life*, 35.
9. De Lauretis, *Technologies of Gender*; Weedon, *Feminism, Theory and the Politics of Difference.*
10. McRobbie, *Postmodernism and Popular Culture*, 70.
11. Ibid., 71.
12. Steinberg and Kincheloe, *Kinderculture*, 12.
13. Cross, *Kid's Stuff*, 2.

14. Kinder, *Kids' Media Culture*; Schor, *Born to Buy.*
15. Kline, *Out of the Garden*; Cross, *Kid's Stuff*; Linn, *The Case for Make-Believe.*
16. Sanders, *A Is for Ox.*
17. Schor, *Born to Buy.*
18. Motz, "Seen through Rose-Tinted Glasses"; Ducille, "Dyes and Dolls"; Urla and Swedlund, "The Anthropometry of Barbie"; and Steinberg, "The Bitch Who Has Everything."
19. Steinberg, "The Bitch Who Has Everything," 217.
20. Driscoll's "Girl-Doll" is a notable exception.
21. Inness, "Anti-Barbies"
22. Scanlon, "Boys-R-Us."
23. Pecora, "Identity by Design."
24. Signorielli, "Reflections of Girls in the Media."
25. Kilbourne, *Can't Buy My Love*, 117.
26. Bordo, *Unbearable Weight.*
27. Inness, "Anti-Barbies," 178 (emphasis added).
28. Pecora, "Identity by Design," 77 (emphasis added).
29. Heilman, "The Struggle for Self," 195.
30. Hall, "Encoding/Decoding."
31. Ibid.
32. Buckingham, *Reading Audiences*; Hall, "Encoding/Decoding"; Morley, "The *Nationwide* Audience"; Radway, *Reading the Romance.*
33. Ang, *Watching Dallas*; Fiske, *Television Culture.*
34. Fiske, *Television Culture*; Hebdige, *Subculture*; McRobbie, "Shut Up and Dance"; McRobbie, *Postmodernism and Popular Culture.*
35. DeVault, *Liberating Method.*
36. Hesse-Biber and Yaiser, *Feminist Perspectives on Social Research.*
37. Haraway, *Simians, Cyborgs, and Women*; Lal, "Situating Locations."
38. De Lauretis, *Technologies of Gender.*
39. Ibid.
40. Buckingham, *Reading Audiences*; Couldry, *Media Rituals*; "Theorizing Media as Practice."
41. Barker, "Television and the Reflexive Project of the Self"; Buckingham, *Children Talking Television*; Cherland, *Private Practices*; Fisherkeller, *Growing Up with Television*; Finders, "Queens and Teen Zines"; Finders, *Just Girls*; Hodge and Tripp, *Children and Television*; Murray, "Saving Our So-Called Lives."
42. Amit-Talai, *Youth Cultures.*
43. Hebdige, *Subculture*, 102.

44. McRobbie, *Postmodernism and Popular Culture*; "Second Hand Dresses and the Role of the Ragmarket"; "Shut Up and Dance."
45. McRobbie, *Postmodernism and Popular Culture.*
46. Fisherkeller, *Growing Up with Television*; Hodge and Tripp, *Children and Television*; Steele and Brown, "Adolescent Room Culture."
47. Buckingham and Bragg, *Young People, Sex, and the Media.*
48. Fisherkeller, *Growing Up with Television*, 105.
49. Cherland, *Private Practices.*
50. Schrum, *Some Wore Bobby Sox.*
51. Massoni, "Modeling Work"; Schrum, *Some Wore Bobby Sox.*
52. Schlenker, Caron, and Halterman, "A Feminist Analysis of *Seventeen* Magazine."
53. Mazzarella, "The 'Superbowl' of All Dates"; Peirce, "A Feminist Theoretical Perspective."
54. Carpenter, "From Girls into Women"; Duffy and Gotcher, "Crucial Advice on How to Get the Guy"; Garner, Sterk, and Adams, "Narrative Analysis of Sexual Etiquette"; Ostermann and Keller-Cohen, "Good Girls Go to Heaven."
55. Durham, "Dilemmas of Desire"; Garner, Sterk, and Adams, "Narrative Analysis of Sexual Etiquette"; Massoni, "Modeling Work."
56. Durham, "Sex and Spectacle in *Seventeen* Magazine."
57. McRobbie, "The Culture of Working Class Girls."
58. Ballentine and Ogle, "The Making and Unmaking of Body Problems"; Currie, *Girl Talk*; Durham, "Dilemmas of Desire"; Kaplan and Cole, "'I Want to Read Stuff on Boys'"; McRobbie, *Feminism and Youth Culture.*
59. Currie, *Girl Talk*, 246.
60. Frazer, "Teenage Girls Reading *Jackie*," 419.
61. Moss, "Girls Tell the Teen Romance."
62. Malik, "Mediated Consumptions and Fashionable Selves."
63. Duke, "Black in a Blonde World."
64. Finders, "Queens and Teen Zines"; *Just Girls.*
65. Radway, *Reading the Romance*, 215.
66. Finders, "Queens and Teen Zines," 74.
67. Finders, *Just Girls*, 59.
68. Ibid., 61.
69. Unless otherwise noted, all demographic statistics in the remainder of this chapter are drawn from the U.S. Census Bureau, Census 2000.
70. Best, *Prom Night*; Cherland, *Private Practices*; Finders, *Just Girls*; Fisherkeller, *Growing Up with Television.*

71. Only one of the girls in this study discussed her own sexual identity. She came out to me as bisexual. Some girls referred to their heterosexuality but generally this did not figure into our discussions. For an outstanding discussion of young lesbians and media, see Driver, *Queer Girls and Popular Culture.*
72. Seiter, *Sold Separately*, 7.
73. Marcus, "Ethnography in/of the World System."
74. Throughout this section I use the term "regional" to refer to the various regions of New York City in which the girls live and go to school.
75. See chapter 1.
76. Whitney, "In Search of the Coveted Teen," 12.
77. "Kids Age Segmentation," 6.
78. Madriz, "Focus Groups in Feminist Research," 836.
79. Wilkinson, "Focus Group Research"; Madriz, "Focus Groups in Feminist Research."
80. Hodge and Tripp, *Children and Television.*
81. Buckingham, *Children Talking Television*, 86.
82. Madriz, "Focus Groups in Feminist Research"; Merton, Fiske, and Kendall, *The Focused Interview.*
83. Lather, *Getting Smart.*
84. Parents' occupation was provided through self-report. Although several participants were unsure of what their parents did for a living, the majority of participants were able to report a job for the parents or guardians with whom they lived. Socioeconomic status was determined by job titles that are, according to the U.S. Department of Labor, Bureau of Labor Statistics, high paying (white-collar professional positions) such as electric engineer ($72,090), lawyer ($107,800), pediatrician ($143,300), moderately paying (blue-collar positions) such as police officer ($44,960), middle school teacher ($44,830), locksmith ($30,540), and lower-paying (working-poor positions) such as waiter ($15,578), truck driver ($26,530), home health aide ($19,180). While these are nationwide statistics and New York City residents generally earn above the national average, the Department of Labor statistics provide a perspective of socioeconomic status of the family (U.S. Department of Labor, 2003, http://stats.bls.gov/oes/2003/may/oes_nat.htm).
85. Douglas, *Where the Girls Are.*
86. Reinharz, *Feminist Methods in Social Research*, 258.
87. Lather, *Getting Smart*, 67.
88. Lal, "Situating Locations," 115.

89. DeVault, *Liberating Method*; Hegde, "A View from Elsewhere."
90. Buckingham, *Reading Audiences*; Kvale, *InterViews*.
91. Hedge, "A View from Elsewhere," 288.
92. Haraway, *Simians, Cyborgs, and Women*.
93. Although Staten Island is New York City's fifth borough, it is not included in this study for two reasons. The first is that I had less access to Staten Island. Unlike the other boroughs, which have subways that shuttle residents between them, Staten Island must be accessed by ferry, car, or bus. Furthermore, this distinction in Staten Island's identity as well as its unique relationship to the city of New York made it a logical delimitation. A recent *New York Times* article sums up Staten Island's relationship to the rest of NYC:

    In a variety of ways, Staten Island is distinct from the rest of the city. Until the Verrazano-Narrows was completed in 1964, the island was connected to New Jersey by three bridges, but to the rest of the city only by ferry. The island has consistently voted Republican for generations. While homeowners make up 30 percent of the city's population and renters seventy percent, on Staten Island the statistics are exactly the reverse." (Berger and Urbina, "Along with Population and Diversity")

    In addition, Staten Island's population of children between the ages of ten and nineteen represents less than 10 percent of the total population of New York City youth in this age group (U.S. Census Bureau, Census 2000).
94. Participants' race and ethnicity were determined by self-report; socioeconomic status was determined by a combination of information on the girls' schools, neighborhoods, and parental occupations. For each public school attended by participants, socioeconomic status of students was determined by percentage of students eligible to participate in the free lunch program. The economic status of a neighborhood was determined by the median household income and the percentage of residents who live below the poverty line as determined by the U.S. Census Bureau in the Census 2000. As a base, readers should be aware that according to Census 2000, the median household income was $41,994 nationwide and was slightly higher in New York State at $43,393 and the percentage of individuals with income below the poverty line was 12 percent nationwide and 15 percent in New York State (U.S. Census Bureau, Census 2000). Finally, parents' occupation was provided through self-report.
95. Fancsali et al., *Where the Girls Are*, ii.
96. Ibid., iv.

97. Girl Scouts of the U.S.A., *Feeling Safe*, 8.
98. Ibid., iv.
99. All participants participated voluntarily and provided informed consent and parental consent. I guaranteed confidentiality with the required caveats that I could encourage, but not guarantee, that other focus group participants keep group discussions confidential, and that I was required by law to report suspicion of harm the participant may commit to herself, to children, and to others. Participants' names and identifying information have been changed while the nature of their life experiences and social locations has been kept intact.
100. Though relatively little research has been done comparing girls involved with Girl Scouting and those not affiliated, there is some suggestion that Girl Scouts may have greater self-esteem and respect for teamwork and leadership than their peers. (Hwalek and Minnick, *Girls, Families, and Communities*; Royse, "Scouting and Girl Scout Curriculum as Interventions.") I recognize that some of the girls' responses may be influenced by their involvement with scouting.
101. This, and all subsequent free lunch data, is referenced in New York City Department of Education, www.nycenet.edu.
102. Although she was vocal in the focus group, Grace had little to say in our individual interview. She does not appear in the study.
103. In this case, African-American includes one participant who recently moved from Africa. There is an ongoing dispute in the African-American community as to whether recent immigrants and their families should be using the term African-American or if this strips it of its initial symbolism of descendents of African slaves in America (Swarns, " 'African-American' Becomes a Term for Debate.").
104. Couldry, "Theorizing Media as Practice," 117.

## 3 Wanna Get Dirrty? Determining Authentic Sexual Subjectivity

1. Williams, "Exclusive Interview: Robin Antin."
2. Fatemeh, "Katy Perry Plays Make Believe."
3. Aapola, Gonick, and Harris, *Young Femininity*, 136.
4. Durham, "Sex and Spectacle in *Seventeen* Magazine."
5. Levy, *Female Chauvinist Pigs*, 30.
6. Tolman, *Dilemmas of Desire*, 3.

7. Kilbourne, *Can't Buy My Love*; Lamb and Brown, *Packaging Girlhood*; Levy, *Female Chauvinist Pigs.*
8. Levy, *Female Chauvinist Pigs*; Mulvey, "Visual Pleasure and Narrative Cinema"; Schor, *Born to Buy.*
9. Dworkin, *Intercourse.*
10. Boston Women's Health Book Collective, *Our Bodies, Ourselves*; Bright, *Susie Bright's Sexual State of the Union*; Friday, *My Secret Garden*; Greer, *The Female Eunuch*; Wolf, *Promiscuities.*
11. Wolf, *Promiscuities.*
12. Baumgardner and Richards, *Manifesta.*
13. Riordan, "Commodified Agents and Empowered Girls," 292.
14. Gill, "From Sexual Objectification to Sexual Subjectification."
15. Ibid.
16. Frith and McRobbie, "Rock and Sexuality," 144.
17. Lewis, *Gender Politics and MTV*; Peterson, "Media Consumption and Girls Who Want to Have Fun."
18. Whiteley, *Women and Popular Music.*
19. Fiske, *Understanding Popular Culture*; Robertson, *Guilty Pleasures.*
20. Emerson, "Where My Girls At?"
21. Wald, "Just a Girl?" 588.
22. Ibid.
23. Lemish, "Spice Girls' Talk"; "Spice World."
24. Schilt, " 'A Little Too Ironic.' "
25. Haynes, "Let the Woman Finally Be on Top," 141.
26. Ibid.
27. Shakira, also biracial, is not simply authentically Latina as Juana suggests; Shakira credits the belly dancing she performs throughout concerts to her Lebanese heritage. What is significant in this discussion, however, is Juana's perception of the belly dancing as authentically Latin.
28. Dougherty, "A Butterfly Takes Wing."
29. Boucher, "Back Atop the Charts, Her Way"; Dougherty, "A Butterfly Takes Wing."
30. Boucher, "Back Atop the Charts, Her Way," A1.
31. Corliss, "A Diva Takes a Dive."
32. "Skeeved me out" is slang for "made me feel sick" or "I felt it was disgusting."
33. Just as Juana mentions that Mariah wanted "to keep up with all the other artists" without specifically naming the other artists, Razia suggests that Mariah is "just like all the other girls." Although neither girl names the artists about whom they are referring, we can

assume from their conversations about popular female music artists that they are talking about the abundance of female artists in girl power media culture for whom sexuality and sexual dress is a central component of their public persona.

34. I am not claiming truth or lies about this narrative. Rather, I am establishing the story that supports Aguilera's claims that she is in control of her sexuality and how this story has been communicated to fans.
35. Valdes-Rodriguez, "Genie behind 'Bottle.'"
36. Harrington, "Christina Aguilera," C1.
37. Ibid.
38. Valdes-Rodriguez, "Genie behind 'Bottle,'" F1.
39. She released a Spanish version of her first album as well as a Christmas album of traditional songs in between *Christina Aguilera* and *Stripped*.
40. "Stripped Intro."
41. Haynes, "Let the Woman Finally Be on Top," 142.
42. Ibid.
43. Ibid.
44. Ibid.
45. Whiteley, *Women and Popular Music*, 137.
46. Durham, "Sex and Spectacle in *Seventeen*," 16.
47. Gill, "From Sexual Objectification to Sexual Subjectification."
48. Rosen, "Big Apple Circus."
49. Hoban, "The Night."
50. Rosen, "Big Apple Circus."
51. Helligar, "Apple's Way"; Hilburn, "What a Drag It Is Being Young"; Schilt, "'A Little Too Ironic," 12.
52. Perry, "Whose Am I?" 145.
53. Ibid.
54. Ibid.

## 4 The Clothed Body: Girls' Social and Emotional Experiences of Style

1. Pomerantz, *Girls, Style, and School Identity*, 47.
2. Ibid.
3. Malson and Swann, "Prepared for Consumption."
4. For example, see Baumgardner and Richards, "Feminism and Femininity"; Durham, "The Taming of the Shrew"; Railton and Watson, "Naughty Girl and Re-Blooded Woman."

5. Bettie, *Women without Class*; LeBlanc, *Pretty in Punk*; Pomerantz, *Girls, Style, and School Identity*.
6. Barnard, *Fashion as Communication*; Craik, *The Face of Fashion*; Driscoll, *Girls*; Hebdige, *Subculture*; Pomerantz, *Girls, Style, and School Identity*.
7. Foucault, *History of Sexuality*; Driscoll, *Girls*.
8. Ewen, *All Consuming Images*, 3.
9. Entwistle, "The Dressed Body."
10. For example, see Hebdige, *Subculture* and Willis, *Learning to Labour*.
11. McRobbie, "The Culture of Working Class Girls"; McRobbie, "Shut Up and Dance."
12. Heilman, "The Struggle for Self," 198.
13. Pomerantz, *Girls, Style, and School Identity*, 64.
14. Lewis, *Gender Politics and MTV*, 219. Though her book is an important ethnographic account of woman within the rock music scene and their fans, Lewis makes grand claims about the potential of style appropriation and shopping.
15. Driscoll, *Girls*; Gonick, "Between 'Girl Power' and 'Reviving Ophelia.'"
16. Skeggs, *Formations of Class and Gender*, 107.
17. Ibid., 90.
18. I have sometimes used first names to discuss media characters and celebrities as this is the way they were referred to by participants.
19. Hunt, "Moving Out of Phoebe's Shadow," E6 and Jones, "Touchingly 'Real' Lisa," I1.
20. For further discussion of teen girls' relationship with feminism see chapter 6.
21. At the time of the interviews Jennifer Aniston was married to Brad Pitt and Courtney Cox was married to David Arquette.
22. Evans and Thornton, *Women and Fashion*.
23. Rose, *Black Noise*, 166.
24. hooks, *Black Looks*.
25. Perry, "Whose Am I?" 137.
26. After an extreme weight loss in 2002, Missy Elliott began wearing more form-fitting and typically feminine clothes but she has, for the most part, continued to resist using her body in a sexualized manner.
27. Adorno and Horkheimer, *The Culture Industry*.
28. Harris, *Future Girl*, 90.
29. For example, see Bloustien, *Girl Making*; Heilman, "The Struggle for Self"; McRobbie, "The Culture of Working Class Girls"; McRobbie,

*Postmodernism and Popular Culture*; Pomerantz, *Girls, Style, and School Identity*.

30. U.S. Bureau of the Census, "2000 Census."
31. Phat is slang for "cool" according to the Urban Dictionary, www.urbandictionary.com.
32. Bloustein, *Girl Making*.
33. Malson, Marshall, and Woollett, "Talking of Taste."
34. Skeggs, *Formations of Class and Gender*, 95.
35. Bettie, *Women without Class*, 48.
36. Skeggs, *Formations of Class and Gender*, 3.
37. Ibid.
38. Postrel, "Inconspicuous Consumption."
39. Bloustein, *Girl Making*, 82.
40. For more discussion on style as a performance see Pomerantz, *Girls, Style, and School Identity* and Bettie, *Women without Class*.
41. For example, see Dwyer, "Contested Identities"; Gilroy, "Between Afro-Centrism and Euro-Centrism"; Malson, Marshall, and Woollett, "Talking of Taste."
42. Gilroy, "Between Afro-Centrism and Euro-Centrism," 4.
43. Ibid., 6.
44. Hall, "New Ethnicities."
45. Dwyer, "Contested Identities"; Malson, Marshall, and Woollett, "Talking of Taste."
46. Hollows, *Feminism, Femininity, and Popular Culture*, 133.
47. Malson, Marshall, and Woollett, "Talking of Taste," 480.
48. Miller, "Consumption as the Vanguard of History," 29.
49. Malson, Marshall, and Woollett, "Talking of Taste."
50. Duits and van Zoonen, "Headscarves and Porno-Chic."
51. Duits and van Zoonen, "Whose Afraid of Agency," 164.
52. Gill, "Critical Respect," 72.
53. Ibid., 76.

## 5 "I Don't Know What I'm Going to Do When It Happens": Independence, Motherhood, Careers, and Imagining the Future

1. Harris, *Future Girl*; Harvey, *The Condition of Postmodernity*.
2. Douglas and Michaels, *The Mommy Myth*.
3. Dodson, *Don't Call Us Out of Name*, 10.
4. Douglas and Michaels, *The Mommy Myth*, 176.
5. Johnston and Swanson, "Undermining Mothers."

6. Vranica, "Marketing and Media."
7. Douglas and Michaels, *The Mommy Myth*, 25.
8. Aapola, Gonick, and Harris, *Young Femininity*, 59.
9. Dow, *Prime-Time Feminism*, 94.
10. Ibid.; Kaplan, *Motherhood and Representation*; Press, *Women Watching Television*.
11. Press, *Women Watching Television*.
12. Dow, *Prime-Time Feminism*.
13. Kaplan, *Motherhood and Representation*.
14. Vavrus, "Opting Out Moms in the News."
15. Harris, *Future Girl*.
16. Vavrus, "Opting Out Moms in the News."
17. Ruddick, *Maternal Thinking*.
18. Lopez, *Hopeful Girls, Troubled Boys*.
19. Way, *Everyday Courage*.
20. Oyewumi, "Ties that (Un)bind."
21. Collins, *Black Feminist Thought*, 119.
22. Cauce et al., "African American Mothers and Their Adolescent Daughters," 105.
23. Oyewumi, "Ties that (Un)bind."
24. Lopez, *Hopeful Girls, Troubled Boys*, 121.
25. U.S. Census Bureau, "American Community Survey 2004."
26. Dodson, *Don't Call Us Out of Name*, 22.
27. Ibid.
28. Harris, *Future Girl*.
29. Aapola, Gonick, and Harris, *Young Femininity*, 73.
30. Harris, *Future Girl*.
31. Ibid., 61.
32. Ibid.
33. Dodson, *Don't Call Us Out By Name*.
34. Warner, *Perfect Madness*.
35. Harris, *Future Girl*; Budgeon, "I'll Tell You What I Really, Really Want."
36. Proweller, *Constructing Female Identities*, 135.
37. U.S. Census Bureau, Census 2000.
38. Proweller, *Constructing Female Identities*, 203.
39. From my own recollection, Cliff Huxtable does not always seem to be working. However, it is Aiyisha's perception here that is of relevance. She perceives that Cliff was able to have children and be an obstetrician but that she would have trouble balancing these two roles.
40. Dow, *Prime-Time Feminism*, 95.

## 6 "If Feminism Is Believing that Women Are Humans, Then I Am a Feminist": Girls Define Feminism and Feminist Practice

1. In actuality DiFranco defines herself as bisexual and Paula Cole, while she has a lesbian fan base and has been married to a man, keeps her sexuality ambiguous.
2. Ibsen, *A Doll's House.*
3. Goldman, Heath, and Smith, "Commodity Feminism," 348.
4. Lees, *Sugar and Spice*; Tolman, *Dilemmas of Desire*; Wolf, *Promiscuities.*
5. Lees, *Sugar and Spice.*
6. Budgeon, "'I'll Tell You What I Really, Really Want'"; Jowett, "'I Don't See Feminists as You See Feminists.'"
7. Dodson, *Don't Call Us Out of Name.*
8. Taylor, "Cultural Stories: Latina and Portuguese Daughters and Mothers" found that the participants in her study of Hispanic and Portuguese teen girls believe that their parents are too strict and treat their sons and daughters differently.
9. Budgeon, "'I'll Tell You What I Really, Really Want'"; Budgeon, "Emergent Feminist?"; Harris, *All about the Girl*; Harris, Next Wave Cultures; Jowett, "'I Don't See Feminists as You See Feminists'"; Lemish, "Spice Girls' Talk"; Proweller, *Constructing Female Identities*; Riordan, "Commodified Agents and Empowered Girls"; Roberts, *Girls in Black and White.*
10. Budgeon, "'I'll Tell You What I Really, Really Want'"; Jowett, "'I Don't See Feminists as You See Feminists'"; Proweller, *Constructing Female Identities.*
11. Jowett, "'I Don't See Feminists as You See Feminists.'" 96.
12. Lopez, *Hopeful Girls, Troubled Boys*, 114.
13. Bulbeck and Harris, "Feminism, Youth Politics, and Generational Change," 225–226.
14. Budgeon, "'I'll Tell You What I Really, Really Want'"; McRobbie, "Notes on Postfeminism and Popular Culture"; Harris, Future Girl; Proweller, *Constructing Female Identities.*
15. There are some exceptions to these findings. See Kearney, *Girls Make Media*, for media production that is influenced, explicitly and implicitly, by collective feminism and Harris, Next Wave Cultures, for discussions of young women involved in subcultural feminism and activism.
16. Weedon, *Feminism, Theory and the Politics of Difference.*

17. Fraser, *Justice Interruptus.*
18. Ibid., 14.
19. Harris, *Next Wave Cultures*, 7.
20. Fraser, *Justice Interruptus*, 23.
21. Judah, "Women."
22. LeBlanc, *Pretty in Punk.*
23. Scott, "Sleek, Tough, Frosted?"
24. While Rice made a few public remarks in support of women's rights in the Middle East, these were largely unreported outside of the feminist community and her associations with an antichoice president certainly marks her as a woman who does not actively fight for women's rights.
25. It is also important to note: In 1997, Ellen Degeneres publicly came out as a lesbian as did her character Ellen Morgan. In 2008, after California passed Proposition 8, changing the state's legal definition of marriage to specify only heterosexual marriage, thus putting the legality of her marriage to Portia de Rossi in question, Degeneres spoke out in support of the rights of gays and lesbians to marry. However, in 2003–2004, when her talk show was in its early years, the entertainer was notably less politically vocal. Similarly, Rosie O'Donnell has recently been vocal about gay rights, the war in Iraq, and gun control in the United States but was much less so during the time of these interviews.
26. Baumgardner and Richards, *Manifesta*, 48.
27. Butler, *Gender Trouble and the Subversion of Identity.*
28. Banet-Weiser, "Girls Rule!"; Dow, *Prime-Time Feminism.*
29. Dow, *Prime-Time Feminism.*
30. Douglas, *Where the Girls Are*, 9.
31. Dow, *Prime-Time Feminism*; Press, *Women Watching Television.*
32. Harris, Future Girl; Taft, "Girl Power Politics."
33. Aapola, Gonick, and Harris, Young Femininity; Harris, Future Girl; Henry, *Not My Mother's Sister*; McRobbie, *Feminism and Youth Culture*; McRobbie, "Notes on Postfeminism and Popular Culture."
34. McRobbie, "Top Girls."
35. Aapola, Gonick, and Harris, Young Femininity; Gonick, "Between 'Girl Power' and 'Reviving Ophelia.'"
36. Budgeon, "'I'll Tell You What I Really, Really Want'"; McRobbie, "Notes on Postfeminism and Popular Culture"; Proweller, *Constructing Female Identities.*
37. McRobbie, "Young Women and Consumer Culture," 547.

38. Harvey, *The Condition of Postmodernity.*
39. Comaroff and Comaroff, "Millennial Capitalism," 305.
40. Harvey, *The Condition of Postmodernity*, 300.
41. Ibid., 300.
42. Comaroff and Comaroff, "Millennial Capitalism."
43. Skeggs, "Women's Studies in Britain in the 1990s."
44. Fraser, *Justice Interruptus*, 27.
45. Weedon, *Feminist Practice and Poststructuralist Theory.*
46. Fraser, Justice Interruptus, 27.

# Bibliography


Aapola, Sinikka, Marnina Gonick, and Anita Harris. *Young Femininity: Girlhood, Power, and Social Change.* New York: Palgrave Macmillan. 2005.

Adorno, Theodor, and Max Horkheimer. "The Culture Industry: Enlightenment as Mass Deception." In *The Cultural Studies Reader*, edited by Simon During, 29–43. New York: Routledge. 1993.

Althusser, Louis. "Ideology and Ideological State Apparatuses Notes towards an Investigation." In *Lenin and Philosophy and Other Essays*, edited by Louis Althusser, 127–186. New York: Monthly Review Press. 1971.

American Association of University Women. *Shortchanging Girls, Shortchanging America: Executive Summary: A Call to Action.* Washington, D.C.: American Association of University Women. 1991.

American Association of University Women. *How Schools Shortchange Girls.* Washington, D.C.: American Association of University Women. 1992.

Amit-Talai, Vered, ed. *Youth Cultures: A Cross-Cultural Perspective.* New York: Routledge. 1995.

Ang, Ien. *Watching Dallas: Soap Opera and the Melodramatic Imagination.* New York: Methuen and Co. Ltd. 1985.

Ballentine, Leslie Winfield and Jennifer Paff Ogle. "The Making and Unmaking of Body Problems in *Seventeen* Magazine, 1992–2003." *Family and Consumer Sciences Research Journal* 33, no. 4 (2005): 281–307.

Banet-Weiser, Sarah. "Girls Rule!: Gender, Feminism, and Nickelodeon." *Critical Studies in Media Communication* 21, no. 2 (2004): 119–139.

Barker, Chris. "Television and the Reflexive Project of the Self: Soaps, Teenage Talk, and Hybrid Identities." *British Journal of Sociology* 48, no. 4 (1997): 611–627.

Barnard, Malcolm. *Fashion as Communication.* New York: Routledge. 2002.

Baumgardner, Jennifer and Amy Richards. "Feminism and Femininity: Or How We Learned to Stop Worrying and Love the Thong." In *All about the Girl: Culture, Power, and Identity*, edited by Anita Harris, 59–68. New York: Routledge. 2004.

Baumgardner, Jennifer and Amy Richards. *Manifesta: Young Women, Feminism, and the Future.* New York: Farrar, Straus, and Giroux. 2000.

Bettie, Julie. *Women without Class: Girls, Race, and Identity.* Berkeley: University of California Press. 2003.

Berger, Joseph and Ian Urbina. "Along with Population and Diversity, Stress Rises on Staten Island." *New York Times*, September 25, 2003, B1.

Berger, Peter L. and Thomas Luckmann. *The Social Construction of Reality: A Treatise in the Sociology of Knowledge.* New York: Anchor Books. 1966.

Best, Amy. *Prom Night: Youth, Schools, and Popular Culture.* New York: Routledge. 2000.

Bloom, Leslie Rebecca. *Under the Sign of Hope: Feminist Methodology and Narrative Interpretation.* Albany: SUNY of New York Press. 1998.

Bloustien, Gerry. *Girl Making: A Cross-Cultural Ethnography on the Processes of Growing Up Female.* New York: Berghahn Books. 2003.

Boland, Katherine. "'That's Not What I Said': Interpretive Conflict in Oral Narrative Research." In *Women's Words: The Feminist Practice of Oral History*, edited by Sherna Berger Gluck and Daphne Patai, 63–76. New York: Routledge. 1991.

Bordo, Susan. *Unbearable Weight: Feminism, Western Culture, and the Body.* Berkeley: University of California Press. 1993.

Boston Women's Health Book Collective. *Our Bodies, Ourselves: A Book by and for Women.* New York: Touchstone. 1976.

Boucher, Geoff. "Back Atop the Charts, Her Way: Mariah Carey Became the Butt of Jokes after She Was Dropped by Her Label in 2002. Mimi Is Emancipated Now, and a Grammy Nod Is Possible." *Los Angeles Times*, December 8, 2005, A1.

Bourdieu, Pierre. *Distinction: A Social Critique of the Judgment of Taste.* Cambridge: Harvard University Press. 1984.

Bright, Susie. *Susie Bright's Sexual State of the Union.* New York: Simon and Schuster. 1997.

Brooke, Jill. "Girl Power." *Adweek*, February 1, 1998.

Brown, Lyn Mikel. *Raising Their Voices: The Politics of Girls' Anger.* Cambridge, MA: Harvard University Press. 1998.

Brown, Lyn Mikel and Carol Gilligan. *Meeting at the Crossroads.* New York: Ballantine Books. 1992.

Buckingham, David. *Children Talking Television: The Making of Television Literacy.* London: The Falmer Press. 1993.

———. *Reading Audiences: Young People and the Media.* Manchester, UK: Manchester University Press. 1993.

Buckingham, David and Sarah Bragg. *Young People, Sex, and the Media: The Facts of Life.* New York: Palgrave Macmillan. 2004.

Budgeon, Shelley. "Emergent Feminist? Identities: Young Women and the Practice of Micropolitics." *The European Journal of Women's Studies* 8, no. 1 (2001): 7–28.

———. "'I'll Tell You What I Really, Really Want': Girl Power and Self-Identity in Britain." In *Millennium Girls: Today's Girls around the World*, edited by Sherrie Inness, 115–143. Lanham, MD: Rowman and Littlefield Publishers, Inc. 1998.

Bulbeck, Chilla and Anita Harris. "Feminism, Youth Politics, and Generational Change." In *Next Wave Cultures: Feminism, Subcultures, Activism*, edited by Anita Harris, 221–242. New York: Routledge. 2007.

Butler, Judith. *Gender Trouble and the Subversion of Identity.* New York: Routledge. 1990/1999.

Carpenter, Laura M. 1998. "From Girls into Women: Scripts for Sexuality and Romance in *Seventeen* Magazine, 1974–1994." *Journal of Sex Research* 35, no. 2 (1998): 158–168.

Cauce, Ana Mari, Yumi Hiraga, Diane Graves, Nancy Gonzales, Kimberly Ryan-Finn, and Kwai Grove. "African American Mothers and Their Adolescent Daughters: Closeness, Conflict, and Control." In *Urban Girls: Resisting Stereotypes, Creating Identities*, edited by Bonnie J. Ross Leadbeater and Niobe Way, 100–116. New York: New York University Press. 1996.

Cherland, Meredith Rogers. *Private Practices: Girls Reading Fiction and Constructing Identity.* London and Bristol, PA: Taylor and Francis. 1994.

Chideya, Farai with M. Rossi. "Revolution, Girl Style." *Newsweek*, November 23, 1992, 84–86.

Christian-Smith, Linda K. "Femininity as Discourse." In *Becoming Feminine: The Politics of Popular Culture*, edited by Leslie Roman and Linda K. Christian-Smith, 37–59. London: The Falmer Press. 1988.

Clough, Patricia. *Feminist Thought: Desire, Power, and Academic Discourse.* Cambridge, MA: Blackwell. 1994.

Coffey, Amanda Jane and Paul A. Atkinson. *Making Sense of Qualitative Data: Complementary Research Strategies.* Thousand Oaks, CA: Sage. 1996.

Cohen, Lizabeth. *A Consumer's Republic: The Politics of Mass Consumption in Postwar America.* New York: Alfred A. Knopf. 2003.

Collins, Patricia Hill. *Black Feminist Thought: Knowledge, Consciousness and the Politics of Empowerment.* New York: Routledge. 1990.

Comaroff, Jean and John L. Comaroff. "Millennial Capitalism: First Thoughts on a Second Coming." *Public Culture* 12, no. 2 (2000): 291–343.

Consoli, John. "Girl Power." *Brandweek* 40 (1999): 27.

Corliss, Richard. "A Diva Takes a Dive." *Time*, August 13, 2001.

Couldry, Nick. *Media Rituals: A Critical Approach.* New York: Routledge. 2003.

———. "Theorizing Media as Practice." *Social Semiotics* 14, no. 2 (2004): 115–132.

Craik, Jennifer. *The Face of Fashion: Cultural Studies of Fashion.* New York: Routledge. 1994.

Cross, Gary. *Kid's Stuff: Toys and the Changing World of American Childhood.* Cambridge, MA: Harvard University Press. 1997.

Currie, Dawn H. *Girl Talk: Adolescent Magazines and Their Readers.* Toronto: University of Toronto Press. 1999.

De Lauretis, Teresa. *Technologies of Gender: Essays on Theory, Film, and Fiction Theories of Representation and Difference.* Bloomington, IN: Indiana University Press. 1987.

Denzin, Norman and Yvonne Lincoln, eds. *The Landscape of Qualitative Research: Theories and Issues.* Thousand Oaks, CA: Sage. 1998.

DeVault, Marjorie L. *Liberating Method: Feminism and Social Research.* Philadelphia, PA: Temple University Press. 1999.

Dodson, Lisa. *Don't Call Us Out of Name: The Untold Stories of Women and Girls in Poor America.* Boston: Beacon Press. 1999.

Doherty, Thomas. *Teenagers and Teenpics: The Juvenilization of American Movies in the 1950s.* Philadelphia, PA: Temple University Press. 2002.

Dougherty, Steve. "A Butterfly Takes Wing." *People Weekly*, March 2, 1998.

Douglas, Susan. "Girls 'N' Spice: All Things Nice?" *The Nation*, August 25–September 1, 1997, 21–24.

———. *Where the Girls Are: Growing University Press Female with the Mass Media.* New York: Three Rivers Press. 1995.

Douglas, Susan and Meredith Michaels. *The Mommy Myth: The Idealization of Motherhood and How It Has Undermined Women.* New York: Free Press. 2004.

Dow, Bonnie. *Prime-Time Feminism: Television, Media Culture and the Women's Movement since 1970.* Philadelphia, PA: University of Pennsylvania Press. 1996.

Driscoll, Catherine. *Girls: Feminine Adolescence in Popular Culture and Cultural History.* New York: Columbia University Press. 2002.

———. "Girls Today: Girls, Girl Culture and Girlhood Studies." *Girlhood Studies: An Interdisciplinary Journal* 1, no. 1 (2007): 13–32.

———. "Girl-Doll: Barbie as Puberty Manual." In *Seven Going on Seventeen*, edited by Claudia Mitchell and Jacqueline Reid-Walsh, 224–241. New York: Peter Lang. 2005.

Driver, Susan. *Queer Girls and Popular Culture: Reading, Resisting, and Creating Media*. New York: Peter Lang. 2007.

Ducille, Ann. "Dyes and Dolls: Multicultural Barbie and the Merchandising of American Culture." *differences* 6 (1994): 48–68.

Duffy, Margaret and J. Michael Gotcher. "Crucial Advice on How to Get the Guy: The Rhetorical Vision of Power and Seduction in the Teen Magazine YM." *Journal of Communication Inquiry* 20, no. 1(1995): 32–48.

Duits, Linda and Lisbet van Zoonen. "Headscarves and Porno-Chic: Disciplining Girls' Dress in the European Multicultural Society." *The European Journal of Women's Studies* 13, no. 2 (2006): 103–117.

———. "Whose Afraid of Agency: A Rejoinder to Gill." *The European Journal of Women's Studies* 14, no. 2 (2007): 161–170.

Duke, Lisa. "Black in a Blonde World: Race and Girls' Interpretations of the Feminine Ideal in Teen Magazines." *Journalism and Mass Communication Quarterly* 77, no. 2(2000): 367–392.

Durham, Meenakshi Gigi. "Dilemmas of Desire: Representations of Adolescent Sexuality in Two Teen Magazines." *Youth and Society* 29, no. 3 (1998): 369–389.

———. "The Girling of America: Critical Reflections on Gender and Popular Communication." *Popular Communication* 1, no.1 (2003): 23–31.

———. "Sex and Spectacle in *Seventeen* Magazine: A Feminist Myth Analysis." Paper presented at the annual convention for the International Communication Association, San Francisco, May 24–28, 2007.

———. "The Taming of the Shrew: Women's Magazines and the Regulation of Desire." *Journal of Communication Inquiry* 20, no. 1 (1995): 18–31.

Dworkin, Andrea. *Intercourse*. New York: Free Press. 1987/1997.

Dwyer, Claire. "Contested Identities: Challenging Dominant Representations of Young British Muslim Women." In *Cool Places: Geographies of Youth Cultures*, edited by Tracey Skelton and Gill Valentine, 50–65. New York: Routledge. 1998.

Early, Frances H. "The Female Just Warrior Reimagined from Boudicca to Buffy." In *Athena's Daughters: Television's New Women Warriors*, edited by Francis H. Early and Kathleen Kennedy, 55–65. Syracuse, NY: Syracuse University Press. 2003.

Early, Frances H. and Kathleen Kennedy. *Athena's Daughters: Television's New Women Warriors*. Syracuse, NY: Syracuse University Press. 2003.

Edmondson, Brad. "The Demographics of Guilt." *American Demographics* 8 (1986): 33–35, 56.

Eisenhauer, Jennifer. "Mythic Figures and Lived Identities: Locating the 'Girl' in Feminist Discourse." In *All about the Girl: Culture, Power, and Identity*, edited by Anita Harris, 79–90. New York: Routledge. 2004.

Emerson, Rana A. "Where My Girls At? Negotiating Black Womanhood in Music Videos." *Gender and Society* 16, no. 1 (2002): 115–135.

Entwistle, Joanne. "The Dressed Body." In *Body Dressing*, edited by Joanne Entwistle and Elizabeth B. Wilson. Oxford, United Kingdom: Berg Publishers. 2001.

Erkut, Sumru, Jacqueline P. Fields, Rachel Sing, and Fern Marx. "Diversity in Girls' Experiences: Feeling Good about Who You Are." In *Urban Girls: Resisting Stereotypes, Creating Identities*, edited by Bonnie J. Ross Leadbeater and Niobe Way, 53–64. New York: New York University Press. 1996.

Evans, Caroline and Minna Thornton. *Women and Fashion: A New Look*. London: Quartet Books. 1989.

Ewen, Stuart. *All Consuming Images: The Politics of Style in Contemporary Culture*. New York: Basic Books. 1988/1999.

Faludi, Susan. *Backlash: The Undeclared War against American Women*. New York: Crown Publishers. 1991.

Fancsali, Cheri, Nancy Nevarez, Kari Nelsestuen, and Alexandra Weinbaum. *Where the Girls Are: What We Know and Need to Know about New York City Girls*. New York: Girls Incorporated of New York City. 2001.

Fatemeh. "Katy Perry Plays Make Believe." http://www.feministe.us/blog/archives/2008/06/30/katy-perry-plays-make-believe/.

Finders, Margaret. *Just Girls: Hidden Literacies and Life in Junior High*. New York: Teachers College Press. 1997.

———. "Queens and Teen Zines: Early Adolescent Females Reading Their Way toward Adulthood." *Anthropology and Education Quarterly* 27, no.1 (1996): 71–89.

Fine, Michelle. "Working the Hyphens: Reinventing Self and Other in Qualitative Research." In *The Landscape of Qualitative Research: Theories and Issues*, edited by Norman Denzin and Yvonne Lincoln, 130–155. Thousand Oaks, CA: Sage. 1998.

Fisherkeller, JoEllen. *Growing Up with Television: Everyday Learning among Young Adolescents*. Philadelphia, PA: Temple University Press. 2002.

Fiske, John. *Television Culture*. New York: Routledge. 1987.

———. *Understanding Popular Culture*. New York: Routledge. 1989.

Foucault, Michel. *History of Sexuality: An Introduction, Vol. 1*. New York: Vintage Books. 1978.

Frank, Thomas. *The Conquest of Cool: Business Culture, Counterculture, and the Rise of Hip Consumerism*. Chicago: Chicago University Press. 1997.

Fraser, Nancy. *Justice Interruptus: Critical Reflections on "Postsocialist" Condition*. New York: Routledge. 1997.

Frazer, Elizabeth. "Teenage Girls Reading *Jackie*." *Media, Culture, and Society* 9, no. 4 (1987): 407–425.

Friday, Nancy. *My Secret Garden: Women's Sexual Fantasies*. New York: Pocket Books. 1973/1998.

Frith, Simon and Angela McRobbie. "Rock and Sexuality." In *Feminism and Youth Culture*, edited by Angela McRobbie, 137–158. New York: Routledge. 1978/2000.

Fudge, Rachel. "The Buffy Effect, or a Tale of Cleavage and Marketing." *Bitch* 10 (1999). http://bitchmagazine.org/article/buffy-effect.

Garner, Ana C., Helen M. Sterk, and Shawn Adams. "Narrative Analysis of Sexual Etiquette in Teenage Magazines." *Journal of Communication* 48, no. 4 (1998): 59–78.

Garrison, Ednie Kaeh. "U.S. Feminism-Grrrl Style!: Youth Subcultures and the Technologies of the Third Wave." *Feminist Studies* 26, no. 1 (2000): 141–170.

Geertz, Clifford. *The Interpretation of Cultures*. New York: Basic Books. 1973.

Gill, Rosalind. "Critical Respect: The Difficulties and Dilemmas of Agency and 'Choice' for Feminism: A Reply to Duits and van Zoonen." *The European Journal of Women's Studies* 14, no. 1 (2007): 69–80.

———. "From Sexual Objectification to Sexual Subjectification: The Resexualisation of Women's Bodies in the Media." http://www.re-public.gr/en/?p=163.

Gilroy, Paul. "Between Afro-Centrism and Euro-Centrism: Youth Culture and the Problem of Hybridity." *Young* 1, no. 2 (1993): 2–12.

Girl Scouts of the U.S.A. *Feeling Safe: What Girls Say: Executive Summary*. New York: Girl Scouts of the U.S.A. 2003.

Gleick, Elizabeth. "Surviving Your Teens: For Troubled Adolescent Girls and the People Who Love Them, the Best Selling Reviving Ophelia Is a Sacred Text." *Time*, February 19, 1996. 73.

Glennon, Will. 200 *Ways to Raise a Girl's Self-Esteem: An Indispensable Guide for Parents, Teachers, and Other Concerned Caregivers*. Berkeley, CA: Conari Press. 1999.

Goffman, Erving. *The Presentation of Self in Everyday Life*. New York: Doubleday. 1959.

Goldman, Robert, Deborah Heath, and Sharon L. Smith. "Commodity Feminism." *Critical Studies in Mass Communication* 8, no. 3 (1991): 333–351.

Gonick, Marnina. "Between 'Girl Power' and 'Reviving Ophelia.'" *NWSA Journal* 18, no. 2 (2006): 1–23.

Gottlieb, Joanne and Gayle Wald. "Smells Like Teen Spirit: Riot Grrrls, Revolution, and Women in Independent Rock." In *Microphone Fiends: Youth Music and Youth Culture*, edited by Andrew Ross and Tricia Rose, 250–274. New York: Routledge. 1994.

Greer, Germaine. *The Female Eunuch*. New York: Farrar, Straus and Giroux. 1970/2002.

Hall, Stuart. "Encoding/Decoding." In *Culture, Media, Language: Working Papers in Cultural Studies, 1972–79*, 128–138. London: Hutchinson and Co. 1980.

———. "New Ethnicities." In *Stuart Hall: Critical Dialogues in Cultural Studies*, edited by David Morley and Kuan-Hsing Chen, 441–449. New York: Routledge. 1996.

———. "The Rediscovery of 'Ideology': Return of the Repressed in Media Studies." In *Culture, Society, and the Media*, edited by Michael Gurevitch, Tony Bennett, James Curran, and Janet Woollacott, 56–90. London: Routledge. 1982.

Haraway, Donna. *Simians, Cyborgs, and Women: The Reinvention of Nature*. New York: Routledge. 1991.

Harrington, Richard. "Christina Aguilera: No Mickey Mouse Pop Sensation." *The Washington Post*, September 8, 1999, C1.

Harris, Anita, ed. *All about the Girl: Culture, Power, and Identity*. New York: Routledge. 2004.

———. *Future Girl: Young Women in the 21st Century*. New York: Routledge. 2004.

———, ed. *Next Wave Cultures: Feminism, Subcultures, Activism*. New York: Routledge. 2007.

Harvey, David. *A Brief History of Neoliberalism*. New York: Oxford University Press. 2005.

———. *The Condition of Postmodernity: An Enquiry into the Origins of Cultural Change*. Cambridge, MA: Blackwell. 1990.

Haynes, Esther. "Let the Woman Finally Be on Top." *Jane*, September 2004, 141–143.

Heath, Joseph and Andrew Potter. *Nation of Rebels: Why Counterculture Became Consumer Culture*. New York: Harper Business. 2004.

Hebdige, Dick. *Subculture:* The Meaning of Style. New York: Routledge. 1979.

Hegde, Radha. "A View from Elsewhere: Locating Difference and the Politics of Representation from a Transnational Feminist Perspective." *Communication Theory* 8, no. 3 (1998): 271–297.

Heilman, Elizabeth. "The Struggle for Self: Power and Identity in Adolescent Girls." *Youth and Society* 30, no. 2 (1998): 182–208.

Helford, Elyce Rae, ed. *Fantasy Girls: Gender in the New Universe of Science Fiction and Fantasy Television*. Lanham, MD: Rowman and Littlefield. 2000.

———. "Introduction." In *Fantasy Girls: Gender in the New Universe of Science Fiction and Fantasy Television*, edited by Elyce Rae Helford, 1–12. Lanham, MD: Rowman and Littlefield. 2000.

Helligar, Jeremy. "Apple's Way." *People Weekly*, November 25, 1996.

Henry, Astrid. *Not My Mother's Sister*. Bloomington, IN: Indiana University Press. 2004.

Hesse-Biber, Sharlene Nagy, and Michelle L. Yasier. *Feminist Perspectives on Social Research*. New York: Oxford University Press. 2004.

Heywood, Leslie and Jennifer Drake. *Third Wave Agenda: Being Feminist, Doing Feminism*. Minneapolis, MN: University Minnesota Press. 1997.

Hilburn, Robert. "What a Drag It Is Being Young." *Los Angeles Times*, October 5, 1997.

Hoban, Phoebe. "The Night: Crying Is Best Done in Public." *New York Times Online*, October 19, 1997.

Hochschild, Arlie. *The Second Shift: Working Parents and the Revolution at Home*. New York: Avon. 1989.

Hodge, Roger and David Tripp. *Children and Television: A Semiotic Approach*. Stanford, CA: Stanford University Press. 1986.

Holcomb, Betty. *Not Guilty!: The Good News About Working Mothers*. New York: Scribner. 1998.

Hollows, Joanne. *Feminism, Femininity, and Popular Culture*. Manchester: Manchester University Press. 2000.

hooks, bell. *Ain't I a Woman?: Black Women and Feminism*. Boston, MA: South End Press. 1981.

———. *Black Looks: Race and Representation*. Cambridge, MA: South End Press. 1992.

———. *Feminist Theory: From Margin to Center*. Boston, MA: South End Press. 1984/2000.

"How Women Have Changed America." *Working Woman* 11 (1986): 129.

Hunt, D. "Moving Out of Phoebe's Shadow." *The San Diego Union-Tribune*, February 13, 2000, E6.

Hwalek, Melanie and Margaret E. Minnick. *Girls, Families, and Communities: Grow through Girl Scouting*. New York: Girl Scouts of the U.S.A. 1997.

Ibsen, Henrick. *A Doll's House*. Mineola, NY: Dover Publications. 1879/1992.

Inness, Sherrie, ed. *Action Chicks: New Images of Tough Women in Popular Culture*. New York: Palgrave Macmillan. 1998.

———. "'Anti-Barbies': The American Girls Collection and Political Ideologies." In *Delinquents and Debutantes: Twentieth Century American Girls' Cultures*, 164–183. New York: New York University Press. 1998.

Inness, Sherrie, ed. *Delinquents and Debutantes: Twentieth Century American Girls' Cultures.* New York: New York University Press. 1998.

Johnston, Deirdre D. and Debra H. Swanson. "Undermining Mothers: A Content Analysis of the Representation of Mothers in Magazines." *Mass Communication & Society* 6, no. 3 (2003): 243–266.

Jones, Lewis. "Touchingly 'Real' Lisa: Lisa Kudrow Plays Dumb Blondes, but She's No Phoney." *The Ottawa Citizen*, September 25, 1999, I1.

Jowett, Madeleine. "'I Don't See Feminists as You See Feminists': Contemporary Britain." In *All about the Girl: Culture, Power, and Identity*, edited by Anita Harris, 91–100. New York: Routledge. 2004.

Judah, Hettie. "Women: Sisters Are Saying It for Themselves Bitch." *The Guardian* (United Kingdom), June 8, 1999, T6.

Kaplan, E. Ann. *Motherhood and Representation: The Mother in Popular Culture and Melodrama.* New York: Routledge. 1992.

Kaplan, Elaine Bell and Leslie Cole. "'I Want to Read Stuff on Boys': White, Latina, and Black Girls Reading '*Seventeen*' Magazine and Encountering Adolescence." *Adolescence* 38, no. 149 (2003): 141–159.

Kearney, Mary Celeste. "'Don't Need You': Rethinking Identity Politics and Separatism from a Grrrl Perspective." In *Youth Culture: Identity in a Postmodern World*, edited by Jonanathan Epstein, 148–188. Malden, MA: Blackwell. 1998.

———. *Girls Make Media.* New York: Routledge. 2006.

"Kids Age Segmentation." *Home Textiles Today*, October 7, 2002.

Kilbourne, Jean. *Can't Buy My Love: How Advertising Changes the Way We Think and Feel.* New York: Free Press. 2000.

Kinder, Marsha, ed. *Kids' Media Culture.* Durham, NC: Duke University Press. 1999.

Klein, Naomi. *No Logo.* New York: Picador. 1999.

Kline, Stephen. *Out of the Garden: Toys and Children's Culture in the Age of TV Marketing.* New York: Verso. 1993.

Kvale, Steinar. *InterViews: An Introduction to Qualitative Research Interviewing.* Thousand Oaks, CA: Sage Publications. 1996.

Lal, Jayati. "Situating Locations: The Politics of Self, Identity, and 'Other' in Living and Writing the Text." In *Feminist Approaches to Theory and Methodology: An Interdisciplinary Reader*, edited by Sharlene Hesse-Biber, Christina Gilmartin, and Robin Lydenberg, 100–137. New York: Oxford University Press. 1999.

Lamb, Sharon and Lyn Mikel Brown. *Packaging Girlhood: Rescuing Our Daughters from Marketers' Schemes.* New York: St. Martin's Press. 2006.

Lather, Patti. *Getting Smart: Feminist Research and Pedagogy with/in the Postmodern*. New York: Routledge. 1991.

Leblanc, Lauraine. *Pretty in Punk: Girls' Gender Resistance in a Boys' Subculture.* New Brunswick, NJ: Rutgers University Press. 1999.

Lees, Sue. *Sugar and Spice: Sexuality and Adolescent Girls*. New York: Penguin Books. 1993.

Lemish, Dafna. "Spice Girls' Talk: A Case Study in the Development of Gendered Identity." In *Millennium Girls: Today's Girls around the World*, edited by Sherrie Inness, 145–167. Lanham, MD: Rowman and Littlefield Publishers, Inc. 1998.

———. "Spice World: Constructing Femininity the Popular Way." *Popular Music and Society* 26, no. 1 (2003): 17–29.

Leonard, Marion. "Paper Planes: Travelling the New Grrrl Geographies." In *Cool Places: Geographies of Youth Cultures*, edited by Tracey Skelton and Gill Valentine, 101–118. New York: Routledge. 1998.

Levy, Ariel. *Female Chauvinist Pigs: Women and the Rise of Raunch Culture.* New York: Free Press. 2006.

Lewis, Lisa. A. *Gender Politics and MTV: Voicing the Difference.* Philadelphia, PA: Temple University Press. 1990.

Linn, Susan. *The Case for Make-Believe: Saving Play in a Commercialized World.* New Press: New York. 2008.

Lopez, Nancy. *Hopeful Girls, Troubled Boys: Race and Gender Disparity in Urban Education.* New York: Routledge. 2003.

Lorde, Audre. *Sister Outsider.* Freedom, CA: Crossing Press. 1984.

Luker, Kristin. *Dubious Conceptions: The Politics of Teenage Pregnancy.* Cambridge, MA: Harvard University Press. 1996.

Mackoff, Barbara. *Growing a Girl: Seven Strategies for Raising a Strong, Spirited Daughter.* New York: Dell. 1996.

Madriz, Esther. "Focus Groups in Feminist Research." In *Handbook of Qualitative Research: Second Edition*, edited by Norman Denzin and Yvonne Lincoln, 835–850. Thousand Oaks, CA: Sage Publications. 2000.

Malik, Farah. "Mediated Consumption and Fashionable Selves: Tween Girls, Fashion Magazines and Shopping." In *Seven Going on Seventeen*, edited by Claudia Mitchell and Jacqueline Reid-Walsh, 257–277. New York: Peter Lang. 2005.

Malson, Helen, Harriett Marshall, and Anne Woollett. "Talking of Taste: A Discourse Analytic Exploration of Young Women's Gendered and Racialized Subjectivities in British Urban, Multicultural Contexts." *Feminism and Psychology* 12, no. 4 (2002): 469–490.

Malson, Helen and Catherine Swann. "Prepared for Consumption: (Dis) Orders of Eating and Embodiment." *Journal of Community and Applied Social Psychology* 9, no. 6 (1999): 397–405.

Marcus, George E. "Ethnography in/of the World System: The Emergence of Multi-Sited Ethnography." *Annual Review of Anthropology* 24 (1995): 95–117.

Marinucci, Mimi. "Feminism and the Ethics of Violence: Why Buffy Kicks Ass." In *Buffy the Vampire Slayer and Philosophy: Fear and Trembling in Sunnydale*, edited by James B. South and William Irwin, 61–76. Chicago, IL: Open Court Publishing. 2003.

Massoni, Kelley. "Modeling Work: Occupational Messages in *Seventeen* Magazine." *Gender and Society* 18, no. 1 (2004): 47–65.

Mastronardi, Maria. *From the DSM to Ophelia: Teenage Girls and the Psychological Complex.* Unpublished doctoral dissertation, University of Illinois at Urbana-Champaign. 1998.

Mazzarella, Sharon. "The 'Superbowl' of All Dates: Teenage Girl Magazines and the Commodification of the Perfect Prom." In *Growing Up Girls: Popular Culture and the Construction of Identity*, edited by Sharon Mazzarella and Norma Pecora, 97–112. New York: Peter Lang Publishing. 1999.

Mazzarella, Sharon and Norma Pecora. "Revisiting Girls' Studies." *Journal of Children and Media* 1, no. 2 (2007): 105–125.

McRobbie, Angela. "The Culture of Working Class Girls." In McRobbie, *Feminism and Youth Culture*, 44–66.

———. *Feminism and Youth Culture.* 2nd ed. New York: Routledge. 1991/2000.

———. *In the Culture Society: Art, Fashion and Popular Music.* New York: Routledge. 1999.

———. "Notes on Postfeminism and Popular Culture: Bridget Jones and the New Gender Regime." In *All about the Girl: Culture, Power, and Identity*, edited by Anita Harris, 3–14. New York: Routledge. 2004.

———. *Postmodernism and Popular Culture.* New York: Routledge. 1994.

———. "Second Hand Dresses and the Role of the Ragmarket." In *Zoot Suits and Second Hand Dresses: An Anthology of Fashion and Music.* Boston, MA: Unwin Hyman. 1988.

———. "Shut Up and Dance: Youth Culture and Changing Modes of Femininity." *Cultural Studies* 7, no. 3 (1993): 406–426.

———. "Top Girls? Young Women and the Post-Feminist Sexual Contract." *Cultural Studies* 21, no. 4,5 (2007): 718–737.

———. "Young Women and Consumer Culture: An Intervention." *Cultural Studies* 22, no. 5 (2008): 531–550.

Merton, Robert, Marjorie Fiske, and Patricia Kendall. *The Focused Interview: A Manual of Problems and Procedures.* New York: The Free Press. 1956/1990.

Miller, Daniel. "Consumption as the Vanguard of History: A Polemic Way of an Introduction." In *Acknowledging Consumption: A Review of New Studies*, edited by David Miller, 1–57. New York: Routledge. 1995.

Modleski, Tania. *Feminism without Women: Culture and Criticism in a "Postfeminist" Age.* New York: Routledge. 1991.

Mohanty, Chandra. *Feminism without Borders: Decolonizing Theory, Practicing Solidarity.* Durham, NC: Duke University Press. 2003.

Moraga, Cherrie and Gloria Anzaldua. *This Bridge Called My Back: Writings by Radical Womenof Color.* NewYork: Kitchen Table Women of Color Press. 1981.

Morgan, Robin. *Sisterhood Is Powerful: An Anthology of Writings from the Women's Liberation Movement.* New York: Vintage. 1970.

Morley, David. "The *Nationwide* Audience: Structure and Decoding." In *The* Nationwide *Television Studies*, edited by David Morley and Charlotte Brunsdon, 111–291. New York: Routledge. 1999.

Moss, Gemma. "Girls Tell the Teen Romance: Four Reading Histories." In *Reading Audiences: Young People and the Media*, edited by David Buckingham, 116–134. Manchester: Manchester University Press. 1993.

Motz, Marilyn Ferris. " 'Seen through Rose-Tinted Glasses': The Barbie Doll in American Society." In *Popular Culture: An Introductory Text*, edited by Jack Nachbar and Kevin Lause, 211–234. Bowling Green, OH: Bowling Green State University Popular Press. 1992.

Mulvey, Laura. "Visual Pleasure and Narrative Cinema." *Screen* 16 (1975): 6–18.

Munk, Nina. "Girl Power!" *Fortune*, December 8, 1997.

Murray, Susan. "Saving Our So-Called Lives: Girl Fandom, Adolescent Subjectivity, and *My So-Called Life*." In *Kids' Media Culture*, edited by Marsha Kinder, 221–235. Durham, NC: Duke University Press. 1999.

Nash, Ilana. *American Sweethearts: Teenage Girls in Twentieth-Century Popular Culture.* Bloomington, IN: Indiana University Press.

New York City Department of Education. http://www.nycenet.edu.

Ono, Kent A. "To Be a Vampire on *Buffy the Vampire Slayer*: Race and 'Other' Socially Marginalizing Positions on Horror TV." In *Fantasy Girls: Gender in the New Universe of Science Fiction and Fantasy Television*, edited by Elyce Rae Helford, 163–186. Lanham, MD: Rowman and Littlefield. 2000.

Orenstein, Peggy. *School Girls: Young Women, Self-Esteem and the Confidence Gap.* New York: Doubleday. 1994.

Ostermann, Ana and Deborah Keller-Cohen. 1998. " 'Good Girls Go to Heaven; Bad Girls…' Learn to be Good: Quizzes in American and Brazilian Teenage Girls' Magazines." *Discourse and Society* 9, no. 4 (1998): 531–558.

Oyewumi, Oyeronke. "Ties that Unbind: Feminism, Sisterhood and Other Foreign Relations." *Jenda: A Journal of Culture and African Women Studies* 1 (2001) http://www.jendajournal.com/vol1.1/oyewumi.html.

Palladino, Grace. *Teenagers: An American History*. New York: Basic Books. 1996.

Pecora, Norma. *The Business of Children's Entertainment*. New York: Guilford Press. 1998.

———. "Identity by Design: The Corporate Construction of Teen Romance Novels." In *Growing Up Girls: Popular Culture and the Construction of Identity*, edited by Sharon Mazzarella and Norma Pecora, 49–86. New York: Peter Lang. 1999.

Peirce, Kate. "A Feminist Theoretical Perspective on the Socialization of Teenage Girls through *Seventeen* Magazine." *Sex Roles* 23, no. 9, 10 (1990): 491–500.

Pender, Patricia. "'I'm Buffy and You're… History': The Postmodern Politics of Buffy." In *Fighting the Forces: What's at Stake in* Buffy the Vampire Slayer, edited by Rhonda V. Wilcox and David Lavery, 35–44. Lanham, MD: Rowman and Littlefield. 2002.

Perry, Imani. "Whose Am I? The Identity and Image of Women in Hip-Hop." In *Gender, Race and Class in Media: A Text Reader*, edited by Gail Dines and Jean M. Humez, 136–148. Newbury Park, CA: Sage. 1995.

Peterson, Eric. "Media Consumption and Girls Who Want to Have Fun." *Critical Studies in Mass Communication* 4, no. 1 (1987): 37–50.

Pipher, Mary. *Reviving Ophelia: Saving the Selves of Adolescent Girls*. New York: Ballantine. 1994.

Pomerantz, Shauna. *Girls, Style, and School Identity*. New York: Palgrave Macmillan. 2008.

Postrel, Virgina. "Inconspicuous Consumption: A New Theory of the Leisure Class." *The Atlantic*, July/August (2008). http://www.theatlantic.com/doc/200807/consumption.

Press, Andrea. *Women Watching Television: Gender, Class, and Generation in the American Television Experience*. Philadelphia, PA: University of Pennsylvania Press. 1991.

Probyn, Elspeth. "New Traditionalism and Post-Feminism: TV Does the Home." In *Feminist Television Criticism*, edited by Charlotte Brunsdon, Julie D'Acci, and Lynn Spigel, 126–137. Oxford, United Kingdom: Oxford University Press. 1997.

Proweller, Amira. *Constructing Female Identities: Meaning Making in an Upper Middle Class Youth Culture*. Albany: SUNY Press. 1998.

Radway, Janice. *Reading the Romance: Women, Patriarchy, and Popular Literature*. Chapel Hill, NC: The University of North Carolina Press. 1984.

Railton, Diane and Paul Watson. "Naughty Girl and Re-Blooded Woman: Representations of Female Heterosexuality in Music Video." *Feminist Media Studies* 5, no. 1 (2005): 51–63.

Reinharz, Shulamit. *Feminist Methods in Social Research.* New York: Oxford University Press. 1992.

Riordan, Ellen. "Commodified Agents and Empowered Girls: Consuming and Producing Feminism." *Journal of Communication Inquiry* 25, no. 3 (2001): 279–297.

Roberts, Kimberley. *Girls in Black and White: The Iconography of Teenage Girls in Post-Feminist America.* Unpublished doctoral dissertation, University of Virgina, Charlottesville. 2002.

Robertson, Pamela. *Guilty Pleasures: Feminist Camp from Mae West to Madonna.* Durham, NC: Duke University Press. 1996.

Rogers, Mary and C.D. Garrett. *Who's Afraid of Women's Studies? Feminisms in Everyday Life.* Walnut Creek, CA: AltaMira Press. 2002.

Rosch, Leah. "Sugar Daddies." *Folio: The Magazine for Magazine Management* 23 (1994): 52–56.

Rose, Tricia. *Black Noise: Rap Music and Black Culture in Contemporary America.* Hanover, CT: Wesleyan University Press. 1994.

Rosen, Alison. "Big Apple Circus." *Time Out New York*, December 8–14, 2005, 15–17.

Rosenberg, Jessica and Gitana Garofalo. "Riot Grrrl: Revolutions from Within." *Signs: Journal of Women in Culture and Society* 23, no. 3 (1998): 809–841.

Royse, David. "Scouting and Girl Scout Curriculum as Interventions: Effects on Adolescents' Self Esteem." *Adolescence* 33, no. 129 (1998): 159–168.

Ruddick, Sara. *Maternal Thinking: Toward a Politics of Peace.* Boston, MA: Beacon Press. 1989/1995.

Sadker, Myra and David Sadker. *Failing at Fairness: How Schools Cheat Girls.* New York: Touchstone. 1994.

Sanders, Barry. *A Is for Ox: The Collapse of Literacy and the Rise of Violence in an Electronic Age.* New York: Vintage. 1994.

Scanlon, Jennifer. "Boys-R-Us: Board Games and the Socialization of Young Adolescent Girls." In *Delinquents and Debutantes: Twentieth Century American Girls' Cultures*, edited by Sherrie Inness, 184–195. New York: New York University Press. 1998.

Schilt, Kirsten. "'A Little Too Ironic': The Appropriation and Packaging of Riot Grrrl Politics by Mainstream Female Musicians." *Popular Music and Society* 26, no. 3 (2003): 5–16.

Schlenker, Jennifer A., Sandra L. Caron, and William A. Halterman. "A Feminist Analysis of *Seventeen* Magazine: Content Analysis from 1945 to 1995." *Sex Roles* 38, no. 11,12 (1998): 135–149.

Schor, Juliet. *Born to Buy: The Commercialized Child and the New Consumer Culture.* New York : Scribner. 2004.

Schrum, Kelly. *Some Wore Bobby Sox: The Emergence of Teenage Girls Culture, 1920–1945.* New York: Palgrave Macmillan. 2004.

Scott, A.O. "Sleek, Tough, Frosted? Must Be Empowerment." *The New York Times Online,* November 3, 2000.

Seiter, Ellen. *Sold Separately: Children and Parents in Consumer Culture.* New Brunswick, NJ: Rutgers University Press. 1993.

Signorielli, Nancy. *Reflections of Girls in the Media: A Study of Television Shows and Commercials, Movies, Music Videos, and Teen Magazine Articles and Ads.* Kaiser Family Foundation and Children Now. www.kff.org/entmedia/1260-gendr.cfm. 1997.

Skeggs, Beverley. *Formations of Class and Gender: Becoming Respectable.* London: Sage. 1997.

———. "Women's Studies in Britain in the 1990s: Entitlement Cultures and Institutional Constraints." *Women's Studies International Forum 18, no. 4 (1995): 475–486.*

Spivak, Gayatri Chakravorty. "Subaltern Studies: Deconstructing Historiography." In *Selected Subaltern Studies,* edited by Ranajot Guha and Gayatri Chakravorty Spivak, 3–34. New York: Oxford University Press. 1988.

Stacey, Judith. "Sexism by a Subtler Name: Postindustrial Conditions and Postfeminist Consciousness in Silicon Valley." In *Women, Class, and the Feminist Imagination: A Socialist Feminist Reader,* edited by Karen V. Hansen and Ilene J. Philipson, 338–356. Philadelphia, PA: Temple University Press. 1990.

Steele, Jeanne R. and Jane D. Brown. "Adolescent Room Culture: Studying Media in the Context of Everyday Life." *Journal of Youth and Adolescence* 24, no. 5 (1995): 551–576.

Steinberg, Shirely R. "The Bitch Who Has Everything." In *Kinderculture: The Corporate Construction of Childhood,* edited by Shirley R. Steinberg and Joe L. Kincheloe, 207–218. Boulder, CO: Westview Press. 1997.

Steinberg, Shirley and Joe Kincheloe, eds. *Kinderculture: The Corporate Construction of Childhood.* Boulder, CO: Westview Press. 1997.

Stewart, David, Prem Shamdasani, and Dennis Rook. *Focus Groups: Theory and Practice.* Newbury Park, CA: Sage. 1990.

"Stripped Intro" (2002). Recorded by Christina Aguilera. On *Stripped.* CD. New York: RCA Records.

Swarns, Rachel L. " 'African-American' Becomes a Term for Debate." *The New York Times,* August 9, 2004, A1.

Taft, Jessica K. "Girl Power Politics: Pop-Culture Barriers and Organizational Discourse." In *All about the Girl: Culture, Power, and Identity*, edited by Anita Harris, 69–78. New York: Routledge. 2004.

Taylor, Jill McLean. "Cultural Stories: Latina and Portuguese Daughters and Mothers." In *Urban Girls: Resisting Stereotypes, Creating Identities*, edited by Bonnie J. Ross Leadbeater and Niobe Way, 117–131. New York: New York University Press. 1996.

Tolman, Deborah. "Adolescent Girls' Sexuality: Debunking the Myth of the Urban Girl." In *Urban Girls: Resisting Stereotypes, Creating Identities*, edited by Bonnie J. Ross Leadbeater and Niobe Way, 255–271. New York: New York University Press. 1996.

———. *Dilemmas of Desire: Teenage Girls Talk about Sexuality*. Cambridge, MA: Harvard University Press. 2002.

Urla, Jacqueline and Alan C. Swedlund. "The Anthropometry of Barbie: Unsettling Ideals of the Feminine Body in Popular Culture." In *Deviant Bodies: Critical Perspectives on Difference in Science and Popular Culture*, edited by Jennifer Terry and Jacqueline Urla, 277–313. Bloomington, IN: Indiana University Press. 1995.

U.S. Census Bureau. American Community Survey 2004. http://www.census.gov/acs.

U.S. Census Bureau. Census 2000. Summary File 1; generated by Emilie Zaslow; using American FactFinder. http://factfinder.census.gov. September 8, 2004.

U.S. Department of Labor. 2003. National Occupational Employment and Wage Estimates. http://stats.bls.gov/oes/2003/may/oes_nat.htm.

Valdes-Rodriguez, Alisa. "Genie behind 'Bottle': Seeming to Pop Out of Nowhere, Ex-Mouseketeer Christina Aguilera Scurries to Top of the Pop Charts." *Los Angeles Times*, July 26, 1999, F1.

van Zoonen, Lisbet. *Feminist Media Studies*. Thousand Oaks, CA: Sage. 1994.

Vavrus, Mary Douglas. "Opting Out Moms in the News: Selling New Traditionalism in the New Millennium." *Feminist Media Studies* 7, no. 1 (2007): 47–63.

Vranica, Suzanne. "Marketing and Media—Advertising: Stereotypes of Women Persist in Ads; Bikinis Still Sell the Suds, as Masculine Views Reign; Agency Gender Gap Blamed." *The Wall Street Journal*, October 17, 2003, B4.

Wald, Gayle. "Just a Girl? Rock Music, Feminism, and the Cultural Construction of Female Youth." *Signs: Journal of Women in Culture and Society* 23, no. 3 (1998): 585–610.

Walker, Rebecca. *To Be Real: Telling the Truth and Changing the Face of Feminism*. New York: Anchor Books. 1995.

Walters, Suzanna Danuta. *Material Girls: Making Sense of Feminist Cultural Theory.* Berkeley, CA: University of California Press. 1995.

Ward, Jane Victoria and Beth Cooper Benjamin. "Women, Girls, and the Unfinished Work of Connection: A Critical Review of American Girls' Studies." *All about the Girl: Power, Culture, and Identity*, edited by Anita Harris, 15–27. New York: Routledge. 2004.

Warner, Judith. *Perfect Madness: Motherhood in the Age of Anxiety.* New York: Riverhead Books. 2005.

Waters, Mary C. "The Intersection of Gender, Race, and Ethnicity in Identity Development of Caribbean American Teens." In *Urban Girls: Resisting Stereotypes, Creating Identities*, edited by Bonnie J. Ross Leadbeater and Niobe Way, 65–81. New York: New York University Press. 1996.

Way, Niobe. "'Can't You See the Courage, the Strength that I Have': Listening to Urban Adolescent Girls Speak about Their Relationships." *Psychology of Women Quarterly* 19 (1995): 107–128.

———. *Everyday Courage: The Lives and Stories of Urban Teenagers.* New York: New York University Press. 1998.

Weedon, Chris. *Feminist Practice and Poststructuralist Theory.* Oxford: Basil Blackwell. 1987.

———. *Feminism, Theory and the Politics of Difference.* Oxford: Blackwell. 1999.

Whiteley, Sheila. *Women and Popular Music: Sexuality, Identity and Subjectivity.* New York: Routledge. 2000.

Whitney, Daisy. "In Search of the Coveted Teen." *TelevisionWeek*, March 10, 2003, 10.

Wilkinson, Sue. "Focus Group Research." In *Qualitative Research*, edited by David Silverman, 177–199. London: Sage. 2004.

Williams, Don. "Exclusive Interview: Robin Antin." http://www.buddytv.com/articles/pussycat-dolls-present-the-search-for-the-next-doll/exclusive-interview-robin-anti-16462.aspx.

Willis, Paul. *Learning to Labour: How Working-Class Kids Get Working-Class Jobs.* New York: Columbia University Press. 1977.

Wolf, Naomi. *Promiscuities: The Secret Struggle for Womanhood.* New York: Ballantine Books. 1998.

Zaslow, Emilie. *"In the Business of Little Girls:" Pleasant Company's Construction of American Girlhood.* Unpublished Master's thesis, State University of New York, Buffalo. 1997.

# Index

CPSIA information can be obtained at www.ICGtesting.com
Printed in the USA
LVOW11s0336090115
422113LV00005B/534/P
9 780230 119963